DARK PERSUASION

DARK PERSUASION

A History of Brainwashing from
Pavlov to Social Media

JOEL E. DIMSDALE

Yale

UNIVERSITY PRESS

New Haven and London

Yale University Press books may be purchased in quantity for
educational, business, or promotional use. For information,
please e-mail sales.press@yale.edu (U.S. office) or sales@yaleup.co.uk
(U.K. office).

Set in Janson type by Tseng Information Systems, Inc.
Printed in the United States of America.

Library of Congress Control Number: 2020951874
ISBN 978-0-300-24717-6 (hardcover : alk. paper)
ISBN 978-0-300-27103-4 (paperback)

A catalogue record for this book is available from the British Library.

10 9 8 7 6 5 4 3 2 1

Contents

PART III INTO THE TWENTY-FIRST CENTURY

Preface

I WAS WORKING IN the library when I bumped into one of my former patients. I hadn't seen her for maybe five years. We sized each other up. I was a retired professor of psychiatry lugging a pile of books. She was a bright young scholar carrying lots of baggage from her past. We chatted for a bit, surrounded by shelves of books in the stacks, and she asked what I was working on. I told her I had gotten interested in brainwashing.

"Umm," she said. "Isn't that kind of a stale, musty topic—Communists, bad science, and all that stuff?" As I said, she was bright and inclined to come right to the point—tact had never been her strong suit. Why was I spending so much time on this arcane topic? Granted, I am eccentric; but what made me think anybody else would be interested in this subject?

Then I came home to watch the evening news, which featured its usual dose of suicide bombers and mass shootings, followed by political leaders making preposterous statements ("Vaccination causes autism," "Global warming is a myth," "The COVID-19 virus is not a problem"). It is bad enough that leaders can propound such nonsense; the bigger problem is that they persuade so many other people to endorse their misunderstandings of the world. I thought about my patient again. How did *she* make sense of a world where people could be persuaded to believe rubbish and follow it up with self-destructive violence?

As a psychiatrist, I should be one of the last people to believe the world operates rationally. I know better. Leaders have all too often been pied pipers, but something new emerged in the twentieth century. I still don't know what to call this phenomenon. *Brainwashing, coercive persuasion, thought control, dark persuasion*—all these terms refer to the fact that certain techniques render individuals shockingly vulnerable to indoctrination.

I don't think brainwashing is a musty topic, although it is one with a long history. I don't think it is a stale one either. Brainwashing blossomed in the twentieth century because of advances in behavioral science, neuroscience, and pharmacology. It will certainly develop further in the twenty-first century. Yes, the Soviet Union was embroiled in this phenomenon, but so were Great Britain, France, Germany, China, North Korea, Canada, Cambodia, the Vatican, and the United States. And yes, the term *brainwashing* is silly and unscientific. No one ever meant it literally, but the metaphor is a powerful one.

Throughout the twentieth century, governments invested so heavily in research on brainwashing that it has come to be known as the "Manhattan Project of the Mind." But it wasn't just military and intelligence agencies that employed the technique; many cults stumbled upon its use as well. We confront this legacy every day.

Even so, I wouldn't have been so interested in this topic if not for my neighbors.

★★★

When we moved to the hills north of San Diego, we were surrounded by dazzling light; groves of eucalyptus, avocado, and orange trees; and a menagerie of coyotes, pheasants, egrets, and peacocks. It all seemed like a brilliant Garden of Eden.

And yet, a few miles away, our neighbors had themselves castrated, and that was only the beginning of it.

They had rented a nine-thousand-square-foot mansion and lived quietly behind their locked gates, regarding themselves as students in a school for spiritual enlightenment. "Some kind of religious commune," the neighborhood thought. But they paid their rent, didn't bother anyone, and supported themselves as website design consultants. For an unconventional religious group, they had very mainstream clients. One of their last design commissions was for the Fairbanks Ranch Polo Club.[1]

They were New Age seekers who felt lost in this world. They felt stranded, believing they had come from another world in the stars and that their bodies were merely "vehicles." They were part of the "away team" from the heavens.

When the Hale-Bopp comet was sighted in 1995, the seekers felt it was sent from heaven and that an unseen spaceship trailed behind, ready to bring them home. They made methodical preparations. If they could exit their earthly body vehicles at the right time—when the comet was closest to Earth—they would be transported to the heavens on the approaching spaceship. Then, they believed, they would graduate to the next level. The

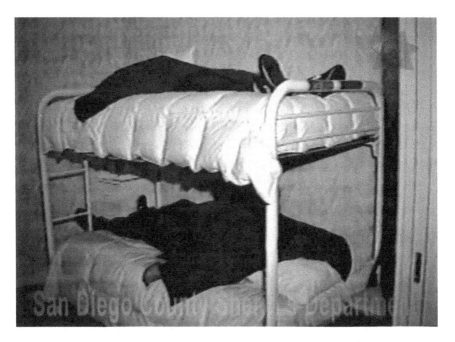

Heaven's Gate bodies cloaked in reverence.
(Courtesy of San Diego County Sheriff's Department, b-roll video.)

date they looked forward to was March 22, 1997. Their website announced: "Hale-Bopp's approach is the 'marker' we've been waiting for—the time for the arrival of the spacecraft . . . to take us home to . . . the literal Heavens. Our 22 years of classroom here on planet Earth is finally coming to conclusion—'graduation' from the Human Evolutionary Level. We are happily prepared to leave this world."[2]

In preparation for their journey, the acolytes wore identical yellow rings on the fourth finger of their left hands, brand-new Nike shoes, and black tracksuits emblazoned with triangular patches reading "Heaven's Gate Away Team."[3] They packed their belongings in duffel bags under their bunk beds, placed their passports and driver's licenses in their pockets, and ate a last meal of vodka and pudding or applesauce that was heavily laced with barbiturates. The medical examiners found a note at the scene describing the group's methodical plans for suicide. "Drink the vodka, eat a few teaspoons of pudding or applesauce, stir in the powder, eat it quickly, drink some more of the 'vodka medicine' and lay back and relax. After the breathing has slowed down use plastic bag to be sure."[4]

To facilitate the transfer to space in an orderly fashion, the group carried out waves of suicide. While the first cohort slept deeply after ingesting the pudding, companions wrapped plastic bags over their dying friends' heads to guarantee suffocation. The corpses were treated with reverence and covered with purple cloths. The next day, the second cohort of believers prepared similarly to exit their bodily vehicles. One day later, the last group overdosed, but there was no one left alive to wrap their heads in plastic or cover them with purple shrouds. Having anticipated this, they ingested extra medication (hydrocodone) to make sure. They all died, and their earthly vehicles were now empty.

The members left detailed records of their beliefs, which I will return to later. Their deaths were very troubling to me. It's one thing when members of a cult kill themselves far away in time and space; it's different when it happens next door. How could people be induced to do such things? What could make them choose castration, assist in killing their friends, and then join them in suicide? The specifics of their beliefs were odd, but people believe many outlandish things. As I struggled to understand what happened at Heaven's Gate, I realized that coercive persuasion is heartbreakingly common. Indeed, it haunted the twentieth century like a recurring nightmare.

★★★

To tell the story of how brainwashing developed, I will discuss a hundred years of observations in fields that range from military history to religious studies and from medicine to the social and behavioral sciences. Given how wide ranging the discussion will be, I'll provide a brief roadmap as a preview. It would be grueling to analyze all instances of brainwashing in the twentieth century; thus, I have focused on the occurrences that seem most informative. Similarly, I have omitted discussing things like hypnosis or mesmerism, which emerged in the eighteenth century rather than the twentieth.[5]

Prior to the twentieth century, coercive persuasion emanated from two unlikely locations—dungeons and churches. Over the centuries, torturers discovered that the psychological aspects of torture were as persuasive as the pain itself, and church leaders learned what factors make people more receptive to religious conversion. In most instances of twentieth-century brainwashing, one can find echoes of torture combined with ecstatic belief.

In the early twentieth century, Pavlov's research on behavioral conditioning and massive stress revolutionized coercive persuasion by introducing scientific experimentation. Pavlov made an unsavory bargain with

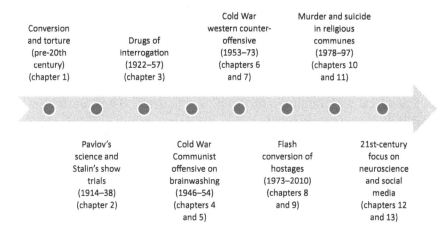

A time line of the evolution of brainwashing in the twentieth century outlined in this book.

Lenin and Stalin to help shape "the new Soviet man" in return for their generous support of his laboratory. Some historians trace the unusual confessions made during Stalin's show trials to the shadowy influence of Pavlov.

In World War II, neither the Nazis nor the Allies were interested in obtaining public confessions. Instead, they rushed to develop drugs that would coerce people to divulge information during interrogation. The military and police worked with doctors to repurpose drugs that had originally been developed to treat obstetrical and psychiatric patients. Meanwhile, academics tried to establish whether the drugs were reliable interrogation agents, and lawyers debated about the ethics of their use.

When the Cold War emerged, it was fought with religious fervor. The goal was almost as much to elicit the enemy's confession and conversion as it was to gain territory. Show trials resumed and defendants once again made improbable confessions.

During the Korean War, American prisoners of war returned home, scarred by their immersion in Korean and Chinese "thought reform" camps, and it was in this context that the term *brainwashing* was born. In reaction, during the 1950s and 1960s, governments frantically accelerated their research on sensory deprivation, psychedelic drugs, group indoctrination, and neuroscience. What kind of dark techniques did the Communists employ? How could we protect our troops from such techniques?

How could we pry information out of the enemy or, alternatively, could we delete memories from our soldiers' minds that were best not recollected? Memories were indeed destroyed using these techniques, and lives were lost.

Research during the Cold War proved that coercive persuasion could be a powerful tool, but it required time and patience. Then, in the 1970s, startling accounts surfaced of *sudden* persuasion among hostages who incomprehensibly started sympathizing with their captors. Data poured in across the world confirming such phenomena. Patricia Hearst's trial for bank robbery obsessed a nation absorbed in whether brainwashing existed and if it could exonerate a defendant.

Religious leaders in places as diverse as the jungles of Guyana and the wealthiest suburbs of America led their congregants to mass murder and suicide. How did they persuade their congregants to take such a course? What were the common practices in these groups that led them to such lethal ends?

A review of the twentieth century reveals countless instances of brainwashing, vague though the term may be. In the context of isolation from outside communication, sleep deprivation, exhaustion, and group confessions, people have been repeatedly persuaded to believe disinformation and to act self-destructively. A peculiarly diverse cast of characters has been involved with brainwashing's evolution in the twentieth century. This recurring nightmare has played out in large cities like Washington, New York, and Montreal, in small towns like Ferris, Texas, and in our most prominent universities. I fear that advances in neuroscience and social media in the twenty-first century will create even more powerful tools of persuasion. It is folly to ignore the perils.

★★★

Some of us write history as a form of therapy, an effort to understand our world. My previous book, *Anatomy of Malice*, studied the psychology of Nazi cabinet leaders.[6] After completing that book, I was left with a new question: how could a country be lured by a charismatic leader into committing atrocities and ultimately its own self-destruction? There are many possible answers, but I started musing about the idea of brainwashing as one explanation. I wrote this book to trace how brainwashing evolved in the twentieth century and to conjecture how it will develop in the twenty-first. My research has taken me to some surprisingly diverse sources: church leaders, criminals, spies, professors, doctors, and charitable foundations. They left records in published books, unpublished archives, and classified documents.

Finally, a confession. I started this work out of intellectual curiosity. Little did I suspect that in the archives I would find my colleagues, professional societies, and universities tied up in all this. This book describes a web of relationships and ideas shared by people who studied brainwashing. I admire some of their contributions and blanch at some of their deeds. Some were patriots and some were opportunists. Some were brilliant, some were rogues. The history of these individuals and the social forces they were caught up in gave birth to brainwashing.

DARK PERSUASION

CHAPTER ONE

Before Pavlov
Torture and Conversion

Persuasion is often more effectual than force.

—AESOP, sixth century BC

[It] is through this material brain that emissaries of God or of
the Devil—dictators, policemen, politicians, priests, physicians
and psychotherapists of various sorts—. . . try to work their will
on man.

—WILLIAM SARGANT, 1957

BRAINWASHING WAS "BORN" IN Pavlov's dog labs in the early days
of the Soviet Union, but it didn't appear out of thin air. While
Pavlov brought in scientific experimentation to intensify persuasion, brainwashing's roots can be traced to traditional practices
in torture and religious conversion.

Torture techniques have existed for centuries. Waterboarding, for instance, did not originate in 2003 at Abu Ghraib; it was used by the Japanese in World War II, the French in Algeria, and the British in Palestine.
It dates back even further than that to the Spanish Inquisition, when it was
called *toca* or *tortura del agua* or, more recently, *submarino*.[1]

There have always been concerns about the effectiveness of torture. When Senator Trent Lott was asked about America's use of torture in 2004, he retorted: "Interrogation is not a Sunday-school class. You don't get information that will save American lives by withholding pancakes."[2] Despite the senator's beliefs, we have almost two thousand years of observations suggesting that torture is unreliable. Not only is the validity of the revealed information questionable, some people are surprisingly resistant to torture. In the third century, Roman jurist Ulpian commented: "[It is a] delicate, dangerous, and deceptive thing. . . . For many persons have such strength of body and soul that they heed pain very little, so that there is no means of obtaining the truth from them . . . while others are so susceptible to pain that they will tell any lie rather than suffer it."[3]

Centuries later, the Catholic Church was also troubled about these differences in susceptibility to torture. It resolved the issue by arguing that individuals who withstood torture and did not confess must have been guilty criminals aided by the devil.[4] Thus, punish them anyway.

French court records from 1510 to 1750 suggest that torture was not guaranteed to elicit confessions, whether genuine or bogus. Out of 625 individuals tortured, 90 percent refused to confess despite waterboarding, crushing of joints, and other horrors.[5]

Interestingly, we have centuries of data teaching us that the *threat* of torture works just as well as the physical torture itself, without the mess. So, if one wants to extract a confession, one could just as well bring in the implements of torture without actually employing them. The victim tortures himself simply with his imagination.

Rulers commonly cite self-defense to justify torture. Stalin commented that since "bourgeois intelligence services use methods of physical influence against the representatives of the Socialist proletariat, . . . why [should] the Socialist intelligence service be more humanitarian toward the mad agents of the bourgeoisie?"[6] Currently, allegations of torture are met with outright denial, claims that it was a one-off instance of aberrant behavior, protestations that the reports were exaggerated, or else justifications that the techniques were not "real torture." This issue of "real torture," incidentally, surfaces repeatedly when authorities try to decide the degree of guilt or responsibility of an individual who caved in under the pressures of coercive persuasion. We will encounter that argument in circumstances as diverse as returning Korean War POWs in the 1950s and Patricia Hearst's trial for bank robbery in the 1970s.

Governments typically dismiss objections against torture as naïve idealism. In 1941 Nazi Germany, Admiral Wilhelm Canaris complained about the torture and improper treatment of Soviet POWs, but he was overruled by General Wilhelm Keitel, who sniped, "These objections . . . are inspired by a chivalric conception of war, but we are dealing here with an ideology. Therefore, I approve and will continue to use these methods."[7]

People often get fixated on torture's monstrous tools and/or the torturers' motivations. What did the torturer experience while inflicting pain and degrading the victim? Was it revenge, sexual stimulation, a gratifying release of pent-up rage? Those questions are important but beyond the scope of this book. We focus instead on the psychological tools that torturers have historically employed in most jurisdictions. Many of these techniques would be incorporated into twentieth-century coercive persuasion.

Before I began my research on brainwashing, I thought the Inquisition relied on standard techniques of torture—whipping, crushing, mangling. In fact, Inquisition practices varied from year to year and by locale. Judges also differed in their willingness to use torture; some were far more severe (*judices malitiosi*, or "hanging judges"). In some jurisdictions, the duration of torture was tightly specified; for example, the prisoner could be tortured only as long as it took the judge to recite one (or ten) Hail Mary's.[8]

The Inquisition's terror was augmented by its secrecy and the victim's inability to confront informers. The Church had elaborate rules and procedures for the Inquisition. While torture was allowed, spilling blood during torture was theoretically forbidden. Torture sessions were meticulously recorded by a secretary, and in many instances a physician was required to be present. Typically, sessions started with stock questions asking for a *discurso de su vida*, or a narrative of your life.[9] "Who are you? Why do you think you have been arrested?" Such required narratives are common in many of today's scenarios of coercive persuasion.

Curiously, it was forbidden to obtain confessions under torture. No, this was not a rule excluding torture but only the timing of torture; only on the day *after* torture was the victim allowed to make a formal confession. Another superficially humane rule was that a person could only be tortured once; when a torture session ended, it could not be resumed. Unfortunately, there was a loophole. If the torture session was merely "suspended," it could resume on another date.[10] Suspension could last for years while people waited, marinating in anxiety, knowing they were under suspicion.

Case histories of torture give vivid evidence of the techniques used to persuade the victim. Historian Carlo Ginzburg recounts one riveting case from sixteenth-century Italy. A miller named Menocchio was an eccentric outspoken man who openly scorned the Church. He held pantheistic beliefs that he shared all too readily, denied the virgin birth of Jesus, and read prohibited books. Anticipating that he would be denounced, Menocchio asked his friends what to do during interrogation. They advised him not to talk too much; remember, they said, the tongue is enemy of the neck.[11]

His first set of interrogations began on February 7, 1584. Disregarding his friends' advice, he incautiously told the Inquisition his beliefs about the beginning of time: "In my opinion, all was chaos, that is, earth, air, water, and fire were mixed together; and out of that bulk a mass formed—just as cheese is made out of milk—and worms appeared in it, and these were the angels. . . . And among that number of angels, there was also God." The inquisitors interrogated him off and on for two years, admonished him to stop blaspheming, and released him from prison in 1586. However, he continued making imprudent public comments and was rearrested in 1599 as a lapsed heretic. This time, the interrogation was unrelenting and months later, he finally conceded that his beliefs were false. The confession did him no good. He was condemned as a heretic and burned alive.[12]

Menocchio's history demonstrates that the Inquisition was not impatient, nor did it rush to employ instruments of torture. Rather, it firmly conveyed to poor Menocchio that there was no escape, and that virtually every word he uttered during his interrogation would be carefully examined by the Holy Office. Had he listened to his friends' advice to keep his mouth shut, the outcome might have been better, but he offered too much. Ginzburg quotes some of the Inquisition's transcript.

> VICAR GENERAL: You say that our souls return to the majesty of God, and you have already stated that God is nothing other than air, earth, fire, and water: how then can these souls return to the majesty of God? . . .
> MENOCCHIO: I don't know. I believe that we men all have a spirit from God. . . .
> VICAR GENERAL: Do you mean that this spirit of God is the one born from that chaos?
> MENOCCHIO: I don't know.
> VICAR GENERAL: Confess the truth and resolve this question; namely, if you believe that souls return to the majesty of God, and that God is air, water, earth, and fire, how then do they return to the majesty of God?[13]

There is a quality to this interrogation that will become familiar as we examine interrogation techniques employed centuries later in so many countries across the world. It is the inexorable weight of a glacier pressing slowly forward.

The practices of the Inquisition bore no resemblance to our ideas of law. There was no presumed innocence; if people were denounced and apprehended, they must have been guilty. Often, the inquisitors did not even bother to disclose the reasons for arrest. Instead, they told prisoners to search their conscience for their sins and confess the truth. Since the defendant's guilt was already established (at least to the Church's satisfaction), the only purpose of an eventual trial was to extirpate heresy, to obtain a very public confession, and submit to authority. Stalin's show trials very much followed in this tradition.

Many of the Inquisition's techniques for eliciting confessions were also used by the czarist Okhrana (secret police).[14] Prisoners were held indefinitely under severe conditions because interrogators observed that confessions were easier to obtain when the prisoner was exhausted, confused, and anxious from a combination of sleep deprivation and malnutrition. While the Okhrana could precisely control the amount of sleep deprivation in jail, the police also let their anxious suspects do the work of self-torment at home, thereby continuing the sleep disruption. Bombarded with contradictory instructions, promises, and threats, prisoners became increasingly confused. As English psychiatrist William Sargant observed, the goal was to try to make prisoners feel so guilty that they longed to be punished to achieve eventual salvation.[15] Sargant's observation harkens back to the Inquisition, which saw its role as punishing in order to achieve atonement through public humiliation.[16]

In the 1970s, the Khmer Rouge developed a primer for novice torturers. Prisoners were interrogated repeatedly and forced to continually write and rewrite confessions. The goal was to obtain adequate confessions before the prisoners' execution. The "Interrogator's Manual" described how this was to be done. Above all else, the novice torturers were instructed, "don't be hasty." More detailed instructions included the following: "Reassure them by giving them something, some food for instance. . . . Terrify them, confuse them in clever ways. Arrange little ploys to make them give up any hope that they will . . . be able to survive. . . . Don't step up the pressure all the time. Say something like 'Don't make us torture you or torture you severely. It's bad for your health, and it makes it harder for us to deal with each other in the future.' If they reveal small

Table 1. Common features of torture and coercive persuasion

Terror
Sleep deprivation
Diaries and confessions
Isolation from family and friends
Patience of the interrogator
Interrogator alternates kindness and brutality
Secrecy
No legal defense

---

matters, encourage them to reveal the big ones. Tell them that if they reveal important matters, . . . [we] will be lenient with them."[17]

For millennia, cultures have relied on torture as an instrument of persuasion. Other than torture's use of agonizing pain, many of its components are discernable in twentieth-century instances of coercive persuasion (see table 1).

★★★

In addition to its origins in torture, brainwashing can trace its roots to traditions in religious conversion. It may seem peculiar that a book on brainwashing discusses religious conversion, but conversions come in many
sizes and flavors—sudden or gradual, grounded in belief or convenience,
brought about by individual decisions or by acts of State. Conversions are
heterogeneous, and some conversions are in fact accompanied by varying
amounts of coercion.

State-mandated conversions have swept up countless millions. Some
people choose to die rather than convert; some go into exile; some adopt
the external appearances of having converted but surreptitiously hold onto
their original faith. Many go along with imposed conversion out of necessity, spinelessness, opportunism, or religious indifference, and some even
come to cherish their new faith.[18]

When conversions are made by personal choice, they are still shaped
by social factors, and here we start to recognize some features shared
with brainwashing.[19] To be sure, brainwashing techniques are more struc-
tured and rigid, commonly entailing physical isolation, fatigue, and abuse.
The impact of these features is amplified when groups exploit individuals' need for approval and their fear of rejection. Brainwashing programs
also include periods of calculated kindness to disarm the subject, as well as
periods of intense study or indoctrination. Despite its dark components,

brainwashing, like conversion, offers the promise of redemption and re-birth into a new social group, frequently after a public confession.

The terror found in coercive persuasion can also accompany instances of religious conversion. Jonathan Edwards's 1741 sermon "Sinners in the Hands of an Angry God" paints a chilling image, even if one is not a be-liever. During such sermons, people became so terrified that they clung to their seats to keep from literally slipping into hell.[20] "God . . . holds you over the pit of hell, much as one holds a spider, or some loathsome insect. . . . The bow of God's wrath is bent, and the arrow made ready on the string, and justice bends the arrow at your heart and strains the bow, and it is nothing but the mere pleasure of God, and that of an angry God, without any promise or obligation, that keeps the arrow one moment from being drunk with your blood."[21]

Both brainwashing and religious conversion rely on strong group pressure. They target people who are exhausted and dejected from exten-sive self-criticism, doubt, fear, and guilt. When potential converts aban-don their old ways of thinking, they feel relief, gratitude, and zeal. They sense a new beginning with a cleansed life. These aspects of conversion are the same whether one is converting to a common established belief or to an uncommon new one. Churches grow and morph; today's traditional or "heritage" church probably was revolutionary generations ago.[22]

There is a long tradition of studying the circumstances that bring people closer to conversion, particularly in the context of revivalist or evangelical churches. In 1859, the Reverend George Salmon observed the trembling, weeping, and swooning that accompanied revival movements of his time and called for empirical studies of conversion to learn how "the mind and body act on one another."[23]

Edwin Starbuck followed Salmon's lead some forty years later with a groundbreaking study of 137 individuals who had conversion experiences, mainly at revival meetings. There were many features common to all the converts. The age of conversion was usually in adolescence or in the twen-ties—as will be seen later, this is also the typical age of victims of brain-washing. Starbuck found that the typical conversion experience was pre-ceded by certain vulnerability factors—feelings of depression, sadness, or rumination (in 70-90 percent of his sample) as well as loss of sleep and appetite.[24]

Starbuck reported that religious conversion was not usually perma-nent. In men, only about 25 percent had a permanent conversion and in women, the rates were about 15 percent.[25] Contemporary studies likewise report the transitory nature of conversion. For example, few converts to the Unification Church remain faithful in the long run. In one cohort of recent converts, only 5 percent were still active in the church after a year.[26] In fact, there is a constant churning in church membership across all denominations, new or old. The key is whether there is freedom of movement in and out of the group. That freedom does not exist in cases of brainwashing.

Writing around the same time as Starbuck, James Leuba observed that those who converted had a sense of sin and a conviction that there was something profoundly missing in their life. He noted that the converted person feels profound joy but also a peculiar sense of passivity regarding the whole process. "They are lookers-on; they attend as spectators the drama that is being played in their consciousness, just as a patient observes . . . the development of his disease."[27]

Conversion offers a path out of the thicket of one's current life. It can be facilitated by physical activities like fasting, vigils, drugs, dancing, and intense exercise. It is also easier if new converts distance themselves from the influence of their families and former friends.[28] In brainwashing, we find similar features, but they have been twisted (starvation, sleep deprivation, drugs, exhaustion, social isolation).

Religious conversion practices have been studied extensively with reference to John Wesley's Methodism—the new religion of the eighteenth century. As a small boy, Wesley quite literally experienced salvation. A fire trapped him on the top floor of his house until he was rescued at the last moment. Years later, at a time of personal disappointment, he found salvation in the belief that Christ had taken away his sins. When he was ordained, he led a small group that prayed for three hours every day, fasted regularly, and visited prisoners to bring them comfort. He found strength in hymns and kept a meticulous diary, hourly charting his religious devotion on a scale from 1 to 9. Perhaps the charting on a 1 to 9 scale was a tad unusual, but in other respects, the faith he espoused does not sound so unusual to us in the twenty-first century.

Wesley took his message of salvation on the road, conducting open-air services. He preached of the joys of a warm heart, singing, fervent prayer, and public confession. His preaching riveted audiences. One of his diary entries testifies to his prowess as a preacher: "Another person dropped down, close to the one who was a strong asserter of the contrary doctrine. While he stood astonished at the sight, a little boy who stood near him was seized in the same manner. A young man who stood up behind him fixed his eyes on him, and . . . soon began to roar out and beat himself against the ground, so that six men could scarcely hold him."[29]

Wesley set up classes for his early followers, urging them to follow "the method"—hence the name "Methodists." Members met regularly in small groups to sing, pray, and confess, hoping thereby to reach salvation. Because conversion was facilitated by the awareness of one's own sins, followers were repeatedly urged to confess their lapses. The confessions could be given orally in front of a group or in written diaries submitted to the authorities.[30] Wesley's followers received formulaic instructions about how to structure their confessions. "What known sins have you committed since our last meeting? What temptations have you met with? How were you delivered? What have you thought, said or done of which you doubt whether it be sin or not? Have you nothing you desire to keep secret?"[31]

Psychiatry has long been interested in the nature of conversion, and Wesley fascinated British psychiatrist William Sargant (1907–88), an influential thinker about brainwashing. His book *Battle for the Mind*, first published in 1957, ranges widely, from his studies of Pavlov to his ideas about the nature of confession. The book's subtitles give a flavor of his interests ("A Physiology of Conversion and Brain-washing" and "How Evangelists, Psychiatrists, Politicians, and Medicine Men Can Change Your Beliefs and Behavior"). Sargant was raised in a strict Methodist family and struggled against his family's assumption that he would become a parson. Instead, he chose psychiatry but maintained a special interest in conversion and the Methodist Church for the rest of his life.[32]

Sargant pops up repeatedly in this book. His ideas about persuasion and religious conversion preoccupied him for decades. He used drugs to restore memories to emotionally battered troops in World War II. The drugs seemed to work, but he found that many of the elicited memories were false. For the rest of his life, he mused about whether drugs can extract truth and how intense emotional excitement can lead to persistent behavioral changes.

Sargant is alleged to have been the in-house psychiatrist with the British intelligence agency MI5. Furthermore, he was a consultant to American and Canadian investigators studying brainwashing. He also provided psychiatric testimony in criminal cases that raised brainwashing as a mitigating defense. Commenting about Sargant's diverse interests and activities, psychopharmacologist Malcolm Lader remarked, "There was a whiff of sulphur about him."[33] I mention all this not just because it is inter-

William Sargant. (Courtesy of Wellcome Library
Archives, PPWWS/A/19: box 2.)

esting, but because it helps provide context for his diverse comments about
potential links between religious conversion and brainwashing.

Sargant began his book by referring to Pavlov's discoveries, suggesting
that they formed the foundation of Soviet and Chinese interrogation and
brainwashing programs. He emphasized that stress and debilitating conditions impair brain functioning, thereby making subjects more susceptible
to conversion or caving in under interrogation. He was intrigued about
the neural aspects of religious belief or, as he put it, the "mechanisms involved in the fixing or destroying of . . . beliefs in the human brain." To
Sargant's way of thinking, religious conversion relied on suggestibility,
which in turn could be enhanced by certain actions: "The leaders of successful faiths have never . . . dispensed entirely with physiological weapons
in their attempts to confer spiritual grace. . . . Fasting, chastening of the
flesh . . . , regulation of breathing, disclosure of awesome mysteries, drum-
ming, dancing, singing, inducement of panic, fear, . . . incense, intoxicant
drugs — these are only some of the many methods used to modify normal
brain functions for religious purposes."[34]

He was keen on demonstrating that conversion occurs during physical debilitation. Reflecting on Saul's conversion on the road to Damascus, he pointed out that many factors were at work. After all, Acts 9:9 plainly states that Saul's conversion was preceded by three days during which he "neither ate nor drank." With this dollop of reductionism, Sargant went on to comment about the power of conversion. Citing William James, Sargant notes approvingly, "Emotional occasions, especially violent ones, are extremely potent in precipitating mental rearrangements. The sudden and explosive ways in which love, jealousy, guilt, fear, remorse or anger can seize upon one are known to everybody. Hope, happiness, security, resolve, emotions characteristic of conversion, can be equally explosive. And *emotions that come in this explosive way seldom leave things as they found them.*"[35]

Although William James would have appreciated Sargant's interests in religion, he would have been put off by Sargant's reductionism.[36] It is unfair to paint Sargant as a kneejerk scientific reductionist, but he was deeply preoccupied with the physiological states that could trigger conversion experiences. He was convinced that terror, guilt, and anxiety were absolutely crucial for conversion experiences and suggested that scientists could learn a great deal about brainwashing and eliciting confessions by studying eighteenth-century American revivalism.[37]

Some of Sargant's ideas, when given a different spin, are consonant with contemporary anthropological insights. Tanya Luhrmann's insightful book about contemporary evangelicals notes that religious experience is commonly accompanied by periods of silence, fasting, hard labor, repetitive hymns, and isolation. Furthermore, converts frequently complete narratives about personal experience of crisis, humiliation, and despair. Luhrmann makes a subtle point about belief, biology, and society that brings us directly back to Sargant's interests in the neurophysiology of religious conversion. "I believe that if God speaks, God's voice is heard through human minds constrained by their biology and shaped by their social community."[38]

★★★

Some may take offense that I have grouped brainwashing, torture, and religious conversion in one chapter. The intent was to point to a common heritage and overlapping interests. However, I have to acknowledge that psychiatrists and psychologists have a unique exposure to the dark side of religious belief. Conversion isn't always positive. I've treated patients who have blinded themselves in religious frenzy or castrated themselves because of guilt over sexual longings.

Psychiatrist John Clark was pilloried because he warned about the risks of cults that regard science and medicine as the enemy.[39] Although he was quick to say that people have the right to their opinions and that cults could well serve as leavening agents in a stagnant culture, critics remember him for his forceful criticisms of absolutist groups that embrace magic and faith healing. He and other clinicians based their observations on their patients who were ex-cult members. Needless to say, people who are happy with their conversion to these new sects do not come to see clinicians. Nonetheless, the clinicians' warnings would become tragically prophetic in the case of some new religious groups.

This chapter was an interlude. We paused here for an overview of persuasion techniques used by torturers and religious groups. With the arrival of the twentieth century, scientific experimentation was coming.

PART I

Government and Academe

CHAPTER TWO

Pavlov's Dogs and the
Soviet Show Trials

Soviet psychology is concerned with adaptations of the . . .
concepts of Pavlov, . . . the belief that men can deliberately be
made to develop predesigned types of thought and behavior
under appropriately controlled environmental conditions.

—CENTRAL INTELLIGENCE AGENCY

THE DOGS WERE RESTLESS. Penned in their cages in the basement of the Institute of Experimental Medicine, they were lonely and weary from their daytime jobs in the professor's laboratory. But it wasn't the dark or the isolation or fatigue that got to them. It was the incessant dripping and lapping of water on the floor of their kennel.

September 22, 1924, started out as a fairly typical day in Leningrad, overcast and raining, but the rain increased throughout the day until the Neva River once again overran its embankment. This time the flood would become the largest in centuries—and it was heading straight for the dogs.

As the water level in the kennel rose, the dogs started barking. At first only their paws sloshed around in the chilly water, but as the hours went by, the water covered their bellies and shoulders until they were half floating in their cages, their nostrils pressed anxiously against the top wire mesh. They howled in fear and desperately snuffled the air while they could get it.

At the last moment, a dog handler raced through the flooded streets to the institute, where he encountered chaos—panicked dogs, floating cages, and the fetid water of the Neva. One by one, he rescued the dogs, but to get them out of their cages, he had to first force their heads under the water. The dogs resisted out of panic.

The dogs were never the same. Their dispositions changed dramatically: the meek became aggressive and the gregarious became shy. It was as if an entirely new "being" inhabited each dog. This was bad enough, but the researchers were also struck by the fact that the dogs had forgotten all the complex learning they had been taught in the laboratory. The dogs' memories were wiped clean.

The staff talked about the dogs' memory loss for weeks and the scientists wrote their colleagues about this strange phenomenon.[1] The occurrence might have been dismissed as a curiosity except that it took place in the laboratory of the Nobel laureate Ivan Pavlov, who had built his career on meticulous observation and experimentation with dogs. For the rest of his life, he talked about the flood, and his comments about traumatic stress and memory reverberated widely, given his relationship with Russia's Communist leaders.

Pavlov demonstrated what every dog owner knows—dogs *learn*—but he also showed how learning affected the dogs' physiological responses. His dogs were irreplaceable to him, and he thought of them as having distinct personalities; in his scientific talks he even referred to them by name ("Beka was a quick learner"; "John was timid"). Pavlov was such an astute trainer that he could teach a dog to respond to a particular musical tone— for example, middle C—but to ignore other notes.

Outside of the laboratory, Pavlov was also an astute observer of Russian society. He disdained the autocratic and incompetent czarist rule but felt this legacy was modifiable.[2] Despite his distaste for the czarist past, he also disparaged the Russian Revolution, partially because he almost starved during the ensuing chaos. While Pavlov was quite open about his political opinions, he was safe from retaliation because he was the first Russian to receive the Nobel Prize in medicine (1904), and the Soviets pointed to him with pride. Like today's scientists, he used his prominence as a bargaining chip to obtain more resources for his laboratory. Even in the midst of the

Ivan Petrovich Pavlov (*center*) in his laboratory, 1914.
(Snark / Art Resource, NY.)

country's severe poverty, his laboratory expanded. As Pavlov begrudgingly acknowledged, "Yes, you must give our barbarians one thing: they understand the value of science."[3]

Although Pavlov wasn't a Communist, he shared certain beliefs with the Communist Party. He was a materialist who believed there was no soul or spiritual uniqueness in human beings. That belief was an advantage in a state that railed against religion. Pavlov was convinced his research on dogs applied to people as well, that change was possible. Given sufficient scientific attention to detail, one could surmount the legacy of centuries of repressive superstitious czarist rule.

The Communists applauded these ideas. In October 1919, Lenin visited Pavlov at the Institute of Experimental Medicine. He stayed for two hours; it was more than just a "photo-op" visit. Lenin hoped that Pavlov's experiments could bolster the State's efforts to mold the New Man. As recounted by one of Pavlov's colleagues, Lenin described the challenges of building the new world of Communism and asked Pavlov's advice. How could he control individualism and shape human behavior so that it would conform to Communist thinking?

PAVLOV: "Do you mean that you would like to standardize the population of Russia? Make them all behave in the same way?"

LENIN: "Exactly. . . . That's what I want . . . and you must help us
. . . by your studies of human behavior."[4]

Lenin was fascinated when Pavlov described the details of how he was
able to shape dogs' behaviors. He immediately grasped the implications of
Pavlov's studies:

LENIN: "Does this mean that hereditary factors can be overcome
by proper education?"
PAVLOV: "Under certain conditions—yes. They can be overcome.
. . . Conditioned reflexes can abolish unconditioned reflexes, or, as
they are called, natural instinct."
LENIN: "That's fine. Excellent. That's exactly what I wanted to
know."[5]

Lenin augmented funding to Pavlov's institute and gave him access to
psychiatric patients so he could test his dog theories on humans. Pavlov
began studying sleep, hypnosis, and how stress affects people of different
temperaments. He pointed out that one could treat even severely resistant patients; all that was required was patience and systematic investigation: "Man is of course a system—roughly speaking, a machine. . . . The
method of investigating the system of man is precisely the same as that of
any other system; decomposition into parts, study of the significance of
each part, study of the connections of the parts, study of the relations with
the environment."[6]

Pavlov observed that intense stress elicits predictable responses. When
dogs were presented with a stimulus that they didn't know how to respond
to or were given inconsistent or conflicting commands, their behavior deteriorated into what he called "transmarginal collapse." Every dog had its
breaking point. In the face of transmarginal collapse, their dispositions
changed: outgoing dogs became shy, shy ones became aggressive. Furthermore, after such collapse, the dogs even changed their preferences for
people: they became friendly to keepers they had previously disliked and
vice versa. In the face of intense stress, some dogs became so quiet they
looked like they were in a hypnotic trance, and Pavlov viewed this behavior as a coping strategy. Pavlov reported that his techniques could reliably
produce experimental neurosis or even psychosis and that such experiments could help evaluate new treatments. He experimented with drugs
(bromides) to make dogs more tractable in such circumstances.[7]

In his studies on people, Pavlov noted that the severely traumatized were not only exhausted but also suggestible, particularly when they were given conflicting instructions. Pavlov went back and forth from the psychiatric hospital to the dog lab, observing that trauma left a hidden vulnerability.

Two months after the severe flood, when his dogs had finally settled down and learned new behaviors, he intentionally exposed one of them to "a small stream of water . . . allowed to trickle noiselessly into the animal's room and form a pool on the floor."[8] The dog froze. In the ensuing days his temperament changed, and he again forgot his learned behaviors.[9] This did not go unnoticed.

After Lenin's death, Pavlov maintained strong ties with the government. The Soviet politician Nikolai Bukharin noted, "I know that he does not sing the '*internationale*.' But . . . he is the leading physiologist in the world, a materialist, and despite all his grumbling, ideologically . . . he is working for us."[10]

Many of Pavlov's ideas helped him garner Stalin's support. In addition to believing that behavior was modifiable, Pavlov thought that acquired behaviors could be inherited. This view of genetics corresponded with Stalin's views, and Pavlov's findings were disseminated throughout the Soviet Union.[11] Stalin vociferously attacked those who said Pavlov's work only applied to animals.[12]

By the end of his life, Pavlov was a professor at the Leningrad Military Medical Academy. The State supported Pavlov's lab handsomely, employing 357 assistants to work on his projects and even renaming the village where his institute was based Pavlova.[13] In 1935, speaking to a group of international physiologists meeting within the walls of the Kremlin, Pavlov described the complex nature of his relationship with the State: "As you know, I am an experimenter from head to foot. . . . Our government is also an experimenter, only on an incomparably higher plane. I passionately desire to . . . see the victorious completion of this historical social experiment."[14]

From traumatized dogs, Pavlov derived a theory of traumatic disintegration, which he then studied in humans. Early Communist leaders were quite taken by Pavlov's ideas, intrigued with the possibility that his techniques could help them shape the new Russia. As *Pravda* put it, Pavlov helped them master nature and achieve unlimited power over the human brain.[15] Stalin's show trials and purges brought millions of people into situations of extreme stress, and most of them disintegrated under the interrogations—exactly as Pavlov had predicted. Pavlov was lucky enough to die a natural death in 1936, just as those show trials were beginning.

★★★

Stalin protected Pavlov despite his pattern of dealing with dissent—whether real or imagined—through torture, exile, or execution. He particularly targeted his closest associates. Of the thirty-three candidate and full members of the Politburo from 1919 to 1938, only a minority survived his purges. The rest were executed, killed themselves, died in prison, or died under questionable circumstances.[16] In 1934, the Central Committee had 139 members and deputy members. By 1938, 90 had been shot or jailed. As Nikita Khrushchev pointed out years later, "Only about ten were brought to trial, the others were shot either after secret trial, or with no trial at all."[17] Stalin also targeted the military, executing more high-ranking military leaders than were killed in all of World War II.[18] His retribution extended beyond the defendants, snaring their spouses, children, and relatives. Somehow, Pavlov escaped Stalin's suspiciousness.

The economy was in ruins from the five-year Russian civil war that followed the Bolshevik seizure of power. Millions died during those years from combat, starvation, typhus, or from Cheka (secret police) executions of "enemies of the people." Industrial and agricultural production collapsed. Command economy interventions like banning private enterprise and rationing of food were failures, kindling resentment and rebellion. In reaction, Soviet economic policies lurched from liberalizing economic regulations to imposing even stricter economic controls. If production declined or the economy was criticized, Stalin blamed it on treason and sabotage rather than his policies.

The international reverberations of the revolution also stoked Stalin's suspiciousness. Stalin had lurking worries that spies had infiltrated the country and that they would never stop until Communism was defeated. His paranoia was also fueled by the looming nightmare of Hitler's rise in Germany. Stalin felt that vigilance and suspicion were crucial for the survival of the Soviet State, noting, "[We] must of necessity be steeped in poison and gall and should not believe in anyone."[19] As the historian Arch Getty perceptively noted: "Criticism was the same as opposition; opposition inevitably implied conspiracy; conspiracy meant treason. Algebraically, therefore, the slightest opposition to the regime, or failure to report such opposition, was tantamount to terrorism."[20]

In this context of a disastrous economy and a beleaguered state, public trials of traitors were enormous media events that served as an excellent distraction from the country's troubles. There was no pretense of dispas-

sionate inquiry. Instead, the courtrooms were decked out in banners reading "TO THE MAD DOGS—A DOG'S DEATH."[21] Courtroom observers reported extraordinary, bizarre confessions, and speculated that the Soviets
had mastered some secret technique for persuading defendants to incriminate themselves. Many suspected that this was Pavlov's handiwork, and
from the show trials of the 1930s to today, Pavlov's name is associated with
brainwashing.

From 1936 to 1938, roughly 1 million people were killed in the Great
Purge, also known as the Great Terror. Stalin's head of the NKVD (Soviet
secret police) commented memorably: "If during this operation an extra
thousand people will be shot, that is not such a big deal."[22] An amaz-
ing mélange of people were swept away in a whirlwind of violence—
intellectuals, Party leaders, peasants, foreigners, and anyone else who
could be branded as anti-Soviet.

Most were killed or sent to the gulag by extrajudicial officers who fulfilled quotas for imprisonment and execution assigned by Stalin.[23] Party
leaders who refused to confess were summarily executed. Typically, they
simply disappeared, but sometimes there were announcements of the cor-
rective effect of their execution. There was also an epidemic of fatal "heart
disease" in the former leaders. Sergo Ordzhonikidze (commissar for heavy
industry) shot himself, but the press announced, "While he was having his
afternoon rest, he suddenly fell ill and a few minutes later died of paralysis
of the heart."[24] When the government acknowledged that some had killed
themselves, Stalin declared that suicide meant people had admitted their
guilt and were merely trying to "cover their tracks" by deceiving the Party
even further.[25]

The routine trials were brief twenty-minute affairs. Even the major
trials rarely lasted beyond a few days. During these major show trials,
there was a religious aura surrounding the courtroom—a kind of public
auto-da-fé to unmask the defendants' betrayal. The pale, nervous prisoners marched into the courtroom, regarding the audience with haunted
eyes. Prosecutor Andrey Vyshinsky hurled insults, calling them "human
garbage, beasts in human form, . . . hideous scoundrels, dregs and scum"
and demanded that the court "crush that cursed reptile."[26] His trial sum-
mations were inflammatory masterpieces. "The guileful enemy must not
be spared. . . . The entire people is trembling with rage. And I, too, as a
representative of the State Prosecutor's office, add my indignant and outraged voice of a State Prosecutor to the roar of the millions! I demand that
the mad dogs be shot—every single one of them!"[27]

The prosecutors realized that if the defendant confessed, there would be no need to try the case, to prove the facts. Instead, one needed only the prosecutor's allegations and the prisoner's confession.[28] No problematic defense cross-examination would be encountered, and the prosecutor's allegations would be unchallenged. This made for efficiency in the proceedings and better drama. But how could you persuade people to confess?

Three trials garnered the most attention. In August 1936, sixteen defendants were tried. They met privately with Stalin and agreed to publicly confess and plead guilty if Stalin promised them clemency. Stalin agreed, the trial proceeded—and then they were promptly shot. In January 1938, seventeen more defendants confessed but this time did not ask for mercy. Indeed, one of the defendants said: "I do not need leniency. The proletarian court should not and cannot spare my life. . . . I want one thing: to calmly mount the execution block and wash away the stain of a traitor to the motherland with my blood."[29] The third trial in March 1938 snared twenty-one defendants, including, most prominently, Bukharin.

The public show trials were reserved for the crème de la crème of Party leaders who willingly confessed to bizarre conspiracies—building spy networks, sabotaging industries, wrecking the economy, trying to overthrow Stalin and replace him with Trotsky. The allegations ranged from unlikely to preposterous. Some Jewish Communist Party leaders, for instance, were charged with collaborating with the Gestapo.[30] Other Party members confessed to sabotaging the agricultural industry by spreading plague among pigs or causing anemia in horses from Byelorussia.[31]

George Orwell satirized the improbable allegations by asking readers to imagine an England in 1938 where Left was Right and Right was Left, where Neville Chamberlain ruled like Stalin and feared an exiled Trotsky-like Winston Churchill. "Mr. Winston Churchill, now in exile . . . , is plotting to overthrow the British Empire. . . . Almost every day some dastardly act of sabotage is laid bare—sometimes a plot to blow up the House of Lords, sometimes an outbreak of foot-and-mouth disease in the Royal racing stables. Eighty percent of the Beefeaters in the Tower [of London] are discovered to be [enemy] agents. . . . And meanwhile the Churchillites . . . never cease from proclaiming that it is *they* who are the . . . [authentic leaders]."[32] As far-fetched as the satire was, the events in Russia were equally improbable.

Stalin's followers regarded him as the font of wisdom, the living embodiment of the Communist revolution. One prominent Soviet author proclaimed ecstatically: "I want to howl, roar, shriek, bawl with rapture at the thought we are living in the days of the most glorious . . . incomparable

Stalin! . . . O great Stalin! Thou art the bright Sun of the people, The Sun of our times that never sets."[33]

Meanwhile, Trotsky warned about the perils of deifying Stalin in a cautionary statement that could just as well apply to some contemporary leaders: "All of these people, starting with Stalin, have been corrupted by their immunity from control or punishment. . . . Since no one dares to criticize him, Stalin gradually has grown unaccustomed to controlling himself."[34]

The Party encouraged people to suppress their doubts and have faith that justice was being done even as more and more people were drawn into the maelstrom of the trials. When high Party officials were removed, documents and photos were doctored accordingly, as Orwell described so vividly in *1984*. One famous photo showed the director of NKVD (Nikolai Yezhov) and Stalin in a friendly pose. After Yezhov himself was purged, he was removed from the photograph, a primitive foreshadowing of what could be done now with deep fakes of news (see figure next page).

Communist sympathizers in the West supported Stalin's actions, praising him for his progressiveness. They regarded the Communist Party as infallible and supported the trials and executions as a means of consolidating the power of the State. Maxim Gorky viewed the labor camps as a "torch of progress" that would cleanse Russia of its repulsive past.[35] Others felt that truth and morality needed to be subservient to the greater good if the Soviet State were to survive. In short, the Stalinists felt that "truth" was a bourgeois luxury.[36] The interrogator Ivanov argues this point in *Darkness at Noon:* "A collective aim justifies all means, and not only allows, but demands, that the individual should in every way be subordinated and sacrificed to the community—which may dispose of it as an experimentation rabbit or a sacrificial lamb."[37]

Courtroom observers had startlingly different impressions. Some presumably astute observers, including *New York Times* reporter Walter Duranty, believed the prisoners' confessions and the prosecutors' allegations. He attributed the confessions to the "stress of a guilty conscience [and] . . . the semi-religious nature of Bolshevist fanaticism, which leads to breast-beating and cries of 'Mea maxima culpa,' when convicted of sin."[38] After reading Duranty's columns, one American pro-Stalinist told his friend that he "could not doubt . . . that such people were . . . mad dogs, criminal oppositionists, heretics, unbelievers, seditionists, driven to conspiracy against the State and murder of the leaders because they had gone against the Party."[39] Duranty's coverage of the show trials has been roundly con-

Kliment Voroshilov, Vyacheslav Molotov, Joseph Stalin, and Nikolai
Yezhov walking along the banks of the Moscow-Volga Canal, April 1937.
(F. Kislov. Part of the David King Collection. Purchased from David King
by Tate Archive 2016. Presented to Tate Archive by David King 2016 /
© Tate, London / Art Resource, NY.)

demned, so much so that years later, the *New York Times* described his reporting as "some of the worst reporting to appear in this newspaper."[40]
Unfortunately, that reassessment came too late to help the victims of the
show trials.

Other reporters were also taken in by the trials, but even Stalin's supporters found the defendants' behavior peculiar. Writing for the *New York
Times*, Harold Denny reported the defendants' incomprehensible behavior: "They supplement their full confessions with eager testimony against
themselves and against each other. They spring to their feet like bright
pupils glad to show how much they know. . . . These doomed men are
marching toward the firing squad. . . . Perhaps it is part of the traditional
Slavic-Oriental indifference to death. One knows that confessions can be
elicited by various subtle pressure. . . . But these defendants do not testify
like men coerced."[41]

The American ambassador Joseph E. Davies believed that the trials

Voroshilov, Molotov, and Stalin: Yezhov has been removed from the original image. (F. Kislov. Part of the David King Collection. Purchased from David King by Tate Archive 2016. Presented to Tate Archive by David King 2016 / © Tate, London / Art Resource, NY.)

demonstrated proof of treason.[42] Writing to his daughter, Davies claimed that his many years as a lawyer qualified him to assess the validity of the testimony and that it indicated the Kremlin's fears were well justified.[43] Other, more sentient observers found the trials unconvincing. American career diplomat Charles Bohlen criticized Davies's naïveté, saying: "I still blush when I think of some of the telegrams he sent to the State Department about the trial."[44]

More thoughtful onlookers were transfixed by the improbable confessions and wanted to know how on earth the Communists had persuaded the defendants to condemn themselves. The show trials were the origin of the twentieth century's preoccupation with what would come to be known as brainwashing.

The Nazis were unnerved by the trials, which suggested that Stalin had developed a new weapon of dark persuasion. Ten years after the show trials, Deputy Führer Rudolf Hess feared that Stalin's fiendish techniques might be used against him. Writing from his jail cell in Nuremberg, Hess

Joseph Stalin, Nikolai Bukharin, Sergo Ordzhonikidze, and
Jānis Rudzutaks on the tribune of the Vladimir Lenin Mausoleum,
Moscow's Red Square, November 7, 1929, celebrating the twelfth
anniversary of the 1917 revolution. None of the three survived
Stalin's purges. (Adoc-photos / Art Resource, NY.)

complained that people around him seemed strange and had glassy, dreamy
eyes, just like the defendants in the Moscow show trials.[45]

★★★

Nikolai Bukharin was the principal target of the third show trial. A prominent Marxist economist, head of Comintern, and newspaper editor, he was
one of the oldest and most popular of the Old Bolsheviks. Lenin viewed
him as the Party's golden boy. From Stalin's perspective, Bukharin might
as well have been wearing a target on his back. Stalin toyed with Bukharin, putting him on trial, releasing him, reinterrogating him, and then re-
trying him. During his extensive imprisonment, Bukharin wrote lengthy
manuscripts and letters that provide a detailed depiction of interrogation
and confession, resistance and yielding.

Bukharin was charged with plotting to assassinate Lenin and Stalin in
order to give Russian territories to Germany, Japan, and Great Britain.

The charges were absurd, so the world was shocked when Bukharin confessed. He wrote that he did not recall any of the plotting but accepted responsibility for it all the same because the only thing positive and enduring was the Soviet Union—something well worth dying for.[46]

Bukharin wrote Stalin a long (seven-page) emotional letter from prison. Among other things, he requested that he be spared the humiliation of a trial and simply be executed instead. He begged for forgiveness and for the opportunity to say good-bye to his family. Then, pages later, he switched course and promised to continue working for Stalin if his life were spared.

> I will say to you from the outset that . . . : a) I have no intention of recanting anything I've confessed; b) I have no desire to make any request of you, nor have I any intention of pleading with you to change matters or divert them from their present course. But I am writing you for your personal information. . . .
>
> I tell you on my word of honour that I am innocent of those crimes to which I confessed during the investigation.[47]

During his ensuing trial, he initially appeared to confess: "Departure from the position of Bolshevism means siding with . . . counterrevolutionary banditry. . . . I am kneeling before the country, before the Party, before the whole people. The monstrousness of my crimes is immeasurable."[48] Then he went off script with sarcasm. "I accept responsibility even for those crimes about which I did not know or about which I did not have the slightest idea."[49]

Arthur Koestler's character Rubashov in *Darkness at Noon* is loosely based on the events of Bukharin's interrogation and contradictory confessions. Koestler masterfully captures the technique of the Soviet interrogators and describes the defendant's belief in the Party's infallibility. "The Party can never be wrong," said Rubashov. "You and I can make mistakes—but not the Party. The Party, comrade, is more than you and me. . . . The Party is the embodiment of the revolutionary idea in history." Revisiting this theme, Rubashov mused: "The individual was nothing, the Party was all; the branch that broke off the tree must wither."[50] The fictional Rubashov's statements mirror Bukharin's comments about the Party in 1936: "One is saved by a faith that development is always going forward. It is like a stream that is running to the shore. If one leans out of the stream, one is ejected completely. . . . The stream goes through the most difficult places.

But it still goes forward in the direction in which it must. And the people grow, become stronger in it, and they build a new society."[51]

How did the Soviets persuade prisoners to confess? We find traces of Pavlov in the ample historical record. Prisoners were offered better food or prison cells if they confessed. The interrogators appealed to their conscience as Party members and their natural concerns for their family. If these appeals did not work the powerful next step for the recalcitrant prisoner was solitary confinement and sleep deprivation for weeks at a time.

The prisoners, kept in isolation in dank cells, felt buried alive. They were typically interrogated at night, with or without accompanying beatings and torture. Some signed confessions found in the archives reveal bloodstains on the documents.[52] The interrogations were unpredictable, sometimes mercifully brief and sometimes going on for forty-eight hours at a stretch. Prisoners could be released to their cells only to be called back for another interrogation moments later, or it might be days before the next summons came. The ongoing sleep deprivation led to bewilderment, confusion, and apathy. Survivors commented about the soul-crushing burden of sleep deprivation.[53]

The interrogator's behavior and demeanor were inconsistent. He could be mild and solicitous, promising leniency, good food, and release, or he could suddenly start yelling. Interrogations were carried out in locations where the prisoner could hear other prisoners screaming during torture. The examinations could continue off and on for months. Survivors described a semiconscious state after fifty or sixty interrogations and no sleep. "A man becomes like an automaton. . . . In this state he is often even convinced he is guilty."[54]

Even a trivial morsel of guilt in thought or deed could become the foundation for a major confession, whether true or not. As in the Inquisition, prisoners were told that the Party did not arrest people without cause and they must rethink what they might have said or done. William Sargant observed, "The prisoner . . . [is] cross examined until . . . he contradicts himself on some small point. This is then used as a stick to beat him with; presently his brain ceases to function normally and he collapses. In a subsequent highly suggestible state, with old thought patterns inhibited, he will readily sign and deliver the desired confession."[55]

Bukharin wrote plaintively from prison: "I cannot go on like this. . . . My legs are failing. I cannot bear the atmosphere that has been created. I am not able to speak in this situation. I have no wish to burst into tears, nor do I wish to faint or give way to hysteria."[56] Another defendant described being dragged about by the scruff of his neck, throttled, beaten with a rubber rod, and tortured for five weeks, during which he slept only two or three hours a day. "They threatened to rip my throat out along with my confession."[57]

The Soviet techniques were similar to those used by the Inquisition and the czarist secret police, but some refinements seemed to follow from Pavlov's playbook. Confessions were readily obtained after bombarding prisoners with contradictory information and eliciting feelings of guilt and anxiety. The prisoners' cognitive functioning was so disturbed by malnutrition, sleep deprivation, and massive anxiety that they readily confessed. By that time, they longed to be punished as a way to obtain salvation.

One victim of the purges vividly described the interrogation process: "I went over the events of the last ten years in my mind. I considered everyone with whom I had been in personal contact, or with whom I had corresponded. . . . Suddenly a long-forgotten incident . . . came to my mind. . . . My God! I thought, that must be it!' [His interrogator then told him:] 'Go home again and come back the day after tomorrow. . . . and tell me when you first got in touch with the enemy and what ideas caused you to go over to his side. If you freely confess and show us that you want to be a loyal Soviet supporter again, we'll do all we can to help you.'"[58]

Stalin choreographed the interrogations and trials. If confessions were not forthcoming, he advised interrogators to increase the torture. "Isn't it time to squeeze this gentleman and force him to report on his dirty little business? Where is he: in a prison or in a hotel?"[59] He also advised the prosecution, "Don't let [the accused] speak too much. . . . Shut them up. . . . Don't let them babble."[60] He hovered over the secret police, reportedly threatening, "If you do not obtain confessions . . . , we will shorten you by a head."[61]

Foreshadowing interrogation techniques that would be used in the 1950s in Korea and China, many prisoners had to write extensive critiques of their lives—their upbringing, accomplishments, and shortcomings. After reading the self-criticism, the interrogator would declare it inadequate and order the prisoner to start all over. Although prisoners were not told exactly what they should write about or even what exactly they were charged with, they were supposed to form a hypothesis as to why they had been apprehended. In the horror of confinement, confusion, and torture, it was natural for the prisoner to wonder if he *had* done something, even something trivial, in opposition to the State. When he confessed to that triviality, he was told that it was not sufficient, that he must search his heart for other acts against the State.

Some prisoners admitted to associating with enemies of the State but denied carrying out any actions against the State. The interrogators responded that associating with enemies of the State, even if only meeting them socially, was helping support the morale of the enemy. The prisoner was told, "Come now, confess. You associated with spies. You must be a spy." Then, in a seemingly nonchalant manner, the interrogator would confuse the prisoner by saying something like: "We don't need your confession. No one will ever find out about you. You are nothing but vermin whom the party will crush."[62]

Interrogators carefully rehearsed the defendants' confessional testimonies, giving prisoners lists of questions that would be asked and stipulating acceptable answers. The defendants were told to memorize the scripts so there would be no last-minute embarrassments.[63] The trials were precisely choreographed and followed a libretto dictated by the prosecution. Party members, conditioned by long and disciplined service to the Party, were prepared to sacrifice their lives. A confession ritual was required. The stage-managing of the trials extended to defendants being instructed where they should look while giving various parts of their testimony.[64] In one trial transcript, prosecutor Vyshinsky feeds the lines to defendant Lev Kamenev:

> VYSHINSKY: What appraisal should be given of the articles and statements you wrote in 1933, in which you expressed loyalty to the Party? Deception?
> KAMENEV: No, worse than deception.
> VYSHINSKY: Perfidy?
> KAMENEV: Worse.
> VYSHINSKY: Worse than deception, worse than perfidy—find the word. Treason?
> KAMENOV: You have found it.[65]

The confessions were filled with ludicrous details. One prisoner testified that he had plotted with Trotsky's son in the Bristol Hotel in Copenhagen in 1932. The problem was that the hotel had been torn down in 1917. The interrogators had constructed a crime to which the defendant would plead guilty, but to fill in the details of the supposed meeting, they asked the Foreign Ministry for names of some likely hotels in Copenhagen where such a meeting *could* have occurred, and also in Oslo, to cover their tracks. In their trial preparations, the interrogators slipped up and mistakenly jumbled the lists. As a result, they instructed the defendant to confess to a fictitious meeting in a hotel that didn't exist (there *was* a Hotel Bristol in Oslo at the time).[66] The defendant testified as directed.

Occasionally, people confessed and then recanted. When this happened, a short recess was called, and the prisoner was tortured until his confession was restated. One prominent defendant returned and told the court: "Yesterday, momentarily overcome by an acute feeling of false shame, . . . I could not bring myself to say I was guilty. . . . I ask the court to record my statement that I plead totally and utterly guilty to all the most serious charges brought against me personally, and I accept full responsibility for my high treason and treachery."[67]

The court appreciated his obliging testimony but executed him all the same.

Some confessed out of loyalty and deference to the Party, which had been the North Star guiding their entire lives. Their surrender was merely the next step in a lifelong pattern of self-abasement to the Party. Prosecuted by the Party they loved, innocent of the crimes they were accused of, they were driven to despair. For them, confession was a final sacrifice to the Party. Who were they to question its wisdom?[68] In his final statement, Arkadii Rozengol'ts, Commissar for Foreign Trade, proclaimed: "There is no other country on earth where there is such enthusiasm for work, where you can hear such happy, joyful laughter . . . , where love is so splendid, and I say, 'Farewell, my beloved country!'"[69] Economic administrator Georgy Pyatakov, longtime member of the Central Committee, prostrated himself in admitting guilt. "I am standing before you, covered in filth, crushed, deprived of everything through my own fault, having lost my Party, without friends, having lost my family, having lost myself."[70]

Historian Yuri Slezkine astutely pointed out the eerie resemblance between such confessions and the story of Job, with Stalin standing in for God. Protests of innocence were as futile for Job as they were for Stalin's victims. The only way out was repentance and faith in the wisdom of the deity. "Some members of the tribe would be put to the sword, devoured by wild animals, or die of a plague . . . but the tribe as such would triumph no matter what."[71] These peculiar reverberations between religion, coercion, and confession recurrently haunted the development of brainwashing in the twentieth century.

★★★

Building upon established techniques of torture, the Soviets added Pavlov's insights that severe stress, sleep deprivation, and meticulous attention to reward and punishment could shape behavior. They successfully elicited outlandish confessions from defendants who were variously exhausted, confused, defiant, and who longed for oblivion. Despite the torture and false confessions, some went to their deaths still secure in their Communist faith.

A troubled world assumed that the Soviets had mastered a powerful new weapon of persuasion. That conclusion worried both the Germans and the Allies as World War II loomed. How could they protect their troops from such crushing interrogations? The converse question was equally compelling: how could these techniques be used to interrogate enemies? When the war began, governments turned to drugs as the shortcut for dark persuasion.

CHAPTER THREE

Extracting Information with Drugs
The Military's Quest in World War II

Any technique that promises an increment of success in extracting information from an uncompliant source is ipso facto of interest in intelligence operations.

—CENTRAL INTELLIGENCE AGENCY, 1993

STALIN'S THIRD SHOW TRIAL had scarcely ended when World War II started. The military had been watching the trials with calculated interest. Had the Soviets developed new techniques to persuade innocent people to confess to crimes, even at the cost of their own lives? Could these methods be used to interrogate enemies more efficiently? When World War II began, these questions about interrogation were no longer hypothetical.

The military wanted tools of coercive persuasion that worked faster than Pavlov's techniques or torture. Rather than wait for sleep deprivation and anxiety to exact their toll on a prisoner's resistance, they hoped that drugs could persuade an enemy to reveal military secrets. Pavlov had used bromides, first synthesized in the nineteenth century, to treat agitation; but bromides have long half-lives and are prone to toxic accumulation.

Both the Nazis and the Allies began looking for something better, and they arrived there via unlikely routes—obstetrics and psychiatry.

So much of medicine is serendipity. Not only are discoveries unpredictable, but newly discovered drugs tend to be used in unanticipated fashions. Drugs for interrogation were originally devised for utterly different medical indications. In a time of warfare, they acquired vastly different applications.

In 1853, Dr. John Snow used chloroform to decrease Queen Victoria's pain during the birth of her seventh child. An editorial in *Lancet* criticized that "dangerous practice" as irresponsible, warning that "royal examples are followed with extraordinary readiness by a certain class of society in this country."[1] The queen was indeed a trendsetter, and the use of anesthetics in labor and delivery increased sharply. Case reports of the risks of chloroform anesthesia started accumulating, but some other observations emerged that piqued the military's interest.

Because chloroform is difficult to administer safely, other drugs were sought for childbirth. Doctors turned to a combination of drugs to alleviate pain and the memory of pain. That might sound odd, but similar combinations of drugs are routinely administered today for colonoscopies and ambulatory surgical procedures. The anesthesia does not need to be so deep if the emotions and memories are also blocked. If the "edge" is taken off the pain with an opiate, and the memory of the pain is interrupted so that the patient has no recollection of it, did the pain really "happen"?

By the beginning of the twentieth century, German obstetricians in Freiburg systematized the use of scopolamine and morphine to decrease the pain of childbirth. As the *British Medical Journal* wrote approvingly, "There is a vast difference between the true so-called 'twilight sleep' as devised [at Freiburg] . . . and the ordinary haphazard . . . treatment which has been freely practiced by many of us."[2] This Freiburg treatment worked so well that some mothers greeted their newborn with amazement because they did not remember even being present at the time of the delivery. German doctors called the intervention *Dämmerschlaf*, or twilight sleep.[3] Their technique was rapidly adopted internationally despite continuing safety concerns and religious objections that it wasn't right to remove the pain of childbirth imposed by God.[4]

In 1916, in a small town near Dallas, Texas, the obstetrician Robert House made a curious observation while performing a home delivery on a mother who had received the twilight sleep regimen. "[Once the baby was born,] we desired to weigh the baby, and inquired for the scales. The husband stated that he could not find them. The wife, apparently sound asleep, spoke up and said, 'They are in the kitchen on a nail behind the picture.' The fact that this woman suffered no pain and did not remember when her child was delivered, yet could answer correctly a question she had overheard, appealed to me. . . . I observed that [in other deliveries under twilight sedation], without exception, the patient always replied [to my questions] with the truth. . . . [It proved] to me that I could make anyone tell the truth on any question."[5]

This was a bit of an inferential leap. Yet Dr. House was a true believer that scopolamine could force people to tell the truth and that it could help exonerate (or convict) prisoners. He thought that scopolamine could be a crucial tool for evaluating testimony, commenting that "one third of the arrests made are shown by statistics to be in error, and not all convictions are warranted by the facts of the case."[6]

As Dr. House describes, in February 1922, the Dallas district attorney asked that scopolamine be administered to two prisoners.[7] Under scopolamine, one prisoner admitted to certain crimes but denied others. He also named members of a gang that had robbed a bank, something he had previously refused to do. His testimony was viewed as demonstrating scopolamine's success in eliciting the truth. A day after the scopolamine interview, the prisoner wrote Dr. House: "I remember the question, but at the same time I was unconscious of how I answered or all that I said. After I had regained consciousness I began to realize that at times during the experiment I had a desire to answer any question that I could hear, and it seemed that when a question was asked my mind would center upon the true facts of the answer and I would speak voluntarily, without any strength of will to manufacture an answer."[8] The other prisoner, about to be tried for murder, emphatically proclaimed his innocence when scopolamine was administered. He was in fact eventually exonerated.

Other cases followed. A group of ax murderers in Alabama confessed after receiving the drug.[9] In Oklahoma, two people were freed after decades in prison because of late-breaking testimony that emerged under scopolamine.[10] But there were problematic cases as well. A Hawaiian chauffeur confessed to murder and kidnapping during a scopolamine interview. Then he recanted during a second interview. In the meantime, the police apprehended a different criminal.[11] The press nonetheless trumpeted scopolamine as a veritable "truth serum."

It wasn't just obstetrics that gave birth to "truth serum" as a tool for interrogation; psychiatry did as well. In the 1870s the German physician

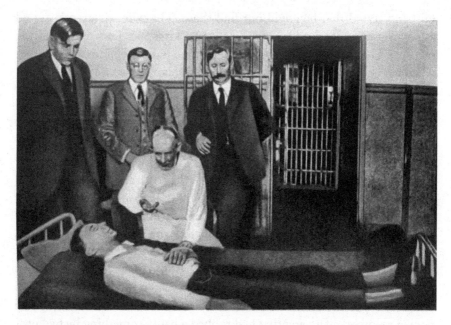

Robert House administering truth serum to a prisoner in a Dallas County jail, 1922, while the prosecutor, a state senator, and the sheriff look on. (From Emilio Mira y Lopez's *Manual of Juridical Psychology* [1932].)

Karl Kahlbaum described severely ill psychiatric patients who were mute, stuporous, and did not interact with their surroundings. Sometimes they stared into space, their bodies frozen in unnatural poses, or they made rhythmic movements, pacing awkwardly; if they spoke at all, it was gibberish.[12] Kahlbaum called the disorder "catatonia."[13] Treatment was problematic. Patients wouldn't eat or drink, so they had to be tube fed, and in the early twentieth century, medications to treat catatonia were limited to bromides and opiates.

Barbiturates are sedating compounds that were first synthesized in 1864, but it took another forty years before their medical applications as sedatives became evident.[14] There are numerous barbiturate compounds, which differ in terms of their absorption rate and length of action.

William J. Bleckwenn of the University of Wisconsin published a curious paper in 1930. Barbiturates were being tested as anesthetic agents. Bleckwenn wondered if one of them—amobarbital (also known as amytal)—might be helpful in treating catatonia. He gave the drug intravenously to fifty psychiatric patients and found that within minutes, the drug was effective in treating severe agitation. Not only that, he observed: "In a few cases there was a lucid interval for one or two minutes just before the patient went to sleep. During this short interval, the patient was rational and had complete insight into his condition. . . . As the initial sleep wore off, the patient appeared dazed . . . [but] the patients asked questions and answered others; they discussed football scores, the duration of the illness, family and relatives, and took nourishment. . . . Several patients recovered rapidly."[15]

One might have thought that a sedative would make such sluggish patients worse, but paradoxically, the catatonic patient "came alive" after receiving an injection of sedating medication. It was as if catatonia implied that the patient was frozen in fear, and that the sedation from the barbiturate "thawed" the patient. The reversal of catatonia with an intravenous barbiturate is about as close to a miracle as one finds in psychiatry.[16]

Amytal was found to be miraculous in treating other psychiatric conditions as well. Occasionally, patients face such tribulation in their lives that they flee their familiar surroundings and lose their memories entirely.[17] This situation is called, poetically, a "fugue" or a flight. One early psychiatrist described the situation of these patients as akin to "the plight of small children who have run away from their parents and are unable to give information about themselves." He reported that the common precipitants were disappointments in love or financial difficulties from which there was no escape.[18]

Today, fugue is commonly referred to as psychogenic amnesia or dissociative amnesia. The disorder is far more severe than normal forgetting. People may not recall their name or occupation, where they live or who their family is, and they may wander for years under a new identity. This amnesia is not attributable to a head injury or drugs but comes on, often suddenly, as a reaction to major stress.[19] Fugues are a never-ending source of fascination in newspapers and movies, particularly when the patient suddenly recovers his or her identity. Newspapers commonly run headlines like "Amnesia Victim's Memory Revived by 'Truth Serum,'" "Man Unable to Remember Is Reunited with Fiancée," or "A Teacher Vanishes Again. This Time, in the Virgin Islands."[20] Although commonly reported in the mass media, fugues are rare. Of the many thousands of patients I have seen, I have treated only two cases of fugue.

Fugue patients have been helped by hypnosis or, more often, anti-anxiety medication, on the assumption that their amnesia reflects profound emotional distress. After a few days the patient's memories start to come back into focus. However, the most dramatic intervention occurs with intravenous amytal. Within minutes, memories and feelings flood back. There is, by the way, an interestingly hazy boundary between hypnosis and amytal; in both, the doctor uses suggestion. With amytal, the doctor typically advises the patient ("suggests") that the drug will help him or her relax enough to restore the memory connections that were previously disrupted by stress. Thus, it is not correct to say that amytal alone acts as some kind of memory reincarnation drug; suggestion itself plays a prominent role.

Catatonia and fugue are relatively rare compared to combat fatigue, also known as shell shock or post-traumatic stress disorder (PTSD). Warfare has always left psychic scars, from the days of antiquity to the present.[21] In World War I, troops were decimated by powerful armaments and static trench warfare, and large numbers of troops became psychiatric battlefield casualties, particularly those who had served longer in the trenches.[22] Some deserted, some refused orders, some "froze" in place. Many developed neurological symptoms like blindness or paralysis even though they had no apparent brain injuries. In World War II a third of the men evacuated from El Guettar in Tunisia were psychiatric casualties.[23]

The military learned that a soldier crippled by battle fatigue was just as much a casualty as a soldier shot by a bullet. Early psychiatric interventions focused on evacuation from the front in the hope that rest and relaxation would help troubled soldiers to recover. Others used a tougher approach—heavy exercise and quasi-punishment drills—to make the soldier "snap out of it" and return to combat.[24] There were few medications to treat shell shock. Old standbys like opiates and bromides had limitations in terms of toxicity, side effects, risks for addiction, and unsatisfactory half-life.

Psychiatrists had observed that patients seemed to "open up" once they had received intravenous barbiturates. Writing from Iowa in 1932, psychiatrist Erich Lindemann described one patient's self-report that the drug made him talkative. "It's funny I am just telling you things which I wasn't going to tell you. . . . No matter what comes to my mind it wants to be expressed too. . . . I don't think I ever talked this way before. . . . The words kind of just come out of my mouth. . . . I know what I am saying and yet I don't know. . . . The little guardian just isn't there. . . . I keep talking and talking. . . . All my reason says to shut up. But I feel like talking and taking a chance." Lindemann noted that the drug gave patients a feeling of serenity and a desire to communicate even about personal matters "usually not spoken of to strangers."[25]

Psychiatrists weren't searching for a truth drug, per se, but they were open to using drugs to help patients so disabled by mental illness that they couldn't talk. While psychoanalysis was proving to be a fascinating way of understanding human behavior, many psychiatrists were impatient with the pace of analysis and questioned whether that approach was helpful for patients with major mental illness.

In England, the psychiatrist Stephen Horsley described an intervention he called "narco-analysis" that combined supportive psychotherapy with intravenous barbiturates. He sometimes repeated the dose over a number of sessions, which he quaintly called "séances."[26] Horsley reported that barbiturates enhanced recollections and that "shyness and inhibition melt away and the patient will volunteer the information that he 'feels [is] confidential.'" In a moving case report, Horsley described curing a shell-shocked World War I veteran who had been suffering for fifteen years from recurrent fugues and amnesia for the whole period of his service in France. Horsley wrote that by using the drug, "in an hour the physician obtains a quantity of relevant information which would not have been obtained in a month by ordinary methods."[27]

Intravenous barbiturates reached their apogee in treating trauma in World War II. They facilitated *abreaction*, or reexperiencing repressed memories. Whether the technique was called *narcosuggestion, narcoanalysis,* or *narcosynthesis*, all these interventions described insights obtained from drug-induced retrieved memories. These techniques were used on thousands of soldiers and civilians caught up in the horrors of war. There was something about expressing these intense memories that was cathartic, even if the memories were not true.[28] That trailing clause "even if not true" was to become enormously important when the drugs were used for interrogation, but the veracity of recovered memories was not so important when the goal was to help a soldier incapacitated by anxiety. However, to recover "truth" under drug-induced interrogation, one has to wrestle with the fact that intoxication does not guarantee precision.

Roy Grinker and John Spiegel vividly described narcotherapy on the battlegrounds of Tunisia in 1943.[29] Their monograph, hurriedly produced by the Josiah Macy Jr. Foundation, was widely distributed by the Air Surgeon, Army Air Forces, to educate doctors about how to treat combat fatigue.[30] The authors didn't describe the drugs as miracle truth drugs, but it was clear that the drugs could help patients retrieve some of their memories and talk about them enough to be helped by a psychiatrist. One patient was a mute infantryman who couldn't even remember his name. After giving him an intravenous barbiturate, the doctors observed:

The patient lay quietly on the bed, without tremor. He was then told that he was in the Kairouan Pass, and that mortar shells were dropping about him. At the moment of the word "shells," he shuddered.... He then ... got out of bed, crying "Steve! Steve, are you all right?." ... He then lurched about the room, looking for something; from time to time he cowered, as if hearing an approaching shell; and then trembling with fear, crouched on the ground. ...

"Just then a mortar came over and landed in a foxhole near me. ... It knocked me down, but I got right up, and went over to the hole. Two men were in there. ... The first sergeant was on top. He was dead, with his head blown open. ... The other man was underneath. He was still alive, but the side of his chest was open, and I could see part of the lung. He was crying; God, I can still hear him crying. I felt sick, and my mind was funny; I couldn't think. I was shaking so I could hardly move. ... The shells were falling all around us. ... I can still hear the sound of the shells. ... I can't go back to the front; I can't take it again. ..."

At this point the patient covered his eyes with his hand and buried his head on the Medical Officer's shoulder. Then he suddenly smiled and said, "I remember my name: it's F ... and I remember where I live. God, what a miracle that I can talk."[31]

***

These observations from obstetrics and psychiatry became intensely interesting to the military. Both sides were riveted by the possibilities of using drugs to facilitate interrogation. Drugs potentially promised a much quicker way of extracting information than traditional interrogation. In addition, if the drugs really did compel "truth," their use would lessen the effects of misinformation during interrogation.

In Dachau, SS Dr. Kurt Plötner wondered whether mescaline could be used to interrogate captured enemy soldiers or spies. On leave from his position as lecturer in medicine at the University of Leipzig, he worked in the medical labs at the Dachau concentration camp, where he subjected prisoners to lethal experiments on the effects of high altitude, hypothermia, malaria, and new formulations of cyanide pills.[32] One of his side studies involved surreptitiously spiking inmates' coffee with mescaline and observing their responses. Some became giddy, some angry, and some drowsy. He then interrogated the prisoners about their "most intimate secrets" and found that they talked carelessly and openly. The intelligence report from Dachau is maddeningly brief. Plötner questioned the pris-

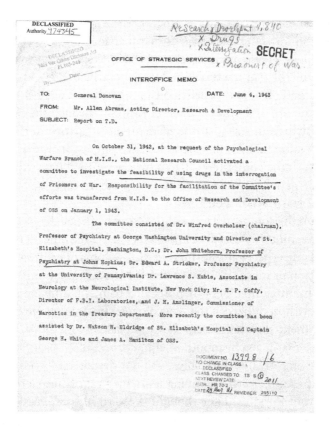

Office of Strategic Services memo cover page, June 4, 1943.
(Record Group 226, entry 210, box 346, WN 13398, National Archives.)

oners about their sexual fantasies and also their rage against the guards. He reported: "Decent persons remained decent during the examination . . . but it could be stated that mental restraints hardly occurred, sentiments of hatred and revenge were exposed in every case." However, he was not satisfied with mescaline's potential military use, noting that "it is impossible to impose one's own will on another person . . . even when strongest doses of mescaline had been given."[33]

While the Nazis were studying mescaline, the U.S. Office of Strategic Services (OSS) convened a special panel to study drugs for interrogating prisoners of war. The group included prominent academics, intelligence agency officials, and, somewhat surprisingly, J. H. Anslinger, the first commissioner of the Federal Bureau of Narcotics.

Anslinger's membership on the committee is curious, given its tenta-

tive endorsement of marijuana as a potential drug for interrogation. Anslinger was an indefatigable critic of marijuana, calling it the "assassin of
youth." He had already gone on record that "every parent owes it to his
children to tell them of the terrible effects of marijuana. . . . There must be
constant enforcement and equally constant education against this enemy,
which has a record of murder and terror running through the centuries."[34]
But his participation was just one of many peculiarities in the committee's membership and findings. Intelligence agent George H. White, a
late addition to the committee, shared his operational field skills with the
panel's academics. He would go on in later years to carry out some of the
CIA's most bizarre studies on LSD.

Although the committee was unimpressed by the evidence that mescaline would be militarily useful in interrogations, three officers volunteered
to try it in January 1943 at a hospital in Philadelphia. The drug did not induce relaxation or cause the men to divulge any information.[35]

The committee members then decided to test marijuana on enlisted
men who were hospitalized at the Neurological Institute in New York City.
They experimented with different doses and delivery methods. When they
administered marijuana by mouth in liquid drops, they observed it elicited
physical discomfort, but the soldiers did not disclose any confidential information. Next, they tried spraying marijuana vapors into a room where
their staff were working. They thought the aerosol spray method offered
some promise and then moved on to try cigarettes containing some marijuana. This also seemed promising: "[It] appeared possible to administer
an amount of the material which would bring about a state of irresponsi-
bility, causing the subject to become loquacious and free in his impartation
of information (some of which it was felt he would certainly not divulge
except under influence of the drug)."[36]

Finally, the committee members commissioned a field study of the
drug—not in volunteers but in real life. In May 1943, they surreptitiously
added marijuana to a cigarette offered to a New York gangster (Little
Augie) who had previously been uncommunicative regarding various
crimes. Indeed, the investigator reported that "the subject prides himself on the fact that he has never been an informer and that he has been
instrumental in killing some persons who have been informants." After
two cigarettes, Little Augie started talking, naming names and providing a
long list of revelations. Among other things, he divulged that he had been
bribing a prominent drug enforcement official for years, that an associate
(Hawkeye) had been bribing a restaurant inspector to permit gambling,

and that two law enforcement officials were blackmailing someone in the liquor business.[37]

Despite this promising observation, the committee had plenty of caveats about marijuana's potential use as a truth drug. For instance, there were wide individual differences in susceptibility to the drug, and thus dosage was critical. On the other hand, in response to a low dose, subjects entered a state of pleasant relaxation in which they started speaking freely and relating "personal anecdotes with abandon and indiscretion."[38] Ultimately, the committee was drawn to the potential capabilities of marijuana—if administered surreptitiously. That suggestion of surreptitious administration would have disastrous consequences during the subsequent CIA-sponsored studies of LSD.

Meanwhile, others in the military became interested in amphetamines as interrogation aids, either on their own or, more improbably, in combination with a sedating drug. The rationale for the combination was that the sedative would lead to relaxation and the amphetamine would produce a rush of talking that would give the prisoner "no time to think or to organize his deceptions."[39] One early report recounted a single case study of a soldier who had gone AWOL and upon his capture claimed he'd had amnesia for the whole period. When methamphetamine was administered and the soldier was interviewed, he started off cocky—sure that he would not be tripped up by the drug. However, as the drug took hold, "he began to realize that he could not hesitate, that he was speaking without thinking or caution, and worse, could do nothing about it." The doctors triumphantly provided a snippet from the interview, showing that the patient in fact remembered everything.

q: Where was your first job?
a: At the —— Grill.
q: How long did you work there?
a: I don't know . . . please . . . maybe two months . . .
q: Didn't you have a social security card?
a: Sure, I did. What has that . . .
q: Where did you get the card?
a: Where does anyone get it? At the post office . . .
q: Didn't they question you at the post office?
a: Sure, they did.
q: Didn't they ask you your age?
a: Sure, but . . .

Q: What did you tell them your birthday was?
A: May 6, 1924 . . . Oh, Jesus . . . [The patient began to wring his hands, weep, and babble incoherently that "they'll throw the book at me now."][40]

The most famous use of truth drug interrogation occurred when Deputy Führer Rudolf Hess was examined in 1945. Years earlier (May 10, 1941), Hess stole a Messerschmitt airplane and flew to Scotland to persuade the British to bow out of the war. His behavior was so peculiar that he was placed in a psychiatric hospital for the duration of the war. There, he attempted suicide, complained of constant pain and itching, and charged that staff members were feeding him nerve poison and the "glandular secretions of camels." When dining, he would suddenly switch plates with his guards because he suspected poison. Hess was also convinced that the British were interfering with his sleep by driving loud trucks past the hospital.[41]

However, Hess's most prominent symptom was his amnesia. During interrogation, he claimed he couldn't remember anything. His memory deficit was decidedly unusual: it twinkled on and off inconsistently and was occasionally too extensive to be believable. Hess claimed, for instance, that he didn't know what skiing was or who Shakespeare was. Prisoners frequently cite problems with their memory in order to cut short interrogation. Was Hess simply malingering, making his amnesia up, or was he dissociating? On May 17, 1945, Hess consented to an amytal interview to help his memory, but nothing useful was elicited.[42]

Hess was subsequently tried for war crimes at the International Military Tribunal in Nuremberg. Even there, Hess continued to claim amnesia. In exasperation, Robert Jackson, the chief prosecutor, tried to compel him to undergo another amytal interview, but Hess refused. So, arguably the most famous trial in the twentieth century tried to use an interrogation drug to compel testimony. It is questionable what new information would have been revealed at Nuremberg, given that Hess's earlier experience with amytal had yielded nothing.

There has been continued dispute about the ethics of drug-assisted interrogation and the veracity of information revealed.[43] In the United States, that issue was eventually resolved in 1963 by the Supreme Court in *Townsend v. Sain.* On New Year's Day in 1954, the Chicago police arrested Charles Townsend for robbery and murder.[44] Townsend was a heroin addict who was high at the time of his initial interrogation. He denied committing the crime. While jailed he went into withdrawal. A jail doctor administered phenobarbital and scopolamine, which helped the withdrawal symptoms. Townsend was then interrogated again and this time he confessed. Both the defendant and the Chicago police agreed to this much of the case.

Townsend, however, alleged that he was beaten by the police and that they had promised to get a doctor to treat him for his severe withdrawal only *if* he confessed. Townsend also stated that after receiving the medication he was dizzy, sleepy, and had blurred vision. He then fell asleep and the next thing he remembered was signing a document that he thought was a bail bond but that turned out to be a transcript of his confession. The police denied these allegations.

The Chicago jury found him guilty and sentenced him to death. After many appeals, the Supreme Court ruled in favor of Townsend on the basis that the lower courts had not properly considered whether the confession was the product of a rational intellect and a free will or coerced.[45] Justice Potter Stewart succinctly stated, "A confession induced by the administration of drugs is constitutionally inadmissible in a criminal trial."[46]

Whether or not they are constitutionally forbidden, the fact remains that confessions obtained under the influence of drugs are unreliable since the drugs can elicit confessions from the innocent. Some people appear to remember things that never happened (aka false memories), whether these stem from their own unconscious or the suggestions of their interrogator.

That recognition was made, oddly enough, by Pope Pius XII in his address to the Sixth International Congress on Criminal Law in 1953. He specifically criticized narcoanalysis, saying that it often produced erroneous results, apparently alluding to forced confessions under Communist rule. He linked his criticism to long-standing Church policy against forced confessions, a policy that had originated eleven hundred years previously.

> The judicial investigation must exclude physical and mental torture and narco-analysis, firstly because they infringe a natural right even if the accused is really guilty, and secondly because all too often they give erroneous results. It is not uncommon for them to succeed [in extracting the] confession . . . not because [the defendant] is actually guilty but because his energy . . . is exhausted and he is ready to make any statements that are demanded. . . . We find abundant evidence in the well-known spectacular trials with their confessions. . . .

Pope Pius XII. (© DeA Picture Library / Art Resource, NY.)

About 1100 years ago, in 866, the great Pope Nicholas I
. . . [maintained that] confession must not be forced, but spontaneous; it must not be extorted, but voluntary. . . . During the long
interval since then, we . . . [wish] that justice had never departed
from this rule.[47]

While the pope positioned himself on the side of the angels in terms
of interrogation, some unexpected personages have defended the use of
interrogation drugs. An unexpected argument arose when the UN Cove-
nant on Human Rights was being drafted in 1950. Delegates had already
agreed that "no one shall be subjected to torture or to cruel, inhuman or
degrading treatment." Then Egypt's delegate, Dr. A. M. Ramadan, asked

to include a ban on truth serums to obtain confessions, referring to their use in Communist countries and in France. Surprisingly, the commission's chair, Eleanor Roosevelt, praised the motives of Dr. Ramadan but "contended that there was too little information yet on the whole subject and that it might be dangerous to specify prohibition of one particular drug."[48] The prohibition against truth drugs never made it into the document.

★★★

Empirically testing putative truth drugs is problematic. Laboratory studies are "pretend models," but the models are still quite interesting, albeit inconclusive. The experiments simulate interrogations but cannot ethically reproduce the conditions that a captured soldier, for instance, would face if examined under a truth drug concerning a topic that must not be disclosed.

In 1924, New Orleans reporters assiduously memorized wrong answers to a series of questions and then were interviewed under scopolamine. Their efforts to provide duplicitous information failed, and they gave truthful answers instead.[49]

Such studies, however, do not prove that the drug works in real-world circumstances. People certainly get tipsy on scopolamine, but can the drug *compel* them to talk? More problematically, once they start talking, will they tell the truth or just blather on? The old expression *In vino veritas* implies that people disclose things when they are intoxicated, but of course people also reveal nonsense when they're drunk.[50] There is also concern that the sedated patient might become more suggestible to the interrogator, revealing what he or she *thinks* the interrogator wants to know as opposed to the truth.

A group of Yale investigators tried a different design.[51] Recruiting volunteers to participate in "an interesting psychological experiment," they asked their subjects to complete a psychiatric evaluation. Some were judged to be "normal" while others revealed various emotional issues like perfectionism or sexual anxieties. The first researcher asked the volunteers to talk about one event they associated with humiliation or guilt. Then, he told them to invent a cover story to disguise the event and to resist telling the true story when questioned by a second investigator. The second interviewer, who was told only the rough theme of the event (for example, "money issues"), then gave the volunteer amytal. Would subjects disclose the real event or would they be able to hold onto their cover story?

One of the nine subjects interviewed, a graduate student, felt guilty about how he was spending the money his financially strapped parents had saved for his education. The true story was that he was spending money on political causes. His cover story was that he used his parents' money to pay for his girlfriend's abortion. Under amytal, he maintained the cover story and did not disclose how he really was using his parents' money.

Three other subjects held onto their cover stories (that is, amytal couldn't extract their true secret). These three individuals were those who had been deemed the healthiest, psychologically, of the bunch. The other subjects, who had various emotional issues, had difficulties maintaining their cover stories. Amytal pierced through the cover story to elicit the true story in two subjects and partially exposed bits of the truth in the other four. The researchers concluded that susceptibility to amytal depended upon the individual's psychological health: "The essential powers forcing us to confess or to resist are within us."

Subsequent investigators ingeniously extended the Yale study. Choosing healthy undergraduates as subjects, they tested the students repeatedly in response to intravenous barbiturates, alcohol, scopolamine, morphine, amphetamines, atropine, and mescaline (whew!). Before they were given any drugs, the subjects were told to write down something personal—like their mother's name—and resist disclosing it during the interview. A research assistant then gave them a plausible-sounding military secret that they were also told not to reveal ("The troops are arriving Tuesday afternoon"). Finally, the investigators used the Yale "cover story" procedure again; the subject was asked to recall a humiliating event but to invent a cover story for it. Over the course of four to eight hours of drug-assisted interrogation, the investigators tried to extract the information from the subjects. None of them gave up the military secret or disclosed the personal history item, but two subjects partially betrayed their cover stories. In other words, within the context of a decidedly artificial experimental situation, truth drugs could not convincingly "crack" the students even though they "became semi-comatose, mildly delirious, panicky, markedly loquacious, euphoric, or underwent transient dissociative reactions."[52]

Another test of amytal took place in an army military hospital in New Jersey.[53] The patients were known to be guilty of various military infractions but denied their guilt. They were interviewed by a psychiatrist who told them that they must submit to an amytal interrogation but that whatever they disclosed during the examination could not be used in court. So, the question was whether the psychiatrist could reliably extract the truth about an actual crime. Note that this study is much closer to a real-world military interrogation than the artificial experiments on college students.

The psychiatrist took pains to build a relationship with the prisoners before starting the amytal. Furthermore, the psychiatrist didn't rush in to query the prisoner about the crime but rather talked around the topic for a while to put the prisoner at ease, saying, "We'll talk about that later."

Even with these efforts, amytal could not be relied upon to compel the truth. Interesting features conspired against amytal's effectiveness. As the authors observed, questioning was not successful unless a good rapport had been established. Even in those cases, however, high doses of amytal were necessary to elicit cooperation, but the result of that was a loss of clarity and a murky dialog because the patient mumbled or embarked on long, tangential fantasies. Even more important, as the authors pointed out, "Testimony concerning dates and specific places are untrustworthy and often contradictory because of the patient's loss of time-sense. Names and events are of questionable veracity. Contradictory statements are often made without the patient actually trying to conceal the truth."

In a classic review of drugs used in interrogation, psychiatrist Louis Gottschalk pointed out some important lessons from the literature.[54] He emphasized that the drugs' effectiveness is not just due to their pharmacological properties. Many people respond to placebos—if told that a drug will have a certain effect, like ameliorating pain or compelling truth telling, 30 percent of people will experience that effect even if the drug is inert. Similarly, the way that the drug is administered is enormously important. Administering the drug in a nonthreatening manner and in low doses (at least initially) helps the subject relax his or her guard. Gottschalk also warned that it is a mistake to leap into talking about explosive topics; instead, interviews are more productive if they focus on relatively benign matters in the beginning, at least until the subject develops some degree of trust.

In another paper, Gottschalk was adamant that "there is no 'truth serum' which can force every informant to report all the information he has." Instead, people can lie or distort the truth while under the influence of drugs. He thought that suggestible individuals, those who are awed by authority or plagued by guilt or depression, might be less successful in withholding information, but they still could unconsciously distort the information and/or confuse fantasies with facts. "It would be very difficult under these circumstances for an interrogator to distinguish when the verbal content was turning from fact to fantasy, when the informant was simulating deep narcosis but actually falsifying, which of contrary stories told under narcosis was true, and when a lack of crucial information coming from a subject under a drug meant the informant had none to offer."[55]

These observations led Gottschalk to believe that training could help military personnel resist interrogation under truth drugs. His suggestions about how to protect troops assumed enormous importance during the peak of the Cold War—in the Korean War and the subsequent decade.

> The informant should know that a drug of itself cannot force him to tell the truth, although it may make him talkative, overemotional, mentally confused, or sleepy. . . . There is no need for the informant to become panicky at any bizarre or uncomfortable reactions he may experience, for these reactions . . . [are transitory]. The informant can confound the interrogator by . . . [simulating] drowsiness, confusion and disorientation early during the administration of the drug. He can revel in fantasies; the more lurid the better. He can tell contradictory stories. He can simulate psychosis. . . . By these devices he can raise serious doubts in the interrogator's mind as to the reliability of the information given by him.[56]

But Gottschalk was mistaken about the very nature of the problem. The government's next challenge was not how to protect our soldiers from revealing secrets; it was the opposite. How could we protect soldiers from an enemy unswervingly dedicated to implanting ideas into them—that is, converting them? That problem emerged five years later in Korea and China.

CHAPTER FOUR

A Cold War Prelude to Korea

In order to eliminate the inevitability of war, it is necessary to abolish imperialism.

—STALIN, 1951

WHEN PEACE CAME IN 1945, the world breathed a sigh of relief, but it was a short sigh. Even as the surrender discussions were under way, the former Allies were preparing for a different sort of war with each other—not a worldwide conflagration but an unremitting battle of ideology and doctrine, punctuated by smaller wars. As Churchill cautioned in 1946: "The United States stands at this time at the pinnacle of world power. . . . When I stand here this quiet afternoon I shudder to visualize what is actually happening to millions now and what is going to happen. . . . A shadow has fallen upon the scenes so lately lighted by the Allied victory. . . . From Stettin in the Baltic to Trieste in the Adriatic, an iron curtain has descended across the Continent."[1]

The Soviets seized Central and Eastern Europe, and all over the world the Soviets and the Americans faced off with proxy wars and efforts to destabilize each other's supporting regimes. The West called the Soviets brutal and totalitarian; the Soviets called the West imperialist and racist.

Stalin was committed to destroying confidence in democratic institutions, which he called "the moderate wing of fascism."[2]

The Cold War was not just about empire, land, and trade. It was also a doctrinal war between liberal democracy and Communism. Secretary of Defense James Forrestal mused that he wasn't sure if the United States was confronting an enemy nation or a religion.[3] The Cold War was a battle of beliefs, where the goal was the conversion of the enemy. Not surprisingly, this long-running battle triggered a burgeoning interest in brainwashing.

To understand the context of how brainwashing developed, it is helpful to review some of the early developments of the Cold War. Table 2 provides a condensed timeline of the initial years of the Cold War.

The post–World War II sense of victory and security evaporated. The dreams of peace that followed World War II seemed to have been a mirage and new nightmares threatened.[4] China was falling to the Communists, and in 1949, the Soviets exploded an atom bomb. By the late 1940s, the Cold War spanned the world. As early as 1945, an extensive Soviet spy ring was exposed in Canada, and American discoveries followed, with revelations about Whittaker Chambers and Alger Hiss. Britain's intelligence service was similarly compromised.

In addition to uncovering numerous nests of spies (on both sides), there was the riveting problem of Communists abducting hostages. Even today, hostage taking is not rare; every year approximately two hundred Americans are held hostage somewhere in the world, typically for money or revenge.[5] In the early Cold War years, the goal wasn't money but rather to seize the enemy, spirit him away, and persuade him to confess or defect to the other side. These abductions were by no means limited to Europe; they took place widely in Japan and South Korea, and even in the United States (for example, the Kasenkina affair in 1948).[6] These abductions were upsetting reminders that the enemy was lurking everywhere.

I was a Cold War child growing up in Iowa in the 1940s and 1950s. Stalin's show trials were a thing of the past, and the world was recovering from a war in which the goal was *elimination* of the enemy. The Cold War, on the other hand, aimed at *conversion* of the enemy. I have shadowy memories of one of those Cold War instances where brainwashing was invoked. I can still "see" the Hungarian cardinal József Mindszenty peering out from a U.S. embassy balcony. An Austro-Hungarian nationalist and rigidly conservative Catholic leader, Mindszenty had been repeatedly arrested by both leftist and rightist forces because he opposed any form of totalitarianism or interference with the Catholic Church. The Commu-

Table 2. Condensed timeline of the early Cold War years

1945	Nazi Germany surrenders
	Atom bombs dropped on Hiroshima and Nagasaki
	Japan surrenders
	Soviet Union occupies Central and Eastern Europe
	Roosevelt dies
	Soviet defector reveals extensive Soviet spying in Canada and United States
1946	Churchill warns that "an iron curtain has descended"
	Stalin states Communism and capitalism are incompatible
	America asserts that domino theory justifies support of Greece and Turkey
	Confrontations in Iran, Dutch East Indies, Latvia, French Indochina
1947	Truman doctrine—assist countries facing Communist takeover
	Voice of America begins broadcasts
	Formation of CIA and Cominform (Communist Information Bureau)
	George F. Kennan strategy of containment against Communism
	Red Scare and loyalty reviews before House Un-American Activities Committee
1948	Start of Berlin blockade
	Soviet jamming of Voice of America
	Soviet coup d'état in Czechoslovakia
1949	Formation of NATO
	Berlin blockade ends
	Mao Zedong defeats Chiang Kai-shek
	Russia explodes atom bomb
	Cardinal Mindszenty show trial
1950	Start of Korean War
	McCarthy era begins
	Rosenbergs indicted for spying
	Klaus Fuchs confesses to spying for Soviet Union
1951	Donald Maclean and Guy Burgess defect from England to Moscow
	Treaties to contain Communism—ANZUS, Mutual Security Act
1952	Truman State of the Union Address—"We are moving through a perilous time. . . . [We are] in the shadow of another world war."
1953	Stalin dies
	Eisenhower takes office
	Armistice to end Korean War
1954	KGB established
	CIA foments coup in Guatemala
	U.S. Senate censures Senator Joseph McCarthy
1955	Formation of Warsaw Pact
	Secretary of State Allen Dulles announces doctrine of massive retaliation

nists tortured him for months before putting him on a show trial in 1949 and sentencing him to life imprisonment. His final detention lasted seven years, four spent in solitary confinement. When the Hungarian Revolution of 1956 broke out, Mindszenty escaped from prison and obtained asylum in the U.S. embassy, where he lived until 1971.[7]

Just before he was apprehended in 1948, he warned his followers that any confession he might make from prison would be a lie because he expected to be tortured. And indeed before his trial, he was subjected to repeated beatings and sleep deprivation; he was malnourished and lost about 50 percent of his weight; and the unceasing screams of other torture victims weighed on him. Nonetheless, he refused to confess. During his interrogations he swore he had committed no acts against the people, to which his interrogator replied, "If that were true you would not be here."[8] The cadence of this dialog thus followed the familiar pattern laid down by the Inquisition and Stalinist interrogations. It would be reprised across the world in subsequent instances of coercive persuasion.

The cardinal worried (appropriately) about being drugged, became apathetic, and developed visual hallucinations in solitary confinement. He was told the beatings would continue until he signed a confession, and if he didn't, his elderly mother would be brought in for questioning. His interrogators alternated between good cop and bad cop, but he adamantly refused to confess. Eventually, however, they wore him down. What got to him was solitude. He wrote: "Noise induces nervousness, but the quiet of solitary confinement also destroys the nerves gradually. . . . The prisoner . . . no longer has a watch; it is therefore difficult for him to follow the passage of time. Inactivity makes solitude worse. . . . The greatest torment in prison is the monotony, which sooner or later shatters the nervous system and wears the soul thin."[9]

Under this duress, the interrogators demanded that he confess to outlandish crimes (like stealing the Hungarian crown jewels) and cited distorted passages from his letters as evidence of his guilt. When they asked him for names of fellow conspirators, he hesitantly offered the names of two individuals he knew were already dead. This partial confession merely encouraged his interrogators. Eventually, he signed a confession but appended a curious abbreviation to his signature: "C.F.," a Latin abbreviation for *coactus feci* ("I have been forced to act"). The old expression has been used repeatedly by the Church, and Mindszenty would have been aware of its use during the Turkish invasion of Hungary when Catholics were forced to sign confessions under duress.[10] It was also used by Pope

Hungarian cardinal József Mindszenty (1892–1975) at trial in 1949,
accused of being a spy. (© Tallandier / Bridgeman Images.)

Clement XIV in the early nineteenth century when he was forced to suppress the Jesuits.[11]

After months of interrogation, Mindszenty confessed to treason and
black-market dealings, and he was subjected to a two-day show trial. His
haunted visage disturbed the West, which became convinced that here was
yet another victim of the mysterious Communist mind control.

In Britain's Parliament, members were shocked that the cardinal had
confessed to such unlikely charges, and there were murmurings that the
Communists must have drugged him. One MP asked: "Is not the de-
meanour of these prisoners in all these trials behind the Eastern curtain
consistent with the administration of a drug which paralyses all will and

all consciousness?"[12] The CIA concurred: Mindszenty's vacant eyes and monotone voice suggested that "he was under the influence of some mysterious mind-bending drug or that he was standing before the dock in a posthypnotic trance."[13] No one used the word *brainwashing* to describe his situation because that term would not be invented until one year later, but from press reports and governmental observations, the conclusion was that something truly remarkable had happened—some instance of cryptic Communist influence.

I am not so sure that the cardinal's confession was the result of some startlingly new form of dark persuasion. After months of harsh treatment, solitary confinement, and torture, it is understandable that someone might succumb to interrogation and confess. Why do we think that people would not? Besides, if he had been successfully brainwashed, would he have added the secret message buried in the signature line of his confession, saying, in essence, "This confession was obtained only under the duress of force"? Finally, the ashen look on his face likely reflected exhaustion. Why conclude that he was a mind-controlled zombie, as in films such as *Cabinet of Doctor Caligari* (1920) or *Frankenstein* (1931)? He looked exhausted, pained, and drained of energy not because of black magic but because he was indeed exhausted, pained, and drugged with concoctions of stimulants and mescaline.[14]

There is, however, a germ of truth to allegations that the Hungarians used a secret Communist technique. His tormentors were methodical and patient. They were also prescient in recognizing that sleep deprivation was one of their most powerful tools. Shakespeare wrote, "He that sleeps feels not the toothache"; he would have been just as accurate to state the converse: "He that sleeps not suffers agonies."[15]

★★★

This issue of secret Communist techniques of persuasion returned even more compellingly one year later as reports started to trickle in from China and then from Korea. Many Western missionaries, scholars, and reporters had remained in China during the protracted civil war. When Mao's forces eventually won in 1949, these Westerners and many Chinese intellectuals were detained by the Chinese. Rumors circulated that the Chinese were using odd methods of interrogation and indoctrination on these prisoners.

There are countless autobiographies by those who were detained, but I find the work of Allyn and Adele Rickett particularly interesting. They were graduate students studying in China when they were imprisoned as spies from 1951 to 1955, but there was something decidedly unusual about how they were treated in custody. The Ricketts were told that the purpose of their imprisonment was not punishment but reeducation. They were to use their time in prison to learn a new outlook on life, to reform their thinking through study and mutual criticism.[16]

The detainees were treated harshly and subjected to protracted interrogation and indoctrination. Interrogators told them that intellectuals were not "of the people," that they would come to realize their crimes, and that Western visitors like them were stooges of imperialism cloaking their true intentions behind a façade of scholarship. The prisoners were asked to write long autobiographies, but whatever they wrote was judged inadequate and they were forced to start all over again. Minute discrepancies in the autobiographies were viewed as evidence of lying.

Much of this treatment followed Russian strategies of interrogation, but the Chinese introduced a new weapon of persuasion—group pressure. Detainees were put in small cells with other prisoners and forced to make daily confessions of their crimes, which were severely criticized by the other prisoners. The groups were quick to recognize insincere confessions and were brutally frank ("Who do you think you're going to fool with that hogwash?"). The Communist cadres encouraged open confessions. "What we want to hear is what you honestly think. Nobody has ever been reprimanded here for being honest. But if you lie and hedge and try to pretend to be something you aren't, then we don't like that. . . . You've committed a serious crime and you'd better start thinking about whether it was right or wrong. Now talk it over among yourselves."[17]

Cut off from the world, with Communist propaganda their only reading material, the Ricketts and the other prisoners were forced to study Communist theory and listen to incessant lectures about Communism. If one prisoner slacked off, everyone in the cell was punished, thereby assuring constant pressures on one another to comply.

After months and sometimes years of such pressure, many confessed and then were freed and banished from China. They gave the world a glimpse of their ordeal through interviews and news stories. Although it was expected that they would renounce their conversions to Communism, not all did. Their views of themselves and the world seemed changed by their experiences in detention. Some even found an appealing quality to the Chinese masses working together to build a better world in comparison to the imperialism and racism of the West. Based on their confessions, McCarthyites threatened U.S. returnees with charges of treason, and as a result, many of the former detainees weren't sure where in the world they belonged anymore.

Upon their release, the Ricketts were forced to see a psychiatrist and subjected to press conferences where they were barraged with questions. Journalists reported that Adele's "mind has been twisted out of recognition." In a surprise statement, Allyn publicly admitted that in a sense his studies in China really were a form of spying and in light of that, he felt he had been treated leniently. This was viewed as further evidence of contemptible cowardice ("Why didn't you stay in China if you liked it so much?").[18]

In addition to detainees' autobiographies, studies of former Chinese prisoners started to emerge. The most prominent study was that of U.S. Air Force psychiatrist Robert Lifton, who interviewed fifteen Chinese scholars and twenty-five Westerners expelled from China in 1951. Based on these extensive interviews (and those he subsequently conducted with returning American POWs), Lifton coined the term *thought reform* to describe the Chinese techniques of persuasion.

While thought reform had similarities to earlier Russian methods, it had a different emphasis. In Russia, confession was followed by purge, exile, or liquidation. In China, the goal of confession was reeducation and rehabilitation. Certainly, there was coercion, but it was mixed with an evangelistic fervor to "wipe out criminal thoughts and establish a new moral code." Lifton likened thought reform to a process of dying and being reborn, characterizing the public confessions as "ecstatic repentance and histrionic remorse."[19]

Lifton suggested that thought reform occurred in phases. Newly arriving Chinese intellectuals in prison were greeted warmly and encouraged to get to know one another. There was a sense of optimism and esprit de corps. Then the detainees were taught about the old society's corruption and shown that they, as intellectuals, had come from such depraved social classes. They were then encouraged to purge themselves of their past to become part of the new society. The Chinese maintained airtight control of this milieu, filtering out what prisoners could learn from the outside world. They demanded purity, confession, and absolute acceptance of their dogma. The cadres used language filled with slogans and dichotomized the world between "the people" versus "the reactionaries." It was a recipe that future cults readily adopted.

Finally, there was a period of conflict (or struggle) when prisoners summarized their life history by criticizing themselves and their fellow students—ever on the lookout for signs of unorthodoxy. There was a long list of what to criticize: "'individualism'—placing personal interests above those of 'the people' . . . ; 'subjectivism'—applying a personal viewpoint to a problem rather than a 'scientific' Marxist approach; 'objectivism'—undue detachment, viewing oneself 'above class distinction,' . . . 'deviationism,' 'opportunism,' . . . 'revisionism,' . . . , 'sectarianism,' 'idealism,' and 'pro-American outlook.'"[20]

As Lifton described it, thought reform led to a compulsion to confess, the more luridly the better, and to revival-like meetings where students rejoiced that the State had washed away all their sins. In his words, "confession amounted to atonement and led to redemption."[21]

In the end, the thought-reformed prisoner acquired a new identity, but would the new ideas persist after release? Lifton noted that prisoners were stunned when they were freed. They staggered out of China with a haunting sense of sadness, confusion about the world, and lingering feelings of guilt and shame. Most of all, they felt like outsiders in their own culture.

POWs in the Korean War had a different experience than the Chinese intellectuals and Western missionaries. With these POWs, the Chinese resorted to more brutality to soften up the prisoners before trying to convert them. I'll elaborate on the techniques used on American POWs in Korea subsequently. But first, it is important to set the historical context because the Korean conflict is arguably one of America's most forgotten wars.

★★★

Most people do not recall details of the war that brought brainwashing into public conversation. It's important to note the geographical context: in Korea, distances are not great—Seoul is only thirty-five miles from the border with North Korea.[22] The Korean peninsula dangles from Manchuria, which has, at various times, been part of China to the west or Russia to the north. Because of its geographical setting, Korean borders have been repeatedly crisscrossed by invading armies. In 1910, Japan annexed Korea and went on to invade Manchuria in 1931 and China in 1937. In those days China itself was in the throes of a civil war, which had to take a back seat during the Japanese occupation.

When World War II ended in 1945, Japan's empire was rolled back and the Chinese civil war resumed, with Mao Zedong ultimately victorious in 1949. Thereafter, China had a loose (and ambivalent) relationship with Russia, and Manchuria was divided between Russia and China. Korea was split at the 38th parallel between a northern sector administered by Russia and a southern sector administered by the United States. The naïve idea

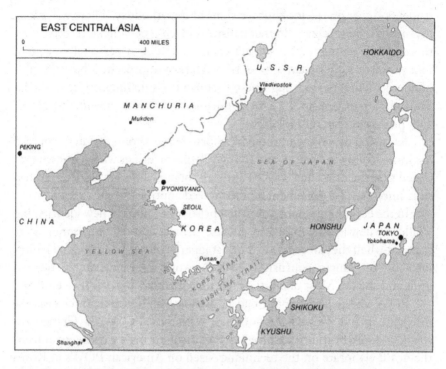

Geographical setting of the Korean War. (From Billy C. Mossman,
United States Army in the Korean War: Ebb and Flow, November 1950–July 1951
[Washington, DC: Center of Military History, United States Army, 1990].)

was that Russia and America would help stabilize and develop Korea after
thirty-five chaotic years of Japanese occupation and then depart after elections took place.

In June 1950, the North Koreans suddenly invaded South Korea and
almost succeeded in seizing the entire peninsula. When the front shifted
north, Chinese troops flooded across the Manchurian border to assist the
North Koreans. Throughout the war, the front lurched repeatedly north
and south. China in particular and Russia, secondarily, supported the
North; the United States and the United Nations supported the South.[23]
During one phase of the conflict, General Douglas MacArthur staged a
brilliant offense into the North—so successful that it threatened to esca-
late the war into a direct conflict with Russia and China. America became
obsessed with the threat of Communism after President Truman fired
MacArthur for insubordination. And the war dragged on.

Millions of people were killed in this vicious war. It is hard to say which season was hardest for combat—blistering summers with monsoon rains or frigid winters. The casualty rate among early prisoners in North Korea was particularly high due to the mountainous terrain and extreme temperatures. The North Koreans had insufficient detention facilities, so they summarily executed many prisoners. The rest were sent north on death marches until they were handed over to the Chinese. Among the dead were some thirty-six thousand Americans.[24] After China took control of prisoners and once cease-fire discussions began in July 1951, the mortality rate of POWs dropped, but it took two years for an uneasy armistice to be reached in 1953.

The behavior of the prisoners during and after their imprisonment was profoundly galling to the U.S. government. What had the Chinese done to the American prisoners to make them confess to waging germ warfare and to participate in antiwar propaganda? Even worse—how had the Chinese persuaded a small number of POWs to refuse to return home after the war? Prisoners were also denounced for dishonorably *dying* in captivity. These events became linked to the idea that prisoners succumbed because American culture was weak and too liberal. Then a magical word appeared to explain everything—brainwashing.

CHAPTER FIVE

The Korean War and the
Birth of Brainwashing

In brainwashing, a fog settles over the patient's mind until
he loses touch with reality. . . . Brainwashing is something
new which is contrary to human nature and inseparable from
communism.

—EDWARD HUNTER, 1956

THE KOREAN CONFLICT WAS a war for territory and ideological conversion of the enemy. All sides bombarded one another with extensive propaganda campaigns. The principal combatants were the South Koreans, supported by the United States and the United Nations, versus the North Koreans, supported by the Chinese and Russians. Given the Chinese involvement, the Nationalist Chinese were also involved in their own blizzard of propaganda against the Chinese. The war dragged on for an extra two years while armistice negotiations stalled, primarily over the question of allowing captured POWs to choose where they wanted to go upon release. The answer to that question had enormous propaganda value. All sides sought to persuade captured soldiers to repudiate their home country and defect to the other side.

The fact that some American troops chose to defect to China was a gut-wrenching blow to the United States. What really happened to the prisoners, and how did it come about? Many voices described that phenomenon and tried to make sense of such decisions. Some voices were shrill, others more nuanced.

The loudest voice was that of Edward Hunter, a journalist who worked for the OSS in World War II as a propaganda specialist in psychological warfare. He brought a real flair to reporting and we owe the term *brainwashing* to his gift of gab and ability to turn a catchy phrase. The Chinese term is *xi nao*, which refers to achieving change by washing or cleansing the heart through retreat from the world and meditation. Now *that* is hardly as catchy as "brainwashing." The philosopher Wittgenstein observed that "a new word is like a fresh seed sown on the ground of the discussion."[1] Hunter's new word flourished like crabgrass.

The book jacket gives a flavor of Hunter's classic *Brainwashing in Red China*.[2] "'Brain-washing' . . . is the terrifying new Communist strategy to conquer the free world by destroying its mind. . . . This is the first book that reveals how the Communists in China are utilizing this combination of misapplied psychology and perverted evangelism. . . . [This book] discloses for the first time new and horrifying extremes in the psychological warfare being waged against the free world and against the very concept of freedom."

Hunter interviewed Chinese intellectuals and Westerners released from Chinese detention and described the brainwashing process as turning the prisoner into a mindless, Communist automaton, "a living puppet—a human robot—without the atrocity being visible from the outside."[3] The expert in propaganda was right; his term was catchy.[4]

According to Hunter, initially, prisoners were subjected to mock executions, near starvation, and sleep deprivation. The Chinese deprived prisoners of everything and then offered a morsel of something, thereby ensuring gratitude. Then, prisoners were forced to memorize and discuss Communist tracts. They were divided into groups in which they criticized themselves and one another. Those who refused were put in solitary confinement. The guards sought confessions, using terms like *reform* and *rebirth* to describe the persuasion of their captives. Hunter, like Robert Lifton, recognized an almost medieval religious quality in this quest for confession, commenting that in the original sense of the term, confessing connotes both cleansing and being in conformity with a larger force (for example, Church or State).

Convinced that brainwashing was an extension of Pavlov's approach,

Hunter called the leaders of the reeducation camps "mystic Pavlovians of high communism" and asserted that the Chinese were conducting mind control behind "a Great Pavlovian Wall." He accused the Communist states of using Pavlov's techniques to produce "the insectivization of human beings . . . [where the] individual [was] replaced by the *we* of collectivity."[5] Hunter was indefatigable, authoring numerous books on brainwashing, testifying to Congress, and speaking everywhere. He wrote with verve in a casual style, with minimal references—and those he provided were sloppy in extreme (for example, "Bible, 273, 276").[6]

Despite his glib style, Hunter did in fact capture many features used by the Chinese, but he also saw the world through deeply held conservative convictions. The House Un-American Activities Committee (HUAC) sought him out as a consultant to explain brainwashing. He gave the committee an earful, not just about Chinese activities but about America's weakness too. He warned HUAC that Communists had turned our leaders into defeatist liberals and intellectuals who believed in peaceful coexistence and converted professors into fools who considered themselves objective historians. He thundered about the liquidation of U.S. moral values. Why did so many American soldiers cooperate with the Communists? Because they were soft, raised on a tradition of getting along as opposed to leading. "There is no such thing as a Communist Party. . . . It is a Communist conspiracy, a Communist psychological warfare organization . . . [based on] the findings of the Russian physiologist, Pavlov."[7]

HUAC members loved him. They had found a man after their own heart. The problem was that virtually none of the psychiatrists who examined the Chinese scholars or American POWs agreed with Hunter's premise. They hated Hunter's florid terminology and rejected his assertion that there was some mysterious revolutionary discovery that guided Chinese indoctrination efforts. The people who *did* agree with Hunter were largely other journalists and those who were obsessed with concerns about Communist conspiracy. Hunter's simple message as an expert in propaganda trumped the academics' expertise.

Dutch psychiatrist Joost Meerloo coined a rival and equally flamboyant alternate term—*menticide*. Having escaped the Nazis as the sole survivor of his family, Meerloo warned that totalitarian regimes inevitably worked toward what he called the rape of the mind, or menticide.[8] He did not feel the risk was confined to Communism alone; rather, "Menticide is an infectious disease that exists everywhere, including the United States, where there is a mass hysteria over communism."[9]

Meerloo noted that forced confessions have been common in history but that there was a peculiarly methodical quality to the Communist indoctrination efforts. These coercive techniques were so powerful, Meerloo thought, that virtually anyone could be worn down by the process. He, like Hunter, traced this back to Pavlov, commenting that Pavlovian conditioning is facilitated when sensory inputs are restricted: "Pavlov . . . [discovered] the conditioned reflex could be developed most easily in a quiet laboratory with a minimum of disturbing stimuli. Every trainer of animals knows this from his own experience; isolation and the patient repetition of stimuli are required to tame wild animals. . . . The totalitarians have followed this rule. They know that they can condition their political victims most quickly if they are kept in isolation."[10]

Allegations about Chinese coercive persuasion tactics were triggered by inexplicable behaviors in the American (and British) POWs who were held by North Korea and China. Most of the American POWs had been captured early in the war and thus spent years in harsh confinement. The war had come as a surprise to the United States, and planning was deficient. The early days of the war were marked by lack of ammunition, and supplies were so short that soldiers were limited to two sheets of toilet paper when they went to the bathroom.[11] It was the coldest Korean winter in one hundred years, and troops had improper clothing for such harsh conditions. When troops were captured, morale was low and conditions in the camps were abysmal. The soldiers were malnourished, received inadequate medical care, and were crowded in huts where they were bombarded by Communist propaganda from loudspeakers.

Most American POWs had been captured by the North Koreans in the first three months of the war and were forced into pitiless death marches to reach the camps. Those caught later in the war bypassed the North Korean brutality, as they were captured by or transferred to the Chinese. If they survived long enough to be handed over to the Chinese, the POWs were stunned to find that their new guards greeted them with a smile, a cigarette, and a handshake, beginning a process of indoctrination that would last about three years.

It was in this context that POWs started confessing to waging germ warfare and participating in antiwar propaganda. Moreover, a small number of POWs refused to come home when the armistice was eventually finalized. America saw the hand of satanic Communism at work.

The germ warfare allegations were explosive, but war always breeds contagion with its chaos, filth, malnutrition, and absence of effective government. In World War II, infections were rampant in the European theater. Furthermore, in World War II, Japanese Unit 731 had experimented with biowarfare weapons on some ten thousand POWs held in Manchuria.[12] In some protocols, the captors inoculated prisoners with bacteria. In others, they tested the infection rate of prisoners tied to stakes at varying distances from bombs laden with anthrax and cholera.[13]

After World War II, infectious plagues were particularly prevalent in postwar Japan, where over 650,000 people suffered from cholera, dysentery, typhoid fever, scarlet fever, or diphtheria, and 100,000 died from these infections.[14] As that war wound down, the United States shielded Japanese germ warfare specialists from prosecution and used their expertise to build a sizable biological warfare program at Fort Detrick in Maryland.

In March 1952, there were reports of anthrax and plague in China and North Korea and also peculiar sightings of insects, even in the dead of winter. Were the Korean outbreaks merely another manifestation of the natural indirect effects of war, or did they reflect more sinister causes? The Chinese believed the infections came from America and persuaded some captured American pilots to confess that they had dropped germ warfare bombs over North Korea.[15] It would have been a major propaganda coup if the North Koreans and Chinese could have tied the Americans to germ warfare. This would link the United States to the hated Japanese occupation in World War II, thereby strengthening the Communist cause and assuring that America would be pilloried worldwide.

From the U.S. side, brainwashing was invoked to explain the fact that half of the seventy-eight captured American aviators confessed to participating in a biowarfare program. The United States vehemently rejected the allegations, labeling them "a tremendous and calculated campaign of lies."[16] The confessions, widely disseminated, were repudiated once the flyers returned to the United States.

Air Force colonel Walker Mahurin described his treatment under the Communist interrogation: "During the heated period of my confession process, when they had begun to affect my thought processes . . . I blurted out that I had visited the Army camp of Detrick. . . . This, of course, was a thing that they wanted, and they pressed me to write the details of my visit. . . . After getting me to break on this information, they began to press me quite heavily to make a total confession."[17]

Other captured pilots reported they had been subjected to extreme duress, isolated in unheated huts or water-soaked holes in the ground, manacled in painful positions, deprived of sleep and food. All the while, they were badgered about China's suffering under capitalism, the faults of imperialism, and the promise of socialism. Upon his return to the United States, Air Force pilot John Quinn described his interrogation: "He [the interrogator] constantly harangued me with stock questions on what was I thinking, what were my feelings, what was Communism etc., etc. I can't write sensibly about what that does to a person when he can't fight back. . . . I hope others . . . may get some vague feeling for what I—and others—have been through. . . . The result is living dead men, controlled human robots, which willingly, as long as they are under the spell, do their master's bidding."[18]

The power of Chinese thought reform appeared to get stronger as the war dragged on. Air Force psychiatrist Louis Jolyon (aka "Jolly") West studied successive cohorts of American POWs who arrived in the Chinese prison camps at different times and examined how many confessed or collaborated. Over the course of just one year, the percentage of American POWs who made bogus confessions tripled from 25 percent to 75 percent.[19] It was the first of many telling observations West would make about brainwashing in a career that spanned from air force prisoners to elephants, LSD, and Patty Hearst.

Years later, scholars tracked down one of the senior Chinese interrogators and asked him how the interrogations were performed. He did not address the brutality but described some of the techniques for grilling prisoners.

> When the prisoners first came to our camp, they filled out a form requiring information about themselves, their family, life prior to joining the armed forces, military career, social activities, and political affiliations. . . . Then after a few days, we . . . called each one in for an interview. It might last an hour or two, all day, or even a couple of days. . . . [We] required them to make a written statement. . . . After we read their paper, we called them back in a day or two and had further discussions, asking them to give more details, to provide a fuller account of themselves. . . . They gave in very easily. . . . One by one, it was very easy to have them say what they knew.[20]

In response to the brutality and the unending interrogation, POWs signed antiwar petitions, authored letters to the editors of their hometown papers, and wrote their families criticizing the war as imperialistic and the United States as racist. Corporal LaRance Sullivan from Santa

Barbara wrote home in November 1952: "I have come to realize that the war is not being fought for the common people like you and I, but for a handful of Wall Streets. . . . I was of the belief when I first got captured that I would be killed. But as you can see, Mama, I am still alive. . . . I am hoping with all my heart that all you folks will stay in the mood for peace—maybe soon all the boys will be back. One thing for sure, Mama, if everyone gets in the move for peace, some day the common people will win."[21]

Other prisoners criticized the war as a senseless waste of lives and asked that their savings accounts be redirected to support Communist newspapers like *New Masses* and *Daily Workers*. They criticized America for hypocrisy and racism and blasted Senator McCarthy and the House Un-American Activities Committee. "I have been in prison for three years, and for the first time in my life, I have seen complete equality for men of all races and colors who worked together and played together. When I see things like this I am reminded of what happened to me in my own country where as children, I and other Negro boys were whipped by policemen because we didn't take off our hats to them." One POW wrote home stating simply: "It is impossible to fight for peace in the United States. Anyone who tries to fight for peace will be prosecuted and even put to death. The Rosenbergs spoke out for peace and look what the United States government did to them."[22]

Many letters didn't "ring true" to their recipients. One private wrote a long letter home criticizing how America was treating the former POWs, but it didn't sound right to his family. His sister commented: "My brother couldn't have written those letters. He was too dumb to write like that. Why, when he went in the Army he was seventeen and still in the eighth grade. . . . Someone addressed it, signed it 'Bud,' and filled in the middle."[23]

Other families noted stylistic inconsistencies in the letters they received, which made them wonder if they were genuine. Private First Class Morris Wills wrote: "It is my understanding that there is a peace movement back there, so tell Father that with all my heart I hope he supports the peace movement to his fullest ability in faith that it will bring me back home, quick and safe." The letter went on, talking about harvesting wheat and of the hired men on the family farm. But his sister said that he had never called his father anything but "Dad" and she pointed out that there were no hired men on the farm and they never planted wheat.[24] The hidden errors in the letter were clues that the letter had been written under duress.

Conditions in many camps were so bad that some prisoners had to sign a peace petition just to get an aspirin.[25] These conditions may have contributed to prisoners' signing propaganda letters and petitions: a quid pro quo to receive slightly better treatment in terms of food, clothing, and shelter.

The question of prisoner repatriation was the key sticking point that mired the cease-fire negotiations.[26] After any war, it is assumed that prisoners will want to return to their home countries. However, after World War II, it was clear that millions of people displaced by the conflict did not want to return to their "homes" for various reasons—because their homes were no more, their neighborhoods and towns were no more, or even their countries were no more. Furthermore, for some, there were risks to returning; many POWs who returned to the Soviet Union were promptly accused of collaboration and shipped off to forced labor in the gulags.

President Truman demanded that all POWs be given a choice of where they wished to be repatriated, knowing that many of the North Korean and Chinese POWs did not wish to be resettled in the North. Their reluctance to return was a potential propaganda disaster for North Korea and China, particularly if Chinese POWs preferred to resettle in Nationalist China.[27] So the armistice discussions dragged on while fighting continued and prisoners languished. Eventually, the armistice agreement allowed prisoner repatriation after a three-month waiting period under the supervision of the United Nations.

That some North Koreans and Chinese did not want to be repatriated was one thing, but what really disturbed the United States was that some U.S. POWs preferred to stay in China rather than come home. The country was floored when twenty-three soldiers declared they did not want to return, although two changed their minds.[28] One mom wondered: "Could it be that Jack is mentally ill? Maybe his headaches started again and they worked on him when he was in that condition. . . . Maybe he has an incurable disease. . . . Jack wouldn't want to be a burden to us. Maybe they threatened his family . . . or maybe they sold him a bill of goods that Communism is going to help humanity." The governor of Maryland sent a taped message to one of the twenty-one asking him to renounce Communism and return to his home and family. "Come home, John, come home to the freedom and dignity of America. The United States has no imperialist ambitions. It is the Communists who are the would-be emperors of the world."[29]

Who were the twenty-one soldiers who refused to return to the United

U.S. POWs who chose not to repatriate after the Korean War.
(Bettmann / Getty Images.)

States? What was their background? The most reliable information comes
from the extraordinary reporting of journalist Virginia Pasley. In a field
that came to be sullied by doctrinaire agitprop articles, her analysis stands
out for its clarity and thoroughness. Crisscrossing the country, she visited
the soldiers' hometowns and talked with their parents, relatives, ministers,
guidance counselors, and teachers. That task would be hard enough today,
but in the 1950s, with no internet to facilitate her detective work, it was a
remarkable achievement.

Most of those who chose not to return grew up in small towns or rural
communities mired in poverty. Only four of the twenty-one had finished
high school; five of them never got beyond eighth grade. Most came from
broken homes, but only three of them were ever in trouble with juvenile

authorities. While many had troubled childhoods, others had remarkably quiet upbringings. One mother wrote about her son: "Jack was always a good child. The only mischief I ever remember him getting into was when he ate a whole tube of toothpaste and broke out in terrible hives."[30]

They were young men; only six were older than twenty-one when captured and three were just seventeen. They were volunteers, not draftees. Twenty had no understanding of Communism other than thinking it a dirty word. Most had no idea what they were fighting for in Korea. Neighbors and classmates described them as withdrawn, lone wolves in school who took no part in activities or sports. Nonetheless, they got along well in the army; some had even been decorated for heroism.

Sergeant Richard Corden's childhood priest described him as "a boy who never had anything, who didn't have much to be happy about. He was a wonderfully bright boy and he showed definite signs of qualities of leadership. But he had little direction. . . . I haven't got the answer but I feel that it is a further development of something he suffered when he was a child. . . . He must be confused now. No boy in his right senses would do what he did."[31]

Pasley's methodical approach can be seen in her extensive description of sources regarding Private First Class William Cowart, who ran away from home before completing high school. One of his teachers said, "He had quite a few emotional problems to solve. It was apparent that he had a chip on his shoulder and . . . didn't get along with his stepfather. He was extremely insecure [and] rather than make friends and fail, he just withdrew from the other boys in the class." Another teacher commented that Cowart's letters from Korea were filled with wistful longing. His principal said, "He was a boy who was hard to know. At times he was easy to talk to and would cooperate. At other times he was silent and resentful—suspicious. He was not a boy I would have picked out as being one who would turn his allegiance from his country." Pasley even tracked down and interviewed a neighbor, who commented: "Billy was a strange boy, never happy or satisfied in his life. I can't say that I ever liked him, though he was in and out of my house most of his life. But when I saw the movies of him over there, I sat down and cried. . . . He was quiet and moody; he tried to be happy-go-lucky but he just couldn't make it. I think he was just too young. They shouldn't have sent him over there."[32]

After the POWs announced their decisions about not repatriating, they had a three-month waiting period while their families tried to persuade them to change their minds. Heartbreaking letters and tapes were sent, but these were typically not even opened or acknowledged by the prisoners. One mother begged her son to come home: "Please son, don't let me down. I can't give you up. I love you." A father wrote his son: "Just imagine, son, that I have my arms around you. Imagine that I am right there by you, kissing you on the cheek. We all want you home, son. I can guarantee you will not be harmed. Tell . . . [them] that you want to come home and they will let you."[33]

The parents faced ostracism in their community for raising disloyal sons. Private First Class Hawkins's mother refused to take the abuse and fought back in the *Oklahoma City Times:* "If you ask me who has disgraced themselves, it is we, who have sat back in apparent helplessness and let those Red devils carry off twenty-one of our American boys and for propaganda purposes of our own say, 'Good riddance to bad rubbish.' One of those boys happens to be mine and I'm not going to let the Communists push me around while I sit idly by and say and do nothing. . . . Let him who is without sin cast the first stone at these boys. Judge not, lest ye be judged."[34]

The war lasted roughly three years and involved about 1.6 million U.S. soldiers. By the time the armistice was concluded, thousands of Americans had died in combat, ninety-eight thousand had been wounded, 38 percent of POWs had died in captivity, and twenty-one soldiers had defected to the People's Republic of China. The death rate among American POWs was higher than that found in the Central Powers' prison camps in World War I (4 percent), among American POWs in Japan (35 percent), or in Vietnam (16 percent).[35] The high death rate in Korea was due to more than just inclement weather conditions; only 2 percent of the Communist POWs died in American captivity.[36]

The remaining POWs returned home to a country unsure whether they were traitors or victims. It was a painful time; the lack of an outright victory in Korea, the heavy losses, and the continuing Cold War confrontations weighed heavily on America. At that fraught moment, the Job's comforters started their harangues.

★★★

It's always good practice to analyze what went wrong with a project, whether you are reviewing a war, building a car, or monitoring a hospital's infection control. This quality assurance mentality works when it is dispassionate and is interested in solving problems rather than casting blame. In contrast, the haranguers in the wake of the Korean conflict were passionate advocates for punishing the wicked. The agitators continued on a course blazed by Hunter at HUAC: American professors and politicians are weak; liberalism has sapped our strength, and so on. *That* is why our soldiers behaved so poorly.

In addition to Hunter, two other agitators were prominent. Major William E. Mayer, an army psychiatrist, reviewed the files of returning POWs and unburdened himself in an interview in *U.S. News and World Report*.[37] Why did so many American prisoners die and why did so many collaborate? American culture and education were to blame. Americans had become too soft; they had no gumption; U.S. soldiers needed to toughen up. POWs who were particularly susceptible to the blandishments of the North Koreans, Mayer said, were those raised in a culture of "momism" — overprotective, smothering mothers who sapped their sons' maturity and independence. Mayer went on a lecture tour where he fleshed in his comments. Why did so many prisoners die? "They died because of some failures and lack . . . of character, the development of loyalties, the development of leadership. . . . [They had] 'Giveupitis,' . . . a disease of the passive, the dependent, the rather inadequate, the kid who was awfully insecure, . . . who cried himself to sleep at night . . . [who] talked about his mother a lot. Who brooded."[38]

Although Mayer denied that Pavlovian conditioning was involved with the troops' poor behavior, he then described the Chinese system as patiently manipulating and rewarding those who complied. Isn't that the essence of Pavlov?

Going off on a tangent (as he frequently did), Mayer continued that Communists "didn't use sex or sexual methods—and this is a question many people ask for the simple reason that we know, for example, in the University of Chicago in the 20s and 30s . . . , there were some groups of sort of alleged free love activities connected with the Young Communist League."[39] In a remarkably restrained rebuttal, psychiatrist Louis Jolyon West commented, "In my opinion, many of Mayer's conclusions are not justified by the available data."[40] In academic parlance, that is a faintly coded denunciation filled with contempt.

The next Job's comforter was journalist Eugene Kinkead. Writing in the *New Yorker* in 1957, he stoked similar themes, starting his essay, "In every war but one that the United States has fought, the conduct . . . of its service men who were held in enemy prison camps presented no unforeseen problems to the armed forces and gave rise to no particular concern in the country as a whole." The essay continues in that vein, asserting that American soldiers did not try to escape, that their discipline and loyalty in the camps were poor, that they had the temerity to die in the camps, and so on. The last straw was that twenty-one soldiers had defected to the Communists. Such things had never happened before, according to Kinkead and the army officials he interviewed.[41]

Warming to his topic, he asserted that one out of three prisoners had collaborated. He added with gratuitous cruelty that "thirty-eight percent of them . . . died in captivity," a statistic he attributed to "the ignorance or the callousness of the prisoners themselves." In other words, according to Kinkead, it was not the Communists' brutal treatment but the soldiers' own weakness that accounted for all the failures.[42] That was just on the first page of his polemic, which he later expanded into a book.

In contrast to these diatribes, the military carried out remarkably careful and thorough analyses of the returnees. The returning GIs were studied extensively on their three-week voyage home from Korea; psychiatrists and psychologists assembled massive dossiers about each soldier, cross-checked against other soldiers' reports. The average POW returned home with 185 denunciations, and one soldier accumulated about 800 complaints about his behavior.[43] In a curious twist on brainwashing and interrogation, CIA operatives also wanted to use amytal interviews on the returning GIs to learn more about the Chinese techniques, but the plans were vetoed by the surgeon general's office.[44]

The soldiers also underwent Rorschach tests and sentence completion assessments. They seemed calm and almost apathetic, but their Rorschach inkblots revealed an underlying turbulence and aggression, as if "they were ready to tear into something in a rage."[45] A common response to one of the inkblot cards was "two men ripping something apart, perhaps another man's chest, from which they were removing his heart."[46]

After all this information gathering, the army concluded that one in three soldiers collaborated on some level and one in seven collaborated more seriously. Participating in propaganda broadcasts or declaring that they were being treated well was considered minor collaboration. Two hundred and fifteen more severe cases were turned over to special investigators, and ultimately forty-seven were referred for court-martial.[47]

Observers acknowledged that this was the first war in which the enemy tried so methodically to manipulate the minds of its prisoners and that the efforts were highly coordinated and focused on demoralizing prisoners. They found "indoctrination" closer to the reality of the experience than "brainwashing."

The military extensively discussed whether the Chinese treatment amounted to torture. Where does one draw the line between torture and brutality? It is a question that troubles us to this day. Some army officials regarded "torture" narrowly, as "pain so extreme that it causes a man to faint or lose control of his will."[48] Merely uncomfortable things, like being repeatedly kicked, beaten, held in painful cramped postures, and exposed to frigid weather, did not, to their way of thinking, count as torture. The army thought that caving in under torture might be forgivable; however, good soldiers should be able to resist collaborating in the face of "ordinary" severe treatment. Good soldiers should be able to resist confessing or collaborating in response to terrible treatment that did not result in unconsciousness. Poor treatment might explain their actions, but it didn't excuse them.

How much interrogation is "too much"? As in Stalin's Soviet Union, the Chinese interrogations were unpredictable in duration and in frequency. Some POWs were interrogated on more than fifty occasions. One pilot was interrogated for twenty hours at a stretch. He was forced to witness the execution of fellow POWs and told that the rest of his crew and his family at home were now targets. During the protracted interrogations his weight dropped by seventy pounds, his memory and logical thinking started to fail him, and after 330 days in solitary confinement, he signed a Korean-dictated confession.[49]

Kinkead disregarded such testimony. To him, the soldiers were weak-willed and "seemed lost without a bottle of pills and a toilet that flushed." This would not have happened if they had been toughened up before combat. Kinkead concluded his censure of these men: "The Army would like to see every American parent, teacher, and clergy man work to instill in every one of our children a specific understanding of the differences between our men and the Communist way of life and . . . give every child, in the blunt, old-fashioned spirit, a firm regard for right and an abiding distaste for wrong."[50]

Thoughtful observers were not so quick to cast blame. Dr. Charles W. Mayo spoke to the United Nations about the torture methods used by the Communists. His remarks were republished verbatim in *U.S. News & World Report*, where he elaborated on the abusive treatment that six American flyer POWs had experienced and described how the Chinese had obtained bogus confessions.

Unlike Kinkead, Mayo did not exonerate the Chinese from charges of brutality. One of the returned flyers, Colonel Walker Mahurin, for in-

stance, was interrogated so brutally for three weeks that he attempted suicide. During his first three months of confinement, he refused to confess
and was then placed in solitary confinement for three more months, during which he was threatened daily with death and roused every night so he
couldn't sleep. This was followed by six weeks of a supposedly "friendlier"
treatment during which he was shown other soldiers' confessions and accusations of his participation in germ warfare. Another soldier was tortured
for four months: "He was stood at attention for five hours at a time, confined eight days in a doorless cell less than 6 feet long; held to the ground
by two guards while a third kicked and slapped him; stood at attention 22
hours until he fell . . . ; interrogated three hours with a spotlight six inches
from his face; ordered to confess while a pistol was held at the back of his
head; . . . left without food three days . . . ; put before a firing squad and
given a last chance; hung by hands and feet from the rafters of a house."[51]

There was a "pattern" to all the interrogation, Mayo told the UN,
which suggested to him that the Communists were using Pavlov's conditioned reflex tricks.

> [The prisoners'] resistance was punished with kicks and slaps in
> the face, . . . with threats of death. . . . Signs of cooperation, on the
> other hand, were rewarded with slight increases in rations, with
> promises of better treatment soon. No wonder that some of our
> prisoners . . . were brought down to that animal level of response
> where resistance was associated with death, . . . and where survival
> on any terms seemed more important than the moral principles
> that distinguish men from beasts. If anything is surprising to me,
> it is that so many of our soldiers—both those who [falsely] con-
> fessed and those who did not . . . somehow continued throughout
> to act like men.[52]

★★★

Many of the future leaders of American psychiatry, psychology, and sociology were actively involved in assessing the POWs, and they took a decidedly different view from their colleague Mayer as well as journalists
Kinkead and Hunter. The scholars' work makes for interesting reading,
but it was, well, scholarly and thus (sadly) ignored. Who wants to read
well-written scientific reports when you can read superbly written and
sensationalist journalism!

The experts hated the term *brainwashing*, resenting its lurid imagery, and strongly denied that there was something radically new in the Chinese brainwashing techniques. Rather, they saw the treatment as a continuation of long-established interrogation practices. They were also less sure that diabolical "Pavlovism" was inherent in the procedure. One scholar commented that people were foolish to regard conversion to Communism as "the demonic machinations of the Doctors Pavlov and Fu Manchu."[53]

If by "Pavlov," one meant some secret and potent technique that his followers possessed, this was ridiculous, said the experts. If, on the other hand, by "Pavlov," one meant patient trial and error, punishing undesirable behavior and rewarding desired behavior, then certainly the experts agreed that was an important element of the interrogations.

To explain the collapse of morale in the POW camps, some pointed to the social setting. Many of the soldiers had been unprepared, in every sense of the word, for the war. Their training and equipment were sub-par. When the Chinese entered the war, the front shifted so rapidly that many UN positions were overrun, and in many cases the leadership of the units was suboptimal. On a more fundamental level, collaboration with the enemy increased because soldiers did not know exactly who or what they were fighting for, in contrast to World War II, where troops fought with allies against a well-known enemy.

When POWs were eventually turned over to the Chinese, they were puzzled by their captors' initial apparent leniency, but it was an "iron-fist-in-a-velvet-glove" type of leniency. The Chinese destroyed the units' leadership structure, segregating the enlisted men from their officers and fomenting distrust among the soldiers by soliciting informants. They interfered with mail, allowing letters from home only if they contained bad news. Many POWs became apathetic, and morale plummeted so low that only 13 percent of the men showed much concern for their fellows; informing on another prisoner was common.[54]

The Chinese were methodical, pacing their endless demands carefully and requiring some degree of participation from the prisoner, no matter how trivial.[55] Their approach relied on what Jolly West called "DDD" (debility, dependency, and dread).[56] They isolated prisoners, depriving them of social support and making them dependent on the interrogator for life-sustaining privileges. Guards imposed a barren monotonous environment. They degraded prisoners by forbidding personal hygiene, hurled incessant insults, and demanded compliance with seemingly meaningless rules.[57] They induced debilitation through semi-starvation, prolonged interrogation, sleep deprivation, and constant threats of death, but they occasionally offered tantalizing indulgences to encourage compliance. Above all, they made it clear that they had complete control over the prisoners' fate and that resistance would be futile.

U.S. Army studies of the prisoners upon repatriation revealed that 15 percent of the POWs chronically collaborated with the Chinese by writing and broadcasting propaganda and informing on fellow prisoners, but few of these collaborators actually converted to Communism. After returning home, 45 percent expressed some "sympathy" toward Communism as a way of life but very few became Communists. Those who collaborated did it for opportunistic reasons (for example, getting better food) rather than ideological ones.[58] Only 5 percent of the soldiers were able to resist the Chinese pressures, and 80 percent were apathetically in the middle; as one researcher described them: "They simply sat by either in apathy or anxiety—and let the conflict rage about them."[59]

The level of collaboration did not differ in terms of soldiers' background characteristics like age, education level, or rank.[60] Did stress have anything to do with caving in? The answer depends upon how you ask the question. One group of investigators, defining "stress" as one profoundly distressing event, reported that high stress elicited more resistance. Another group, which defined stress in terms of chronic pressure and harassment, found the opposite.[61]

According to Kinkead, in previous wars there had never been so many POW defections and instances of collaboration with the enemy. Actually, that is not true. Wartime collaboration was not unique to the Korean War. In her usual incisive writing, Rebecca West described the collaboration of British POWs with the Nazis. "There were also the children among the traitors, the ones who thought like children, and felt like children, and were treacherous as children are, without malice, only because someone was giving away sweetmeats or because the whole gang was chasing the dog."[62] Ten percent of Germans captured by the Russians during World War II developed some sympathy for Communism, and many more collaborated to receive better treatment.[63] In World War I, Germans assumed that Irish soldiers serving in the British military would be excellent targets for collaboration or defection.[64] Soldiers defected in the War of 1812, and about five thousand "reconstructed rebs" went over to the Northern ranks in the Civil War. As neurologist Harold Wolff mused, maybe those "reconstructed rebs" were nineteenth-century equivalents of brainwashed prisoners of war.[65] Even George Washington once complained that some of his troops lacked "public spirit."[66] A certain percentage of soldiers always behave badly, but this time, with Korea, Kinkead et al. invoked national moral decay as the cause rather than an individual soldier's weakness.

Kinkead argued that collaboration was unusually extensive in Korea, as if collaboration were a black-and-white dichotomy. Thirty-nine percent of the POWs admitted to signing propaganda petitions, and 16 percent made some kind of propaganda recordings. How do we classify these soldiers? The army concluded there were gradients of collaboration with the enemy. On some level, every prisoner must comply with his jailers, whether the prison is in Los Angeles or Manchuria. How much compliance is acceptable? The military wrestled with such questions and tried to define a range of responses.[67]

When all was said and done, only ten out of the returning four thousand troops were tried and found guilty of collaboration. Many soldiers both collaborated *and* resisted the Chinese. Kinkead had no patience for such subtleties in evaluating collaboration, but the distinctions are important. Some prisoners, for instance, made mock confessions, knowing that the nuance would be lost on their interrogators (for example, "I promise that I will never again *be caught* stealing the property of the People's Volunteers").[68]

Kinkead asserted that no American POWs tried to escape.[69] There actually were a few escapes, but keep in mind the setting. The closest neutral nation was Burma—two thousand miles away, and it wasn't as if Americans could blend in with the Koreans. Even among the 436,000 German POWs held in the United States during World War II, only twenty-eight escaped without capture, and *they* could presumably blend in more easily than the Americans held in Korea.[70]

Both Kinkead and Mayer assert that the poor morale and defections stemmed from soldiers having been raised in soft conditions. Let's look at that closely. Most of the POWs were about twenty years old in 1950. One could hardly describe the living situation during the depression and World War II as "soft." Furthermore, many had enlisted in the army because it promised (as it still does) education and an escape from poverty.

Kinkead alleged that, in comparison with the American POWs, the two hundred Turkish POWs in China functioned admirably, maintained their esprit de corps, resisted indoctrination, and did not allow themselves to die. The difference may well have been due to the timing of the POWs' capture. The brutality and living conditions were worst in the first year of the war; 99 percent of the 2,634 U.S. Army soldiers who died in captivity died in that first year.[71] Many Turks were captured later in the war and, more to the point, the Chinese had so few Turkish translators that it was impractical to indoctrinate Turkish troops.[72] In order for the Chinese to communicate with the Turks in some camps, the translation required four steps: from Mandarin to Korean, from Korean to English, from English to German, and finally from German to Turkish.[73] Not exactly optimal for brainwashing.

It is difficult to compare global rates of survival given the wide differences in treatment throughout the war, geographically and chronologically. I doubt that moral fiber could explain why the mortality rate for New Hampshire POWs was 62 percent whereas for Hawaiian POWs it was only 16 percent.[74] Kinkead was merely stereotyping Americans with little regard to the complexity of the wartime experience.

★★★

As far as popular culture had it, brainwashing was a demonic new force that could be imposed on anyone. There were fears about sleeper agents among the returning POWs and suspicions of rampant spies in high government positions. Communism, it was believed, had a fearsome new weapon that could strike anywhere. In *The Manchurian Candidate*, the long shadow of Pavlov is invoked. Sergeant Raymond Shaw is ordered to murder one of his fellow prisoners. The evil Dr. Yen Lo, portrayed as a graduate of the USSR's Pavlov Institute, explains to the rapt audience of Communists, "We have trained Americans to kill and then have no memory of having killed. . . . [The prisoner's] brain has not only been washed, it has been dry-cleaned."[75]

The experts dismissed brainwashing as a Gothic horror story, but they did believe that coercive persuasion techniques were powerful and that the United States would need to defend against them. The experts had good data about the breaking point of soldiers. After eighty-five days of uninterrupted combat, shelling, sleep deprivation, and the like, 50 percent of soldiers would break down; 75 percent could be expected to break down by combat day 140, and 90 percent by combat day 210.[76] In other words, there was a "dose response curve" concerning soldiers' breaking point.

But what could help a soldier resist the dark persuasion efforts of an enemy? Air Force psychiatrists thought that survival training was necessary for future troops.[77] They had to be taught what to expect—brutal conditions, coercive interrogation strategies—by experiencing analogs during their training period. They had to overrule their squeamishness about eating vermin, if that was all that was available. They needed to be better educated about American history and government, who the enemies were, and why they were fighting them. Such training might inoculate soldiers to be less susceptible to coercion at the hands of the enemy. However, as the noted neurologist Harold Wolff cautioned, even such inoculation would not always work because "the affective life of some individuals is inherently thin, and their capacity for love, devotion, faith, and loyalty of a low order." [78]

The Chinese built on existing knowledge of interrogation and extended it by recognizing the enormous power of social influences on resistance and collaboration. While acknowledging that *brainwashing* was a distorted, hyperbolic term, the U.S. government *was* interested in discovering new options for confronting the Communist menace. If "they" had the weapon, then "we" had better have one at least as good.

Thus began the sordid story of Project MKUltra. Governments started partnering with scientists to obtain data. Harold Wolff and Lawrence Hinkle, working as consultants to the Department of Defense, founded the Institute for Social Ecology at Cornell to use science to study coercive persuasion. [79] They revealed their goals for this new discipline of social ecology in 1956. "Individual man . . . [is] a living system entirely dependent upon maintaining a satisfactory relationship with his total environment. A man's life is dependent upon . . . a satisfactory intake of food, fluids and air; . . . and a satisfactory amount of rest and activity. It is equally necessary for him to maintain a satisfactory relationship with the other human beings in his environment, and especially with those humans who . . . have acquired a special meaning for him." [80]

That benign-sounding preamble introduced an uneasy collaboration between the scientists' institute and the CIA's MKUltra program. It would become a disaster.

CHAPTER SIX

The CIA Strikes Back
Dead Bodies

We must . . . learn to subvert, sabotage, and destroy our enemies
by more clear, more sophisticated, and more effective methods
than those used against us.

—*Commission report to President Eisenhower*, September 30, 1954

FOLLOWING STALIN'S SHOW TRIALS and the recriminations about
the Korean War POWs, the United States was determined to
mount a brain war offense. CIA director Allen Dulles laid out the
challenge: "[The Russians] take selected human beings whom
they wish to destroy and turn them into humble confessors of crimes they
never committed or make them the mouthpiece for Soviet propaganda.
New techniques wash the brain clean of the thoughts . . . and, possibly,
through the use of some 'lie serum,' create new brain processes and new
thoughts which the victim, parrot-like, repeats."[1]

Independent commissions advised President Eisenhower on the need
for the United States to take a proactive role in the quest for efficacious
brainwashing methods.[2] The fear was there, and the political posturing
was there, but there was very little science to move the program forward.

The experts—the psychiatrists and psychologists who treated the Korean War POWs—knew that the Chinese used powerful tools for indoctrination and persuasion, but they also knew that the techniques were not revolutionary breakthroughs. However, those same experts were quite happy to receive grants during the Cold War while the government searched for new weapons.

To the government, brainwashing represented a threat that had to be carefully evaluated and that, incidentally, kept the country focused on fighting Communism with a strong, well-funded intelligence agency. The Soviets seemed to want more than just global conquest; with their massive disinformation campaigns and hidden agents, they aimed to undermine confidence in the West. How could the West respond? One CIA writer, musing about Cardinal Mindszenty's trial, observed: "The style, context and manner of delivery of the 'confessions' were such as to be inexplicable unless there had been a reorganization and reorientation of the minds of the confessees. . . . Basic changes in the functional organization of the human mind cannot be brought about by the traditional methods of physical torture. . . . Newer or more subtle techniques had, therefore, to be considered."[3]

Agency analysts speculated that such inexplicable confessions might have been brought about by psychosurgery, electrical shock, or drugs, and thus the CIA turned to academia to explore such possibilities. Academia was poised to defend the country as long as government funding was provided. Grants to some eighty universities poured in from Bluebird, Artichoke, and MKUltra—code names for the CIA's behavioral research programs that flourished in the 1950s and 1960s.[4] Bluebird was phased out in favor of Artichoke in 1951 because of security concerns; people were getting too familiar with the program.[5] As a shorthand, I'll refer to all these studies as MKUltra-funded projects. Called by some a "Manhattan Project of the Mind," these various programs spent billions of dollars in clandestine studies that focused on behavioral control, social influence, and propaganda.[6] Proposals focused on "the evaluation and development of any method by which we can get information from a person against his will and without his knowledge. . . . Can we get control of an individual to the point where he will do our bidding . . . ? How could we counter such measures if they were used against us?"[7]

Even though most of the MKUltra documents were shredded, ample documents survive describing the goals of these partnerships between the CIA and academe. One set of contractors was told

Assess . . . personnel in order to accurately predict their . . . susceptibility to defection and/or indoctrination techniques.

Precondition selected agent personnel to accept clandestine missions.

Induce selected agent personnel to perform acts . . . , the effects
of which may be . . . dangerous to his being; [and] contrary to
any previous consciously expressed intentions and interests. . . .

Build into agent personnel a durable motivation which will resist
hostile interrogations and political indoctrination.[8]

MKUltra supported the brightest behavioral scientists in America
(Margaret Mead, B. F. Skinner, and Carl Rogers, to name a few). Ironically, it was the CIA-supported psychologist Carl Rogers who warned
about the risks of governments using behavioral control: "We can choose
to use our growing knowledge to enslave people in ways never dreamed
of before, depersonalizing them, controlling them by means so carefully
selected that they will perhaps never be aware of their loss of personhood.
. . . [Or we] can choose to use the behavioral sciences in ways . . . which
will develop creativity . . . ; which will facilitate [individuals' finding] . . .
freshly adaptive ways of meeting life and its problems."[9]

If researchers needed funding for basic research, they turned to the
government, not only NIH but also intelligence agencies and the military. Private foundations also supported research, but many of them were
covertly funded by the government ("cutouts," or intermediaries for the
security agencies). The CIA recognized that some researchers were re-
luctant to conduct research for the agency, but when funding followed a
more circuitous route (for example, from a foundation that supported all
kinds of research, related and unrelated to the CIA mission), the reluctance diminished. Such non-CIA mission grants, or "cover grants," helped
to build legitimacy for the various foundations.[10] Some scholars, whether
they deliberately turned a blind eye or were simply naïve, claimed they
were unaware that the CIA was their funding source.[11] Even Erving Goff-
man, prominent critic of social norms and controls, was on the payroll.[12]

Cornell's Institute for Social Ecology was one of the key conduits
for transferring CIA funds to university researchers. Its origins reveal a
remarkable backstory, peopled by remarkable individuals. CIA director
Dulles's son, Allen Macy Dulles Jr., came home from the Korean War disabled by a major head injury. Dulles turned to Cornell neurologist Harold
Wolff (1898–1962) to help his son. Wolff tried to rehabilitate the wounded

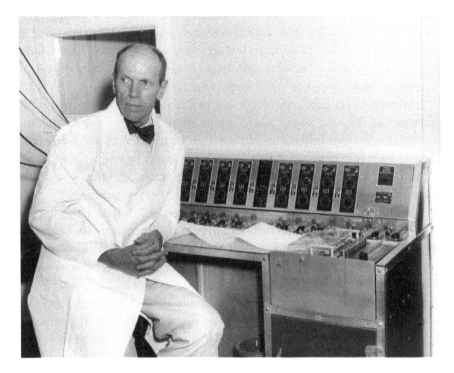

Harold Wolff. (Courtesy of Medical Center Archives, NewYork-
Presbyterian / Weill Cornell Medicine.)

Dulles, even giving him various odd jobs in his department.[13] Wolff had
already been vetted by the CIA because of his service to OSS during World
War II and, at least according to one colleague, Dulles also chose Wolff
"because he had been a student of Pavlov's."[14] Wolff was one of America's
most prominent neurologists. An expert in headaches and the subtle inter-
play of brain and behavior, he was also editor in chief of the *Archives of
Neurology* and president of the American Neurological Association.

Wolff was a broad thinker, a riveting lecturer, and a caring physician who was convinced that stress and emotional response influenced
the course of most diseases. Obsessed by research, he posted a revealing
maxim in his office: "No day without its experiment."[15] He was also an
austere, autocratic, humorless, and fiercely competitive man who could
be quite intimidating. Wolff personally suffered from migraines. In his
description of the typical migraine patient (ambitious, successful, perfec-
tionist, efficient, and with unrealistic expectations), one suspects he was

describing himself as well.[16] Wolff had such a one-track mind when it came to work that one of his close colleagues wryly observed, "If a dog came in and threw up on the rug during a lecture, he would continue."[17] But, flaws and all, he gathered around himself the leaders of psychosomatic medicine in a group nicknamed the Wolff Pack.

Seventy years ago, neurology and psychiatry were not as distinctly different as they are today. One branch of psychiatry—psychosomatic medicine—tried to bridge the gap between neuroscience, psychoanalytic theory, and biological psychiatry. Wolff was a leader in this psychosomatic movement, bringing to it a training pedigree including studies with the most prominent neuropathologists and psychiatrists of the time.[18]

Dulles, grateful to Wolff for treating his son, offered to support Wolff's research if he would help identify other outstanding investigators who might be able to advance the CIA's research agenda. Wolff turned to his colleague Lawrence ("Larry") Hinkle (1918–2012), professor of medicine at Cornell, to help establish the Institute for Social Ecology. I knew Larry Hinkle and found him a bit off-putting; he was a big, gruff, sardonic man who had no tolerance for fools and carried himself with a military bearing. He used to haunt the back of lecture halls at national meetings and hurl rapier-like questions at hapless presenters. Thankfully, I never attracted his attention. But behind that exterior, he had a delightfully warm, if peppery, sense of humor.

Hinkle was a brilliant internist who made major contributions in cardiovascular epidemiology. Like Wolff, he believed that stress had potentially deadly effects and thus he emphasized the importance of studying disease in the context of the social environment. So the name "social ecology" referred to legitimate scientific interests in how humans relate to their social environment. Except that in this instance, the institute's focus on "social environment" meant it supported research on interrogation, brainwashing, and drugs that might coerce secrets from the enemy.

In the early days of their collaboration, Wolff and Hinkle worked as consultants for the Department of Defense reviewing Communist interrogation techniques. Their superb monograph reached an intriguing conclusion that explains the origins of their new institute's name. "Man is a social animal. His health is as much dependent upon the maintenance of satisfactory relationships with his associates as it is upon his food and drink. . . . Some sort of psychological modus vivendi leading to a degree of acceptance is necessary for any man who exists in a group of other men."[19]

Wolff and Hinkle founded the Institute of Social Ecology at Cornell in 1953. It was initially located in a locked room in a student dormitory. Over the years, it relocated to a variety of New York townhouses while Wolff and the CIA communicated using unlisted phones and mail drops.

Air Force colonel James L. Monroe, an expert on impaired brain functioning, joined the institute in 1956. As its executive director and treasurer, Monroe extended support to researchers outside of Cornell. Carl Rogers joined the board of the Human Ecology group and received funding for several studies on emotion. Years later, explaining his involvement, he noted that he was having trouble getting funded but that after receiving support from the institute, he found it easier to obtain other research support. Looking back on this period in his career, Rogers commented that he would never again touch covert funding "with a ten-foot pole."[20] To some extent, his involvement with the institute gave it more cover as a legitimate foundation. Although the CIA may have been using Rogers, it was also intrigued by his work on interviewing and influencing behavior. Meanwhile, the Institute for Social Ecology funded a vast portfolio of other research—on LSD, sensory deprivation, and isolation—until 1965.[21]

Hinkle became progressively disillusioned with the Institute for Social Ecology, complaining that the CIA was increasingly in the driver's seat and was fundamentally interested in its own operational problems rather than basic research about human ecology.[22] Furthermore, he had reservations about some of the CIA staff detailed to the institute. Years later, Hinkle tried to explain where the institute went awry: "From the outset, it was evident to me that there was an irreconcilable conflict between the high intellectual and humanistic aims of Harold Wolff's concept of 'human ecology' and the scientifically naïve and essentially amoral operation of the professional intelligence men. This conflict was only enhanced by Dr. Wolff's efforts to ignore it."[23]

Hinkle complained, but Wolff "was impervious to any concerns other than his own once he had made up his mind about what he was going to do."[24] As a result, in July 1956 Hinkle left the board. An exchange of letters between intelligence operative George White and Dr. Wolff later that year perfectly encapsulates Hinkle's concerns about the agency men they were working with. White wrote, "What is the possibility of working out a graph indicating the state of panic of the enemy, based upon the varying degree of pressure used?" Wolff smoothly replied, "Yours is a very provocative notion and I am sure it could be documented. Warm regards."[25]

So, who was playing whom? Was the CIA using innocent, naïve academics to pursue agency objectives or were the academics steering the agency where *they* wanted to go? Obviously, it depends upon the details of each collaboration, but in the case of Harold Wolff, he was no defenseless pawn. When Cornell, years later, assessed the checkered history of the Institute for Social Ecology, the review committee ruefully acknowledged how forceful Wolff was. The committee chair said: "From my own recollection . . . , Harold Wolff was the kind of fellow who did exactly what he wanted to do. I don't think the CIA laid out any program for him. If his program were in concurrence with what the CIA wanted, I'm sure that would have been fine with Harold, but I couldn't imagine Harold being told what to do by the CIA." To which Larry Hinkle replied, "He couldn't even be told what to do by the administration [of this university]."[26]

The social ecology work would have continued for many more years with MKUltra funding were it not for the unexpected death of Dr. Harold Wolff in 1962. He was interrogating the former U2 pilot Francis Gary Powers at CIA headquarters when he was felled by a stroke.[27]

While the liaison between CIA and Cornell's Institute for Social Ecology was the most notorious front for supporting brainwashing research, the CIA had relationships with a number of other foundations as well. To this day, it is common for governmental agencies to partner with foundations in supporting shared interests. The Macy Foundation— with its interests in consciousness, neuroscience, wartime psychiatry, and LSD—supported studies that were closely aligned with the agency's brainwashing portfolio.

In the 1930s and 1940s, Kate Macy Ladd, the founder of the Josiah Macy Jr. Foundation, was interested in religion, mind and body, health (particularly migraines), and promoting interdisciplinary research. Her foundation supported the development of psychosomatic medicine and worked to improve military psychiatry by focusing on fitness for duty and improved treatments for combat fatigue. A 1940 Macy conference on war neurosis focused on William Sargant's research on drugs to treat combat fatigue. These Macy conferences were prestigious interdisciplinary forums open only to invitees, including many scientists supported by MKUltra. From 1946 to 1953, they were shepherded by Macy's medical director, Frank Fremont-Smith, who focused attention on cybernetics, conditioned reflexes, hypnosis, and LSD—all with CIA encouragement.[28] In 1958, the foundation partnered with the National Science Foundation to focus on Pavlov's research and its reverberations on other Russian behavioral science research.[29]

Harold A. Abramson, an early pioneer in LSD research, repeatedly thanked the Macy Foundation for supporting his studies revealing that LSD facilitated disclosure of information in psychotherapy. Under LSD, patients in longtime psychotherapy with Abramson started revealing material they had previously withheld—like homosexual fantasies and racist thoughts.[30] The CIA wasn't particularly interested in psychotherapy but was very intrigued to learn that the drug might facilitate the disclosure of information. There would be ill-fated consequences of Abramson's LSD expertise and his association with the CIA.

Macy Foundation funds also supported Louis Gottschalk, a key researcher who studied drugs of interrogation.[31] Harold Wolff received Macy support for his studies of headaches (Mrs. Ladd's lifelong malady) as well as instruments to measure pain. John Lilly received Macy support for his studies of sensory deprivation flotation tanks. Macy supported Margaret Mead's scholarship on cults. The list is extensive; for one reason or another, Macy was "interested" in the work of all the leading scholars who might have something to say about brainwashing.

Charles Geschickter (1901–87) provided another unlikely source of funds for CIA behavioral research. A prominent Georgetown University pathologist who studied breast cancer, he also funneled funds from the CIA into the Geschickter Foundation from 1953 to 1972. These funds supported studies of interrogation and the use of LSD and other hallucinogens on prisoners. Geschickter funded LSD research by Harold Abramson in New York and Jolly West in Oklahoma and at UCLA. The foundation's other interests included discovering toxic compounds in mushrooms and ways of incapacitating people or inducing sleep.

When the scandal about the CIA's research eventually broke, a Senate committee interviewed Dr. Geschickter about his foundation's involvement with the CIA. When Senator Edward Kennedy asked Geschickter why the agency wished to have a hospital-based safe house to conduct research, Geschickter replied evasively: "I have not the slightest idea. . . . I have no idea what their plan was for giving the money." Geschickter attributed it all to the university's sloppy bookkeeping or claimed he couldn't remember. In fact, the agency was studying emotional stress, working on knockout drops, searching for compounds to trigger toxic psychoses, studying how amnesia could be induced by concussions, and using radar to cause sleep. That *last* study Geschickter remembered, noting that it really worked but that the dose was tricky. If you gave too much radar, "you injured the heat center of the brain the way you cook meat."[32]

Eventually, the Human Ecology Foundation (the name of the group changed slightly over the years) moved from New York to Washington, conveniently sharing the same building with the Geschickter Fund for Medical Research. It must have made things easier for the CIA to keep track of its two flagship cover foundations in the same building.[33]

Numerous universities accepted funds from MKUltra through one account or another. When this information emerged in the 1960s and 1970s, there was outrage, perhaps a degree of outrage that is hard to understand today. Then, we were mired in the Vietnam War and had a visceral wariness of authority. "CIA-military-Nixon-assassination-conspiracy" was one giant monster, and those associated with any of this were distrusted and tarred. As will be evident, some of the MKUltra-sponsored research richly deserved this notoriety, but there is no sin per se in receiving research support from the CIA. The issue has to do with the details of the research and the strings attached to the funding.

Some researchers proposed questionable studies. Wolff's proposal still makes one gasp, decades later: "Potentially useful secret drugs (and various brain damaging procedures) will be similarly tested in order to ascertain their fundamental effect upon brain function and upon the subject's mood, thought, behavior conditioning, memory and speech mechanisms. As these drugs are investigated, a concurrent search for antidotes or counter measures will be conducted. *Where any of these studies involve potential harm to the subject, we expect the Agency to make available suitable subjects and a proper place for the performance of necessary experiments.*"[34]

Classified research has its pluses and minuses. It can make rapid progress because it is mission driven. With a goal of deterring war or guarding national security, bureaucratic impediments can be reined in, and the sponsors are often willing to consider startlingly original ideas. On the other hand, mission-driven, classified research is not a panacea. Basic research regards *all* knowledge as valuable, and sometimes a mission-driven approach fails to appreciate original ideas that initially appear unrelated to the mission. It is difficult to predict which ideas will pan out. "Startlingly original" can frequently turn out to be "daft." Good science is remorselessly critical; if scholars can't talk about their research, others can't discover the potential flaws. However, in classified research we can't examine and criticize the methods, the statistical analyses—all the things not reported—and thus it is hard to judge the value of the product. Sometimes details of methodology are intentionally withheld; sometimes they are inadvertently omitted—and what is unmentioned can sabotage replication.

This process of criticism and replication is blocked in classified research. Anyone familiar with borrowed recipes knows the problem; they are unduplicable unless ingredients and techniques are thoroughly disclosed.

***

When Albert Hofmann discovered LSD's hallucinogenic effects in 1943, intelligence agencies across the world began to turn an appraising eye at this and similar compounds. This was a logical extension of the World War II era's inconclusive investigations on drugs of interrogation. Maybe LSD could be used to facilitate coercive persuasion? It was no accident that MKUltra became so intent on supporting classified research on hallucinogens.

While governments wanted to know if drugs could accelerate interrogation, scientists wondered if these drugs could provide a model for understanding psychosis or if they could fuel human growth and creativity. The CIA's portfolio of classified studies about hallucinogens was vast, including projects that attempted to define the effective dose of LSD, how it could be surreptitiously administered to someone, and whether it could trigger psychosis or incapacitate or embarrass a government leader. MKUltra studies examined if one could develop tolerance for the drug or if an antidote could be effective. Harvard's Henry Beecher wondered if LSD could be slipped into a military target like a battleship or, for that matter, a city's water supply.[35] The water supply threat recurred during the Chicago Democratic Convention in 1968 when yippies threatened to pour LSD into the water supply, prompting Mayor Richard Daley to order twenty-four-hour surveillance at all city reservoirs.[36]

The LSD research had literally fatal flaws. Fearing backlash from an outraged public, the agency started cutting back on the MKUltra LSD projects because its experiments were carried out on unsuspecting subjects who had never volunteered. Throughout the United States, people found themselves on surprise LSD trips. These surreptitious dosings variously led to hilarity, enlightenment, panic, psychosis, or suicide. Investigators studied drug responses in students, prisoners, addicts, psychiatric patients, and children. A former prisoner, Marvin Williams, described his experience: "I didn't know what I was getting into. . . . We kept getting handed a glass of what looked like water . . . drink it, they said, and then blam, I don't know what. The roof and the sky exploded. Crazy things happened. I mean really crazy, like not real, but happening. It was like I was in a jungle someplace with wild animals all around me; all these crazy beasts trying to kill me and . . . Never again, man, never again."[37]

One of the CIA's most colorful agents, George White, worked on many LSD projects with MKUltra and Harold Abramson. A colleague said of him, "George could charm the hide off from a rabid dog."[38] White was a balding man who stood five feet seven and weighed two hundred pounds. He was an old-school OSS agent whose rough-and-tumble persona appealed to the shady side of some American scientists.

In White's notorious "midnight climax" project, he rented an apartment on Telegraph Hill in San Francisco and hired prostitutes to slip LSD in their customers' drinks to see if they would confide information more readily. One CIA agent disclosed, "If we were scared enough of a drug not to try it on ourselves, we sent it to San Francisco," where White would experiment with it.[39] They tried aerosolized LSD at a party in Marin County, but it was all for naught—the wind dispersed the drug. These various escapades surreptitiously drugged people and observed their responses. It was a long-term program of study that extended, off and on, for fourteen years.[40]

But there were scientific reservations about the quality of the research itself. In 1963, the CIA inspector general questioned if these drug studies were scientifically well grounded.[41] After all, in many of the studies, the observers were agents who were not scientifically trained, and they observed their subjects only for a few hours. Thus there was insufficient information about long-term effects, and the lack of medical backup created a dangerous situation.

Even with all of its funding, it was not so easy for the CIA to attract researchers to do its bidding. One intelligence leader commented that the trick was to appeal to the "Bad Boy beneath the surface of every American scientist and to say to him, 'Throw all your normal law-abiding concepts out the window. Here's a chance to raise merry hell.'"[42] Occasionally, the agency got more than it bargained for when it worked with scientists who were indeed Bad Boys. Richard Wendt, chair of psychology at the University of Rochester, claimed he had invented a drug mixture "so special that it could make a dumb man talk," but he refused to reveal the ingredients unless the CIA took him and his mistress to Europe to supervise the testing on purported spies. The drug mixture failed, and the CIA was exasperated when it eventually learned that the so-called new ingredients were merely a combination of barbiturate, amphetamine, and marijuana.[43]

News of the MKUltra programs did eventually leak out, and at a Senate hearing in the 1970s Senator Edward Kennedy spoke for the nation in lambasting the program for jeopardizing the lives and well-being of people who were surreptitiously tested: "Certainly, no one would question the need for drug experimentation if there is to be progress in this field, but no one should experience what we have heard here today in terms of the gross misrepresentation about potential side effects . . . , the complete failure of notification in terms . . . of those that participated, so they are completely unprepared to cope or deal with these tragic after effects."[44]

In addition to its obsession with drugs, MKUltra also focused on the effect of social isolation in shaping behavior. Experiments on healthy normal subjects revealed that after two or three days of sensory isolation, subjects began to hallucinate, were unable to think clearly, and were easily indoctrinated. But this knowledge was not acquired just to learn how to "break" people; the scientists also found tangible clinical implications. The sensory deprivation studies led researchers to speculate that the distress in polio patients on iron lungs might be partially attributable to their sensory isolation. Similarly, clinical researchers started questioning if the confusion and delirium encountered so frequently in intensive care units might be partially attributable to sensory isolation.

MKUltra was drawn to neuroscience questions like how memories are shaped and erased and what biological factors drive violence. Much of this work on the neuroscience of memory and the effects of sensory isolation culminated in a disastrous series of studies in Montreal, which will be discussed in the next chapter.

In all of these research areas, government agencies and scientists used one another to promote their own agendas. The scientists struggled for research funds and tried to make the case that their ideas were not only important but also relevant to the funders' goals. The funders were not naïve; they understood the game and carefully considered the applications' scientific merit and relevance to their needs.

The MKUltra program administrator, Sidney Gottlieb, was a brilliant, eccentric PhD chemist. His colleagues affectionately called him "The Beast" or "Merlin."[45] He has been compared to Q in the James Bond series and, less charitably, characterized as a mad scientist straight out of a pulp novel.[46] Gottlieb was introduced to LSD in 1951 by Dr. Abramson, and subsequently Gottlieb personally experimented with the drug more than twenty times.[47] But he didn't experiment only on himself: when he was in the office, he routinely slipped LSD and other drugs into his staff's food, drinks, or cigarettes. Frequently, the results were "interesting" or "enchanting," but sometimes bad trips ensued. One surreptitiously dosed CIA agent fled the building in terror, reporting afterward that "every automobile that came by was a terrible monster with fantastic eyes. . . . It was hours of agony. It was like a dream that never stops—with someone chasing you."[48]

It is important to understand that the effect of LSD varies greatly depending on the setting in which it is taken. In the early days, when it was administered as an adjunct to psychotherapy, therapists reported that bad trips were rare and that the drug promoted insight and euphoria. On the other hand, when LSD was administered in threatening surroundings or, worse yet, given surreptitiously, terror ensued. John Lennon and his wife Cynthia went to a dinner party where their host spiked their coffee with LSD. Cynthia reported, "John was crying and banging his head against the wall. I tried to make myself sick, and couldn't. I tried to go to sleep, and couldn't. It was like a nightmare that wouldn't stop, whatever you did. None of us got over it for about three days."[49]

When news of the MKUltra programs leaked out, accompanied by lawsuits and congressional inquiries, Gottlieb explained the rationale for MKUltra to Congress.

> In the judgement of the CIA, there was tangible evidence that both the Soviets and the Red Chinese might be using techniques of altering human behavior which were not understood by the USA and which would have implications of national survival. . . . It was felt to be . . . of the utmost urgency for our intelligence organization to establish what was possible in this field on a high priority basis. . . .
>
> [We used the foundations as] an attempt to harness the academic and research community of the United States to provide badly needed answers to some pressing national security problems, in the shortest possible time, without alerting potential enemies to the United States Government's interest in these matters. . . . [This] country was involved in a real covert war. . . . I considered all this work . . . to be extremely unpleasant, extremely difficult, extremely sensitive, but above all, to be extremely urgent and important.[50]

Gottlieb in some fashion apologized, while at the same time reminding Congress of the threats the agency faced in decades past. General Vernon Walters, acting director of the CIA in 1973, was not so deferential. "Americans have always had an ambivalent attitude toward intelligence. . . .

When they feel threatened they want a lot of it, and when they don't they tend to regard the whole thing as somewhat immoral."[51]

It might be instructive to examine two notorious studies in the MKUltra portfolio. Both were lethal experiments with LSD.

★★★

People often think that science is conducted by loners working in isolation. In fact, science is intensely social in nature. Researchers always know each other even in obscure areas like those pursued by the MKUltra crew studying LSD. Some of the researchers continued to play a role in the brainwashing story long after the 1960s.[52]

When I was a resident at Massachusetts General Hospital, I was fortunate to work with Chester ("Chet") Pierce. This tall, graying, African American psychiatrist radiated humor, gentle warmth, and pragmatism. He was a font of stoic wisdom, and it is largely due to his influence that I embarked on decades-long studies of the physiological toll of racial discrimination. I say all this not just to remember a revered friend and teacher, but also to put in context the strange story he told me one day. "Did I ever tell you about the time Jolly West and I killed an elephant in Oklahoma?" Huh?

Chet and I had been talking about the capriciousness of funding, our careers, and the many blind alleys in research. It was a typical conversation about some of Chet's favorite themes—the unpredictability of life and the necessity of humility—at least until he brought up the elephant.

Dr. Jolly West was one of the leading military psychiatrists to study returning Korean War POWs. Even during those early Air Force years, he was recognized for his boundless energy and broad interests in social issues and biological psychiatry. He became the chair of psychiatry at the University of Oklahoma, continued to study topics of interest to the military, and received funding from MKUltra's foundations.

Jolly wondered about LSD. In fact, the whole field of psychiatry was mesmerized by the drug. How could such a minute dose so profoundly disrupt attention and perception? What might that tell us about the origins of schizophrenia? Were there biological roots to this devastating illness? The CIA wasn't particularly interested in the physiology of schizophrenia but it was very interested in drugs that might affect agitation. Maybe LSD could be used to brainwash the enemy?

Male Asian elephants go through recurring bouts of musth once or twice a year, during which they run berserk and become exceedingly aggressive. Oklahoma City's zoo had a fourteen-year-old male elephant,

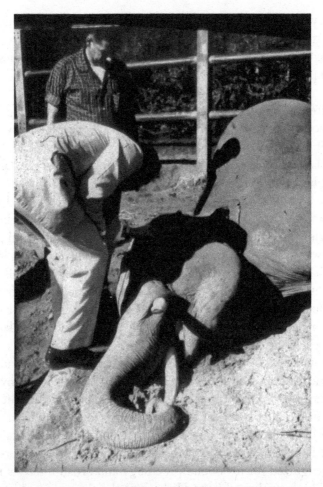

The death of Tusko. (Louis Jolyon West Papers [Collection 590], box 5.
Library Special Collections, Charles E. Young Research Library, UCLA.)

Tusko. Could LSD elicit musth-like behavior in Tusko and could that
teach us something about agitation?

Thus, Jolly, Chet, and veterinarian Warren Thomas designed the
(in)famous elephant experiment. On the day before administering LSD,
they shot Tusko with a dart containing penicillin, as a kind of placebo control. The elephant looked up in surprise, trumpeted in protest, and was
restless for two to three minutes before returning to his typical activities.
The next day, they planned to give him LSD, but how much? They knew
that a dose of 0.025 milligrams of LSD could trigger hallucinations in

humans, but no one had the slightest idea how much to give to an elephant. You can't assume that because an elephant weighs thirty times as much as a human the dose should be thirty times larger; different species metabolize drugs differently. The researchers miscalculated dreadfully and shot Tusko with a dart containing 297 mg of LSD, or almost twelve thousand times the human dose. The authors described what happened in an article in *Science* in 1962: "Tusko began trumpeting and rushing around the pen, a reaction not unlike the one he had shown the day before. However, this time his restlessness appeared to increase for 3 minutes after the injection; then he stopped running and showed signs of marked incoordination. His mate (Judy, a 15-year-old female) approached him and appeared to attempt to support him. He began to sway, his hindquarters buckled, and it became increasingly difficult for him to maintain himself upright. Five minutes after the injection he trumpeted . . . [and] collapsed."[53]

In his private diary, Jolly described how incredulous he felt while watching Tusko die. "Just shot him (Tusko) with the LSD. He whirled around to face the source of attack. . . . He's very aggravated, very restless and running around trying to shake the syringe out. . . . Judy [his companion elephant] seems to be making an effort to comfort him. . . . She has brought some food over and put it down near him in a way that she knows from past experience would interest him." As Tusko moved toward a respiratory arrest, Jolly helplessly mused, "A little mouth to mouth resuscitation would appear to be in order, but I'm afraid only Judy could do that." He concluded his diary entry, "Elephants . . . can be said to possess a fantastic sensitivity of the central nervous system to lysergic acid diethylamide and this may suggest something about the chemical nature of the annual . . . phenomenon of . . . *musth*."[54]

The study was designed by brilliant people with good intentions, and arguably it had a valid purpose—to determine if drugs could elicit psychotic-like behaviors. Still, it was a hare-brained scheme and it brought us no closer to understanding the biological bases of schizophrenia or the induction or treatment of agitation. To answer those questions, one needed human studies, and, here at least, Dr. West was appropriately cautious.

At a 1959 conference extolling the virtues of LSD, West listened incredulously to a presentation claiming that LSD led to excellent results in treating drug addicts, schizophrenics, children, suicidal patients, manic depressives, people with brain injuries, obstetrical patients, and on and on. West interrupted: "At the risk of being branded forever as an incurable skeptic, . . . it is absolutely incredible to me that . . . in every single instance, . . . [patients had an excellent response]. Either LSD is the most phenomenal drug ever introduced into treatment in psychiatry, or else the results were evaluated by . . . enthusiastic, if not positively prejudiced, people."[55]

The CIA was also very enthusiastic about the use of LSD and had no qualms about testing it on humans. I wish I could have said, "testing LSD on human volunteers," but there was very little "volunteering" associated with the testing, and there were lethal consequences. The CIA was eager to test LSD to determine its effectiveness as an immobilizing agent that could subdue large swaths of the population and also, crucially, as a tool to employ in interrogation. Could the drug discombobulate an individual so much that he or she might talk? The agency had some other interests as well. Could it so strikingly change a person's thinking that he or she might defect? If LSD were slipped to a foreign leader in advance of a public appearance, could it embarrass or discredit the leader? Such questions were important for both offensive and defensive reasons.

The agency embarked on a series of studies via its affiliated foundations. It was particularly drawn to administering the drug to unsuspecting individuals. Sometimes the agency used its scientists as guinea pigs, but sometimes the drug was given to psychiatric patients, drug addicts, prisoners, suspected spies, and innocent bystanders.

In the 1960s there was wild enthusiasm about the use of LSD as an adjunct to psychotherapy and a route to personal growth. Dr. Harold Abramson was one of its earliest boosters. As an allergist, he had perhaps an unusual background to be involved in the MKUltra studies of LSD. Furthermore, Abramson should have known better about the risks of surreptitiously dosing people with LSD, given his own first experience with the drug. He was working in his laboratory when he, unknowingly, was accidentally exposed to the drug. Years later, he wrote about what happened over the next few hours. "I was confused. . . . [and thought] I was going to die. . . . I started to think of my life insurance premiums, and I was really quite upset." Once he realized that his experience was due to inadvertent exposure to LSD, he thought, "Well, this is nothing. I will be over this in a few hours, and I went right to sleep."[56]

Abramson continued to evangelize about the drug, pooh-poohing the dangers and claiming he had never seen an adverse effect with LSD and that incidental adverse events were more common with penicillin or cortisone. He did, however, acknowledge that when he gave LSD to his psychotherapy patients, he occasionally provided Seconal (a barbiturate sedative) if they felt the experience was too intense.[57]

Frank Olson in happier days, with his wife Alice and son Eric.
(Courtesy of Eric Olson.)

The most notorious LSD-induced adverse event involved a lethal experiment on Dr. Frank Olson, a bacteriologist doing classified research at Fort Detrick. An enormous amount has been written about this case, but I will focus on what the CIA intended to study and how the agency dealt with the situation.[58]

On November 19, 1953, Olson and colleagues attended a retreat in Deep Creek Lake, Maryland. Sidney Gottlieb spiked the attendees' Cointreau with LSD and Dr. Olson had a severe adverse reaction. He became agitated and depressed, felt that others were making fun of him or criticizing him, and thought he had made a fool of himself. He returned home and for the next few days continued to feel these symptoms. On November 24, his wife took him to CIA headquarters.

The agency flew him to New York to consult with Dr. Harold Abramson, who met with Olson late that afternoon. That evening, Abramson made a house call to the hotel where Olson was staying, and Olson, accompanied by CIA agents, returned to see Dr. Abramson in his office on November 25. Abramson thought Olson would calm down if he went home for Thanksgiving, so the next day, Olson was flown home to Washington. However, he decompensated so alarmingly upon arrival that the agents flew him back to New York for another consultation with Dr. Abramson. Olson agreed to admit himself as a voluntary psychiatric patient to Washington's Chestnut Lodge Hospital the next day. Then he returned to the Statler Hotel, accompanied by his CIA watchers. During the night he "fell" to his death from his room on the tenth floor. I put "fell" in quotes because there was uncertainty at the time whether it was an accidental fall or a suicidal jump. Or it might even have been murder.

It has been alleged that the agency murdered Olson because it feared he might reveal secrets in his confused state. Some, most notably his son Eric, believe he was pushed out of the window because the CIA felt he was a security risk—and not just because of his confusion following the surreptitious dosing with LSD. Olson had been shaken after witnessing some CIA activities in Europe that left him conscience-stricken. He met with William Sargant in London to discuss this, and Sargant informed his superiors in the British intelligence service that Olson could be a security risk. They, presumably, notified American colleagues.[59]

Today, it is unknowable whether he jumped, fell, or was pushed out of that window. What is indisputable is that the LSD dosing was covered up by the agency, which manufactured a history of Olson's mental illness and asserted that the suicide was the logical consequence of that (nonexistent) condition. Agency reviewers bickered about his prior mental illness and whether LSD administration could be blamed for his psychosis and suicide: "It is perfectly possible that the suicide grew out of a pre-existing state which was not affected by the experiment. However, we have taken the position officially that the experiment at least 'triggered' the suicide. . . . Yet [some individuals] are insistent that it is practically impossible for this drug to have any harmful after effects."[60]

A peculiar detail in this story involves the choice to take Olson not to a psychiatrist but to Dr. Abramson, an allergist. But there were reasons for this irregularity. For one thing, this catastrophic choice exemplifies the sorts of problems that emerge when a VIP patient receives treatment.[61] The VIP is assured rapid and confidential assessment, but all too often the wrong physician is selected, or one who is more concerned about the implications of a public relations fiasco than about the patient's welfare.

Most psychiatrists would have immediately hospitalized Dr. Olson, given the duration and severity of his agitation. Abramson, however, opted to have Olson's colleagues watch over him for several days while arrangements were made to transfer him to a psychiatric hospital that could accommodate CIA patients. But Abramson's progress note to the CIA indicates the severity of Olson's condition. He wrote that Olson was agitated, sleeping poorly, and had persecutory delusions and auditory hallucinations. Furthermore, Olson was troubled by guilt and had a profound "sense of inadequacy, with special reference to the scientific performance of his duties. He was obsessed with the idea that his memory was poor, that his work was inadequate, and that he failed his family and his comrades."[62] Things are always clearer in retrospect, but with those symptoms, I cannot imagine a psychiatrist who would *not* have hospitalized Dr. Olson immediately.

Abramson and Olson knew each other from previous agency work on aerosols, so it was thought that Olson would be more amenable to talking with someone he knew. Abramson was also an "agency" man who had a longtime affiliation with the CIA. From 1943 to 1946 he worked for the U.S. Army's Chemical Warfare Service, and his research on aerosolized penicillin was judged so important that he received the Legion of Merit from the Armed Forces for "exceptionally meritorious conduct in the performance of outstanding services and achievements."[63] He knew how to keep secrets, both as a physician who did psychotherapy and as an intelligence officer. The other reason for choosing Abramson was that he was arguably the best-informed expert on LSD in the United States. The Macy Foundation had funded him to convene consensus panels on LSD research, and the CIA supported his studies on the drug.[64]

The events behind Dr. Olson's death were kept from his wife and children for twenty years. The CIA did not tell the family about the covert LSD dosing but merely reported that Olson had fallen or jumped out of the hotel window, ostensibly in confusion or agitation. The agency expressed its sincere condolences and helped with funeral arrangements and insurance. Meanwhile, agency director Allen Dulles issued a mild rebuke to Dr. Gottlieb, the orchestrator of the Cointreau LSD dosing: "This is to inform you that it is my opinion that you exercised poor judgment in this case."[65]

It is patently clear that, at a minimum, Dr. Olson's LSD dosing ex-

emplified badly planned research with a lack of ethical controls and inadequate medical care. In another context, Carl Rogers cautioned that it
was naïve to believe that behavioral scientists could work toward benevo-
lent ends when collaborating with members of military intelligence. He
compared them with "German rocket scientists. . . . First they worked
devotedly for Hitler to destroy the U.S.S.R. and the United States. Now,
depending on who captured them, they work devotedly for the U.S.S.R.
in the interest of destroying the United States, or [vice versa]. If behavioral scientists are concerned solely with advancing their science, it seems
most probable that they will serve the purposes of whatever individual or
group has the power."[66]

The Olson family learned about Dr. Olson's surreptitious LSD drugging years later when CIA secrecy was pierced by revelations of another
set of human brainwashing disasters—this time in Canada.

CHAPTER SEVEN

Dead Memories

The Canadian Legacy of Ewen Cameron

The human mind is the most delicate of all instruments. It is so finely adjusted, so susceptible to the impact of outside influences that it is proving a malleable tool in the hands of sinister men.

—CIA DIRECTOR ALLEN DULLES, 1953

W AIT. CANADA?
I have always regarded Canada as civilized, liberal, and humane. How could Canada have been involved in one of the most devastating experiments in behavioral science? The Canadian MKUltra studies made their way into fiction in Robert Ludlum's books and movies about Jason Bourne. In Ludlum's fiction, the CIA takes a young man to a special institution where a kindly psychiatrist wipes all memories from his brain and then reprograms him to become Jason Bourne, the consummate assassin. I suppose *that* would qualify for brainwashing. The plot (aside from the assassin training) was based on true events in Montreal under the aegis of the Social Ecology Program and the CIA. The psychiatrist's name was Ewen Cameron, but there were many other Montreal neuroscientists whose work was related to brainwashing.

Montreal's world-renowned neuroscience program included researchers who revolutionized our understanding of the brain. Dr. Cameron took
ideas from his colleagues and applied them, frequently to their conster-
nation, to his own work. It is interesting to trace the intellectual currents
that preceded Cameron.

Neurosurgeon Wilder Penfield (1891–1976) started it all by founding
the Montreal Neurological Institute in 1934. He used neurosurgical procedures to destroy small parts of the brain that were causing intractable
epilepsy. Although it sounds gruesome, the operations were performed
under local anesthesia and the patients were awake during the procedure
so that Penfield would know which areas were safe to destroy. By moving
his stimulating electrodes up and down the surface of the brain, Penfield
literally mapped thoughts, sensations, and memories on the surface of the
human brain.[1]

Penfield collaborated with psychologist Donald Hebb (1904–85), who
studied learning and how neurons communicated. The first paragraph of
Hebb's master's thesis refers reverently to Pavlov: "[I propose] to present
a theory of the functioning of the synapse based on the experimental work
of Sherrington and Pavlov on reflexes and inhibitions."[2]

Hebb brought on board his brilliant graduate student Brenda Milner
(1918–). Milner, one of the founders of cognitive neuroscience of memory,
tracked memory disruptions to a small area of the brain called the hippo-
campus. She observed that when this structure was damaged on both sides
of the brain, catastrophic memory problems followed. Patients could still
walk, talk, drive, work on puzzles—do pretty much anything, in fact, except learn new material or remember the past.[3] For military intelligence,
the idea that you could strap down an enemy agent, needle the right spot
in his brain, and force him to talk was a riveting possibility—as was its
converse, that you could "protect" (that is, destroy) the memory of one of
your own agents while allowing him to live. That work would come later.

There were other aspects of Hebb's work that had a special relevance
to the science of persuasion. Hebb reasoned that brains receiving little
sensory input would behave aberrantly, noting that impoverished environments led to dulled intelligence whereas enriched environments led to
greater intelligence.[4] It is ironic that Hebb's studies provided a rationale
for programs as diverse as Project Head Start and MKUltra.

In 1951, Canadian and American intelligence officials met with Hebb
to ask what he thought might account for brainwashing in Korea. He theo-
rized that brainwashing was facilitated by sensory isolation in the prison

camps because people deprived of sensory inputs don't think clearly and become susceptible to persuasion. The agents were intrigued by his theory and asked him to expand upon the idea. Hebb continued: "[By] cutting off all sensory stimulation . . . , the individual could be led into a situation whereby ideas, etc. might be implanted."[5] This "implant" analogy was enticing—he rapidly received funding for secret studies on sensory deprivation. Parenthetically, note the word *implanted*. It would return to haunt the Montreal community.

Hebb recruited healthy young students and put them to bed in a small experimental chamber where they were isolated from environmental stimuli. He wrapped their arms in tubes and put gloves on their hands so that tactile sensations would be reduced. He covered their eyes with translucent goggles and piped white noise into the sensory deprivation chamber. Research staff gave the subjects monotonous food and helped them to the bathroom but otherwise did not talk or interact with the subjects. The idea was to study them for six weeks, but most of the subjects couldn't stand it for more than two or three days. They became anxious, moody, and reported that they could not think straight. They had troubles with mental arithmetic, thinking—even their handwriting deteriorated. Some experienced auditory, visual, and tactile hallucinations.[6]

Volunteers were told to draw a geometric shape by free hand, with instructions such as "Make a straight line from right to left for three inches and then make a right angle and extend the line up by two inches." The figure (next page) shows the correct shape as described in the instructions, the one that the volunteers drew in response to the instructions, and the drawings obtained after progressively longer sensory isolation. Clearly, isolation had toxic effects on perception and motor skills.[7]

These observations on perception were not particularly exciting to the intelligence agencies, but the CIA grew very attentive when Hebb and others started examining if isolation might make subjects more suggestible. Investigators placed subjects in isolation chambers and tried to interest them in all kinds of things.[8] They played tapes promoting dental hygiene or discouraging smoking, tapes that discussed poltergeists or current events in Turkey. When subjects had nothing else to do but listen to such things, they became quite absorbed in them, and investigators reported that after the experiments had concluded, subjects remained interested in those topics.[9]

Some students were easily swayed by tapes they listened to. One study followed subjects who had been exposed to tapes about telepathy, clairvoy-

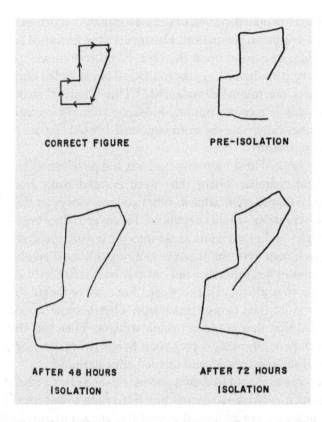

CORRECT FIGURE   PRE-ISOLATION

AFTER 48 HOURS   AFTER 72 HOURS
ISOLATION   ISOLATION

The effects of isolation on perceptual and motor skills.
(From Woodburn Heron, "Cognitive and Physiological Effects of Perceptual
Isolation," in *Sensory Deprivation: A Symposium Held at Harvard Medical School*, edited
by Philip Solomon, M.D., Philip E. Kubzansky, M.D., P. Herbert Leiderman, M.D.,
Jack H. Mendelson, M.D., Richard Trumbull, Ph.D., and Donald Wexler, M.D., Cambridge,
Mass.: Harvard University Press, Copyright © 1961 by the President and Fellows of
Harvard College. Copyright © renewed 1989 by Philip Solomon.)

ance, and poltergeists while they were in the sensory deprivation chamber. Three or four days later, some of the college student volunteers reported they had become engrossed in the idea of ghosts and made excursions to the library to read about them. One became frightened of ghosts and another reported that he tried telepathy to help his poker game.[10] The funding agencies were riveted by such observations and wanted to learn more about who was vulnerable to being persuaded by the tapes.[11]

From his Korean War experience, internist Larry Hinkle was also convinced the brain did not function normally when deprived of sensory stimulation. He believed that Hebb's approach provided the ideal way to break down a prisoner, because it created "precisely the state that the interrogator desires: malleability and the desire to talk, with the added advantage that one can delude himself that he is using no force or coercion."[12]

While there are disputes about the extent of Hebb's involvement with the CIA, he certainly knew that he was doing classified military research and, as discussed in the previous chapter, he was hardly alone in that respect.[13] Furthermore, he openly acknowledged that his classified work "began, actually, with the problem of brainwashing. We were not permitted to say so."[14]

Regardless, Hebb was an immensely careful researcher who allowed subjects to leave his studies if they chose. In both of these respects he was different from the evil genius portrayed in the Jason Bourne books and from Ewen Cameron, the template for that genius.[15]

Before meeting Dr. Cameron, it is important to introduce one other outstanding Montreal researcher. After escaping from Nazi Germany, psychiatrist Heinz Lehmann (1911–2000) settled in Montreal and started his pioneering work in psychopharmacology. Desperate to make a difference in patients' lives, he studied all kinds of things by trial and error—purported remedies like prolonged sleep therapy, fever induction, and high doses of caffeine—but he never let his hopes blind him to the data.[16] He was meticulous with his experiments and honest in disclosing the numerous failures. Then he hit pay dirt. He was the first investigator in North America to conduct careful clinical trials on chlorpromazine (Thorazine) for treating schizophrenia and imipramine for depression. He became one of the founders of psychopharmacology, and he, like Hebb and Penfield, was a rival of Cameron's.

★★★

Because Montreal was such an important neuroscience center, it made sense to build a major psychiatric institute in the city. McGill University joined forces with the Royal Victoria Hospital to establish the Allan Memorial Psychiatric Institute. They formed a search committee to look for a leader. Such search committees typically have a tough task. All too often institutions don't have a clear idea of what they are looking for. They want someone who can walk on water as a star clinician, educator, researcher, and administrator—someone who won't cost too much and someone who is available to move now (although that can raise questions: why is he or she available?). With senior positions, there are surprisingly

The Allan Memorial Psychiatric Institute. (Photograph by author.)

few candidates who match these criteria (even when you drop the require-
ment for walking on water).

In 1943, the committee selected Ewen Cameron as the founding director of the Allan Institute for Neuropsychiatric Research (also known
as the Allan Memorial Psychiatric Institute). There were some red flags.
One letter writer praised Cameron's scientific papers but went on to say
obliquely he was "not so sure on the personality side and its adjustment to
McGill conditions."[17]

With considerable start-up funding from the Rockefeller Foundation,
the Allan Institute was endowed with faculty positions, laboratory facilities, and a clinic on the edge of McGill's campus. All were housed in a
seventy-two-room rather intimidating limestone mansion called Ravens-
crag. The building lived up to its appearance under Dr. Cameron's leader-

ship. Even when the new labs and sensory deprivation chambers were installed in the mansion's stables, the building still seemed ominous.[18]

On paper, Cameron was a logical choice. He was a researcher who was a vocal advocate for improved treatment of mental illness and had an international reputation. He had even been consulted by the Nuremberg International Military Tribunal to examine Deputy Führer Rudolf Hess.[19]

Cameron grew up in Scotland, the son of a stern Presbyterian minister, and had a fraught relationship with the church and authority his entire life. After completing his medical and psychiatric training in Glasgow and London, he obtained further training with Adolf Meyer at Johns Hopkins and then trained in Switzerland. In 1929, he moved to the Brandon Mental Hospital in Manitoba, where he began writing papers. He loved new gadgets and was game to try just about anything to help his patients—dehydration therapy, heat therapy, exposure to red light, cod liver oil, carbon dioxide inhalation, ketogenic diet.[20] None of these were particularly efficacious, but at least he tried something rather than relegating patients to chronic institutionalization. He wrote about these disparate efforts, but his methods were imprecise. When he said that a marker was correlated with clinical improvement, the definition of "improvement" was solely subjective. From his point of view, patient self-report was the least reliable method of tracking progress. Instead, he viewed improvement in sleep as a harbinger of impending cure, but "cure," of course, could only be identified by him.

Cameron longed to move treatment out of the enormous provincial hospitals and to establish clinics serving remote communities and farms in Manitoba. In 1936, he moved to Massachusetts, where he became director of research at Worcester State Hospital. Ever on the lookout for new treatments, he introduced insulin shock therapy at Worcester—its first use in North America. One of insulin's hazards is that high doses elicit such profound hypoglycemia that convulsions and coma result. Cameron deliberately induced comas for two to five hours at a time and repeated the process for up to fifty days in treating severely ill psychiatric patients. Sadly, he found that even this intensive and dangerous process was not particularly effective. He concluded that insulin didn't work because he was treating people too late in their illness; the challenge was to treat people early and very aggressively so that they never became chronic patients.[21]

Two years later, he left Worcester and became professor of psychiatry and neurology at Albany's medical school, where he studied blood pressure and heart rate as well as amytal for treatment of anxiety. Thus, he had

D. Ewen Cameron. (Reprinted with the permission of the American
Psychiatric Association Foundation, Melvin Sabshin, M.D. Library &
Archives [Copyright © 1953]. All Rights Reserved.)

five jobs between 1925 and 1938—a testimony to what? Brilliance? Dedication? Careerism? Personal instability?

When he came to the Allan, he built a large department that embraced
research in anthropology, psychoanalysis, and biological psychiatry. He
vowed to bring together clinical care, education, and research under one
roof by opening the first nonlocked psychiatric facility in Canada and the
first psychiatric day hospital in North America.[22] He was a reformer who
advocated building halfway houses and improving education about mental
illness in the medical curricula.

All of this fulfilled the promise of his recruitment, but there were
some peculiarities. He was aloof and authoritarian in his style, but he had
high energy and he did get things done. The patients vied for his attention,
feeling privileged that the tall, self-assured professor was treating them.[23]
Despite his quirks, he cared for his patients: he saw them twice a day and
phoned the nurses on weekends and holidays to check on their progress.[24]

Cameron rejected religion as superstitious rubbish and believed that religious orthodoxy was producing guilt-stricken patients trying to be "nice" instead of developing healthy assertiveness. He called for humanism rather than moralism. This blew up in a very public confrontation with the Anglican Church in 1951. To espouse humanism so vociferously in Montreal in 1951 (and in the midst of a fund-raising drive for the Allan Institute!) was not prudent. Church leaders blasted him for "frightful heresy" and fired back: "Since all the problems which perplex the world are basically human problems, every attempted solution is doomed to frustration which fails to take into account the 'fallen' condition of mankind, and . . . the vital need of redemption from sin."[25] Cameron's fulminations even elicited an unusual alliance between the Catholic and Anglican Churches of Montreal, otherwise so frequently at odds with each other.[26]

Cameron's colleagues paint a complex picture of his many contradictions. He was described variously as "warm, distant, dedicated, evil, heroic, pathological, vindictive, and fair almost to a fault. A tyrannical, democratic, eagle-beaked loner who brooked no opposition, welcomed the view of others, and pushed forward the frontiers of psychiatry while ruthlessly expanding the psychiatric empire he was building in Montreal. He had an almost magical clinical touch with his patients and an addled persistence for wrong-headed therapy."[27]

Cameron was impatient with the slow course of psychotherapy and thought things would proceed far more efficiently if he could start with a *tabula rasa*, or blank slate.[28] Plato originally used the term *tabula rasa* to describe how memory works: "I want you to suppose, for the sake of argument, that our souls contain a waxen block . . . and that we imprint on it whatever we wish to remember from among the things we see or hear or the thoughts we ourselves have . . . as if we were making impressions from signet rings; whatever is imprinted on the block, we remember and know for as long as its image is in the wax, while whatever is wiped off . . . we have forgotten and do not know."[29]

Cameron's idea was that old memories were troublesome and should be obliterated with electroconvulsive treatment, insulin-induced coma, and drugs. Once this was accomplished, he believed the solution for mental health lay in prolonged sleep therapy and sensory deprivation, supplemented by "psychic driving," repeated messages played back to the patient over a tape loop. This combination of ill-conceived interventions was nothing less than a *furor therapeuticus*, a desperate intervention that stopped at nothing. Perhaps one might be more tolerant of his efforts if he had focused only on severely mentally ill patients who had failed all treatments and been relegated to custodial care or on patients who knowingly volunteered for this extreme treatment. But Cameron used this approach on all sorts of patients: housewives with mild anxiety and depression, executives with anxiety, alcoholics, and chronic schizophrenics. Tucked away in the foreboding Allan Institute, he set up a ghastly assembly line that he thought would conquer mental illness.

Meanwhile, his reputation flourished. He became president of the American Psychiatric Association in 1952 and frequented Washington lobbies and cocktail parties, where he advocated for improved treatment of mental illness and drew attention to his innovative approach to obliterate memories. Cameron, Harold Wolff, and William Sargant were on the same cocktail circuit, where they frequently encountered CIA director Dulles. Dulles's numerous extramarital affairs (at least a hundred, according to his sister Eleanor) created a problem with his wife.[30] Mrs. Dulles was disconsolate about these constant affairs. The CIA suggested that she meet Cameron to see whether his special treatment in Montreal might help her forget about her husband's dalliances. They discussed this over lunch at the Mayflower. She declined the treatment.[31] Aside from his marital issues, Dulles was enchanted by Cameron's theories for professional reasons as well. Electroconvulsive therapy seemed to promise a quick way to shake up an enemy spy and make him more likely to talk.

In 1961, at the peak of his career and before questions started being asked about his work, Cameron stirringly addressed the World Congress of Psychiatry: "Everywhere men move forward on their great adventures—to the understanding of matter—to the opening up of space. Nowhere does enterprise demand more—nowhere does it give more promise—than in the understanding of man. . . . His mind is in the unraveling of the atom and it is his mind no less which may destroy mankind. These are the days and ours are the occasions that summon up determination, fire the imagination and drive us."[32]

Cameron's imagination was fired by aggressively treating mental illness with every tool available. Many of his techniques were in use at that time, but what Cameron did differently was to use all of these interventions to excess, cloak the interventions in a scientific veneer, and remain blind to the failures.

Cameron advocated for convulsive therapies, particularly electroconvulsive therapy (ECT). Although ECT has sometimes been abused as a technique of behavior control, it is an extremely effective treatment for depression. Today, it is used worldwide to treat patients with refractory depression and to offer relief to those who cannot tolerate antidepressants.

For almost a century, psychiatrists had observed that patients with severe mental illness appeared to improve, at least transiently, after a convulsive seizure. They wondered if patients would get better after seizures that were intentionally induced. The first interventions were with insulin. In 1927, high doses of insulin were used to trigger severe hypoglycemia and seizures. The technique was complex and dangerous; if blood sugar levels were lowered too much or for too long, severe brain damage would result.

Because of these problems with insulin coma therapy, doctors searched for other ways of eliciting seizures. In the 1930s, they induced seizures with Metrazol, but the drug was unsatisfactory. A couple years later, Italian psychiatrists used ECT to produce sudden unconsciousness, seizures, and a short period of confusion after the treatment. Modern ECT is administered after the patient has been anesthetized, and medications are administered to lessen the severity of the seizure. The amount of electrical current is carefully controlled and there is accordingly less confusion and long-term memory disruption. Today, one typically administers ECT only to one side of the brain for six to twelve treatments administered over a few weeks.

During Cameron's days, ECT was administered bilaterally for ten to twenty sessions and at higher voltages, but he was a hawk for even higher doses. At the end of World War II Cameron had even proposed using ECT to denazify Germany by administering ECT to every German above the age of twelve.[33]

Aside from these interesting foreign policy thoughts, Cameron was also enthusiastic about an unusual way of administering ECT. English psychiatrists Lewis Page and Robert Russell began experimenting with intensified ECT in the mid-1940s. Their treatment involved giving patients multiple electrical shocks daily, increasing the voltage and duration after each shock.[34] The Page-Russell technique fit in entirely with Cameron's worldview. If some ECT was good, then more ECT must be better and furthermore, the memory disruptions that were side effects of ECT were actually one of the goals of Cameron's approach. One of his papers even claimed that "where amnesia persists, there is no return of schizophrenic symptomatology."[35] He administered hundreds of electroconvulsive shocks to some patients using the Page-Russell protocol and occasionally supplementing ECT with insulin coma. Once ECT had destroyed memories and regressed patients back to their infancy, it was then a simple matter to repattern them.

Cameron also used all kinds of drugs on his patients—amphetamines, barbiturates, chlorpromazine, PCP, and LSD. He called them his "talking-out capsules."[36] He was a bit of a magpie in his approach, employing combinations of drugs, new and old. Typically, patients would be dosed with five or six different drugs simultaneously that sedated them, stimulated them, and made them hallucinate. Patients did not have a choice in the matter. Despite Cameron's strong advocacy for unlocked wards, he was adamant that patients needed to follow his orders regarding medication.

At the start of the twentieth century, sleep therapy with sedatives like bromides and barbiturates was popular in the Soviet Union. The approach had older roots, based on observations that agitated patients improved after sleep and that sleep provides some respite or oblivion from mental suffering. The rationale was muddled, but in Russia, sleep therapy was justified by referring to Pavlov's ideas that sleep would help a brain exhausted by mental illness and no longer able to control or inhibit primitive neuronal circuits.[37] Typically, patients were sedated for two weeks at a time with transient awakenings for toileting and feeding. It was a risky business; without careful nursing care, there was a risk of pressure sores, pneumonia, or pulmonary embolism. One author dubiously claimed that such treatments led to successful cures in one-third of severely ill psychiatric patients.[38]

At the Allan Institute, sleep was maintained with a mixture of barbiturates and chlorpromazine. Patients were wakened periodically, given insulin to make them hungry, fed, toileted, and then sedated again to resume their long-term sleep. Meanwhile, the nurses changed the patients' positions to prevent bedsores. Patients were kept deeply asleep or groggily asleep twenty hours a day for about three weeks. One report from the Allan claimed that 60 percent of patients were successfully treated—patients with schizophrenia, patients with manic-depressive disease, severe obsessive compulsives, addicts, and patients with character disorders. The report did not describe how the diagnoses were made or how the treatment effect was quantified, and it acknowledged in passing side effects like pneumonia, liver damage, seizures, and parkinsonian symptoms. The report also emphasized another benefit of combining sleep therapy with convulsive therapies. By having all of the patients asleep on drugs, the staff could very efficiently move from bed to bed, administering ECT rapidly. A former resident at the Allan proudly claimed that with this setup, they could treat twenty patients an hour.[39] Altogether, according to Cameron and his followers, ECT, drugs, and sleep would increase the patients' regression, facilitate the recollection of forgotten memories, and resolve repressed conflicts.[40]

Cameron had little patience for psychotherapy. Early on, he started taping sessions with his patients, editing what he believed to be the crucial tidbits, and playing them back for his patients to study. He required them to write out their thoughts about the tapes and bring the journal to their sessions. He called this "automated psychotherapy," or in later years "psychic driving." Gradually, he started linking all of these various steps together—memory ablation with drugs and convulsive therapy, sleep learning, and psychic driving—into one toxic cocktail. In a 1956 paper he asserted that psychic driving invariably produced responses.[41]

Aldous Huxley anticipated psychic driving in *Brave New World* (1931). His dystopian novel describes how small children were brought to "Neo-Pavlovian Conditioning Rooms," where they were programmed in their sleep to adapt to their future role in society. Speakers over the cribs would repeatedly broadcast messages like: "Alpha children wear grey. They work much harder than we do, because they're so frightfully clever. I'm really awfuly [*sic*] glad I'm a Beta, because I don't work so hard. And then we are much better than the Gammas and Deltas. Gammas are stupid. They all wear green, and Delta children wear khaki. Oh no, I don't want to play with Delta children. And Epsilons are still worse."[42]

In 1932, Max Sherover acquired the U.S. rights to Linguaphone, a device that purported to teach foreign languages during sleep. The company pushed an appealing concept: one could painlessly acquire grammar and vocabulary during sleep. The company promised that sleep learning would "reclaim a third of your life for self-improvement, learning and personal enrichment."[43] The method did not seem to work out so well in practice, however. One investigator tried and failed to teach Morse code to sleeping soldiers. Another claimed that sleep learning might cure nail biting in boys. After hearing the repeated message "My fingernails are terribly bitter," some boys improved after 16,200 nighttime repetitions during their two-month summer camp session. However, the investigator cautioned that he was not too confident in an intervention tested on only twenty boys and besides, only eight of them improved.[44] That kind of honest skepticism was not in Cameron's genes.

Cameron saw an advertisement for Linguaphone and thought such a device would be a powerful tool for therapeutic brainwashing. He broadcast tape recordings through pillows while patients slept or through a helmet while patients were awake. Cameron was convinced that by playing the appropriate messages, he could change his patients' thoughts about themselves and their relationships. He tried to distill each patient's core issue into a succinct tape loop, believing that if patients listened to this loop repetitively, they would get greater traction in their subsequent therapy sessions.[45]

He called these tape loops "dynamic implants" and described them mechanistically, saying they were almost like injections that "depatterned" patients so that they would think about things differently and change their behaviors.[46] He maintained that the intensity of the implant could be strengthened by suitable reinforcement and that it was safe and easy to administer. No wonder the CIA was enchanted by this process.

The patients didn't like the procedure—neither the repetitiveness nor the messages themselves—and Cameron found he could get better compliance by playing the tape loops while the patients slept and/or while they were disinhibited on drugs. He claimed that the approach led to major breakthroughs. As he acquired more experience, he pushed the dose higher and higher, delivering psychic driving ten to twenty hours a day for ten to fifteen days, with patients in a quasi-sensory isolation room.[47] He also experimented with filtering the tapes—adjusting the treble and bass, varying the volume, introducing echo—to make the patient listen more intently, reminding his readers that this variability evokes a Pavlovian orientation reflex.[48]

One of Cameron's colleagues recalled a patient forced to listen to: "No. It's not true that my mother-in-law is trying to poison me. She is a very nice woman." Maybe that sounds like a sensible message to emphasize, but Cameron had other ideas as well. He thought that a patient's defenses had to be torn down before a new constructive message would take root. A woman admitted for postpartum depression had to listen to this tape: "Do you realize that you are a very hostile person? Do you know you are hostile with the nurses? Do you know that you are hostile with the patients? Why do you think you are so hostile? Did you hate your mother? Did you hate your father?"[49]

He would play such negative messages repeatedly for seven to ten days and then switch to more positive statements for a few weeks. For one patient with severe panic attacks, Cameron's positive message was: "It's all right to be myself. I am affectionate and warm-hearted. It is good to be affectionate and warm-hearted. . . . I don't need to drive myself. People like me as I am."[50]

The messages went on and on for weeks and sometimes months, bombarding patients with alternating criticism and support: "Janine, you are running away from responsibility! Why? You don't want to take care of your husband! Why? You don't want to take care of your children! Why? . . . You *like* to take care of your children, Janine! You *like* to take care of your husband!"[51] Or, "Madeleine, you let your mother and father treat you as a child all through your single life. . . . You never stood up for yourself against your mother or father but would run away from trouble rather than make a stand. . . . You must let your feelings come out. It is all right to express your anger, we all do."[52]

Research is costly and Cameron had pretty much run through his initial dowry of funds from the Rockefeller Foundation. Furthermore, his prickly interactions with colleagues like Hebb and Penfield (as well as the Anglican Church) more or less poisoned the well for him to get much funding from Canadian sources. Fortunately for him, he came to the attention of the CIA, which encouraged him to apply for funds to continue his work on psychic driving. In January 1957, he applied for support from the Society for the Investigation of Human Ecology, and the proposal was rapidly approved as MKUltra subproject 68 and supported for three years. It is important to add that there was not that much new in the proposal. Cameron had been drugging, shocking, and brainwashing patients with his psychic driving for years without CIA support and probably would have continued doing so in any event.

★★★

Cameron was sure that his techniques were helping patients but acknowledged that "assessment has been a matter of singular difficulty."[53] The data looked good to him, exceptional even, but his charts and tables had no real foundation. It's not that he falsified records; he just disregarded evidence to the contrary. In this sense, he was not unusual. As the saying goes, "Nothing is so difficult as not deceiving oneself."[54]

He made every kind of mistake that contemporary clinical trials are designed to forestall. He was inconsistent in his eligibility criteria for the study and enrolled people with vastly different diagnoses as well as people who had received or were receiving other treatments in addition to depatterning. He hired a psychologist to pre-test patients prior to treatment, but he was selective in identifying which patients should be tested. If patients didn't respond to treatment, Cameron dropped them from the study as if they had never been enrolled. When staff complained that this was not the way to do research, Cameron replied, "If you don't want to be associated with it, you don't have to," and the staff moved on to other jobs.[55] When the psychological tests gave the "wrong answers" about treatment effects, Cameron simply overruled them, saying that his clinical experience and judgment were the ultimate arbiters. Furthermore, he was incredibly vague about how he defined a treatment's success.[56] Today, these research deficits would be deplorable, but in the 1950s this was not so unusual for medical research.[57] Perhaps what makes Cameron's actions stand out is that they were performed by one of the most prominent academic psychiatrists of his time and they had such devastating effects on his patients.

The goal of the treatment was to erase patients' memories and bring them back to a regressed state where they were incontinent and unable to take care of themselves. Then the patients were to be changed with psychic driving, administered while awake or asleep. All would agree that Cameron was successful in achieving his first aim. The problem was that some people were left robot-like, with vast chunks of their memories obliterated. As to the second goal, implanting new ideas via psychic driving, it wasn't so clear that this worked either.

Despite Cameron's early reports claiming success, people started having doubts. William Sargant regarded the work as "bordering on the criminal."[58] The Human Ecology group (Wolff and Monroe) decided to make a site visit to Montreal. Cameron gave them a tour, showed them charts, and introduced them to patients lying in their beds, staring off into space. Harold Wolff asked incredulously, "Are these [patients] typical of your successes?" Cameron replied that they were indeed representative of the success of psychic driving. Monroe was astounded: "We were distinctively living in two worlds. His and the real one." The site visitors told Cameron not to expect more funding from Human Ecology, and the CIA concluded that his intervention "didn't seem to really live up to the expectations that we had hoped might come from it."[59]

In his presidential address to the American Psychopathological Association (1963), Cameron described how he had developed the psychic driving program with the conviction that he was on the right track, regardless of obstacles like inconsistent data and curtailed funding. "If this thing [psychic driving] worked after thirty repetitions, it was only common sense to see what would happen if the repetition was increased tenfold, a hundredfold or even more. . . . We soon found, however, that it did not work out quite as we had planned it. . . . We found it was possible for the individual to be exposed to the repetition . . . a quarter to one-half million times and yet be unable to repeat these few short sentences. . . . But we have made a beginning."[60]

Science depends upon keeping an open mind. Resolute to the end, Cameron could not conceive that he might be wrong. He recognized neither his faulty research nor its flawed ethics.

Cameron's successor, Robert Cleghorn, tactfully summed up the state of psychiatric research in the 1950s. "[In Cameron's days] . . . diagnosis was imprecise, hospitalization was unenlightened, teaching and training were woefully inadequate. All these he tackled and improved but his entrepreneurial style, so successful in organization, was not so applicable in research."[61]

Upon Cameron's retirement, Dr. Cleghorn formed a committee to evaluate the depatterning program. The hospital located seventy-nine patients who had received intensive psychic driving and compared their fates with other patients treated around the same time at the Allan. First off, there was little to suggest that Cameron's intervention achieved glowing success in terms of long-term outcomes. Both groups required further psychiatric hospitalizations, had impoverished social adjustment, and only a minority of the patients were actually symptom free. More important, about a quarter of the psychic driving patients had significant physical complications, and their memory tests showed troubling findings.[62] Memory impairments were seen primarily in those patients who had received multiple convulsive treatments over short intervals. Upon follow-up, 60 percent of Cameron's patients reported that they could not recall vast swaths of their memories in intervals ranging from six months to ten years prior to treatment.[63]

His scientific colleagues were not particularly surprised about the negative findings. Hebb, who had squabbled with Cameron for years and resented Cameron's adoption of the sensory isolation model, skewered him much later: "Cameron stuck to the conventional experiments and paper writing for most of his life but then he wanted that breakthrough. That was Cameron's fatal flaw—he wasn't so much driven with wanting to know—he was driven with wanting to be important—to make that breakthrough—it made him a bad scientist."[64] Cameron had all the flaws Hebb enumerated; he was a mixture of bright, opinionated, caring, and ambitious. To borrow a phrase from Shakespeare, Cameron longed to "pluck from the memory a rooted sorrow [and] raze out the written troubles of the brain," but he failed colossally.[65]

In a 1993 lecture in honor of the fiftieth anniversary of McGill's psychiatry department, the speaker reminded the audience that Cameron lived in a different time and that considerations of informed consent in behavioral science became more prominent after Cameron's days. Similarly, Cameron's glowing descriptions of the psychic driving experiments exemplified that era's typical shortcomings in research design. Finally, the nature of the relationship between doctor and patient was characterized then more by blind trust and authority than informed consent and therapeutic alliance.[66]

Donald Hebb was not so charitable. "Cameron was irresponsible — criminally stupid, in that there was no reason to expect that he would get any results from the experiments. Anyone with any appreciation of the complexity of the human mind would not expect that you could erase an adult mind and then add things back with this stupid psychic driving."[67]

Cameron died suddenly in 1967, but it was another ten years before the scandal blew up and the lawsuits started.[68] Lawyers obtained Cameron's proposals to Cornell's Society for the Investigation of Human Ecology and traced the funding from there to MKUltra and then to the CIA. The CIA connection upset people, but ultimately it was Cameron's application itself that was so damning. He had crisply proposed "the breaking down of ongoing patterns of the patient's behavior by means of particularly intensive electroshock . . . ; [supplemented by] intensive repetition (16 hours a day for 6 or 7 days) of the prearranged verbal signal . . . [during which] the patient is kept in partial sensory isolation [and then placed] . . . into continuous sleep for 7–10 days."[69] With this unnerving combination of interventions, Cameron destroyed patients' memories but failed to implant new thoughts, feelings, and behaviors.

If this was the best that academic research could do in the 1950s and 1960s, brainwashing as a tool seemed unpromising for the intelligence agencies. Instead of having a powerful weapon to use against enemies, the agencies were targeted with litigation and bad publicity. The précis of the lawsuit against the CIA summarized the essence of the damages that resulted from Cameron's experiments. "Beginning in 1957 . . . the CIA paid Cameron to conduct behavior control and brainwashing experiments at McGill University on unsuspecting psychiatric patients. . . . In the period from 1957 through 1963, plaintiffs sought psychiatric therapy and medical treatment from Cameron, and instead were used as unwitting subjects in brainwashing and behavior control experiments paid for by the CIA. As a consequence of their involuntary participation in these federally financed experiments, plaintiffs have suffered serious and permanent injuries and seek damages."[70]

Although the treatment occurred in the 1950s, it was not until 1988 and 1992 that the lawsuits were settled by the U.S. and Canadian governments — and further lawsuits are still pending.

Cameron's studies were variously characterized even at the highest levels of the CIA as culpably negligent, professionally unethical, bordering on illegal, repugnant, and totally abhorrent.[71] Cameron was the model for the bogeyman lurking in the Jason Bourne books, but we will encounter *far worse* individuals in the brainwashing saga, individuals who had no aspiration of, to quote Shakespeare again, "ministering to a mind diseased."

Meanwhile, it became apparent that brainwashing was no longer just in the province of government agencies and academe.

PART II

Criminals and Religious Groups

CHAPTER EIGHT

Flash Conversion of Hostages

Stockholm Syndrome and Its Variants

It was the hostages' fault. They did everything I told them to do.
. . . Why didn't any of them attack me? . . . There was nothing to
do but get to know each other.

—JAN-ERIK OLSSON

F ROM ROUGHLY 1915 TO 1965, governments and universities tried
to develop tools for brainwashing. They weren't exactly successful. Torture did not persuade people to adopt different political beliefs, nor did it elicit reliable information. Any number of
drugs could sedate, stimulate, or confuse people, but they were not effective in interrogations or persuasion. Group pressures, sensory isolation,
and sleep deprivation were promising tools for persuading people, but
these required time and finesse.

In the 1970s and 1980s two unlikely players emerged to demonstrate
new techniques in dark persuasion—kidnappers and clerics. While some
kidnappers were able to radically change their hostages' behavior, usually
this did not reflect the kidnappers' deliberate intention. Rather, the
changes were a by-product of what one hostage called "the constant and
palpable threat of death."[1] Paradoxically, hostages wound up liking their

captors and defying their rescuers. The kidnappers thus demonstrated a powerful, if inadvertent, type of dark persuasion. Clerics would show an ability to wield even more alarming influences.

How are hostages supposed to behave? If they are rescued, what should their feelings be toward their captors? The assumption is that rescued hostages would not only feel grateful to their rescuers but would look forward to their assailants' punishment. However, two bank robberies revealed that hostages' feelings and behavior could be radically different from our expectations. The first case gave rise to the term *Stockholm syndrome*. The second, which we will turn to in the following chapter—Patty Hearst's bank robbery in San Francisco—kindled worldwide interest in hostage behaviors. In both these instances, the question of brainwashing was on everyone's mind.

On August 23, 1973, an intelligent and highly experienced robber, Jan-Erik Olsson, entered the Kreditbanken bank in Stockholm wearing a disguise and makeup. He intended to seize hostages, get his friend Clark Olofsson released from prison, rob the bank, and escape. Firing a submachine gun into the ceiling of the bank, he captured four bank employees, herded them into the bank vault, tethered them on leashes (!), and began to negotiate. There was a no-man's-land corridor in front of the vault where the toilets were and where the police and robbers could confer on terms. Little did Olsson know that this robbery would dominate the news worldwide and capture the attention of intelligence agencies.

The police surrounded the bank and began negotiations. Authorities released Jan Olsson's buddy Clark Olofsson, who joined Olsson and the hostages in the bank. Meanwhile, the police set up surveillance microphones and cameras so they could eavesdrop on the abductors and their hostages. They also began drilling holes into the ceiling of the vault, ready to pipe in tear gas if necessary. The grainy images from the surveillance camera capture the drama of the situation.

What was supposed to be a quick negotiation and another successful bank robbery for Jan turned into an exhausting six-day standoff. Even Sweden's prime minister, Olof Palme, participated in the negotiations via telephone. While the experience was terrifying to the hostages, the robbers treated them with some consideration. One young woman, Kristin Ehnmark, commented that Olsson was very kind because he let her go to the bathroom off leash. On the way, she saw police hiding in the corridor. They asked her how many hostages were in the vault and she showed them by holding up her fingers. She remembers, "I felt like a traitor. I didn't know why."[2]

Police surveillance photograph of hostages and robber in the Kreditbanken robbery, 1973. (Courtesy of Stockholm Police Authority Archives.)

During her captivity, hostage Birgitta Lundblad spied an armed policeman approaching and screamed out, "Don't shoot!" Warned of the intruder, Olsson shot and wounded the policeman. The robbers negotiated for a telephone and encouraged their hostages to call their loved ones. Birgitta, unsuccessful in reaching her husband, began to cry. Olsson touched her cheek comfortingly, saying "Try again; don't give up." On another occasion, he consoled her by drawing her to his knees. As Birgitta reported after her release: "The robber told me that everything would be all right if only the police would go away. I agreed with him then. Yes, I thought, it is the police who are keeping me from my children."[3]

At other times Olsson's behavior was more menacing. Once, impatient with the delays, he grabbed Elisabeth Oldgren by the throat and threatened to kill her immediately unless the government guaranteed their get-away. Later, when Elisabeth was chilled and shivering in the bank vault, Olsson draped his coat around her. She later recounted that he presented an unlikely combination of brutality and tenderness.[4]

The government requested that the police be allowed to examine the hostages to verify their well-being, and the robbers agreed. The police were flabbergasted at what they found. The hostages greeted them with sullen hostility and Olsson, relaxed and easygoing, had his arms around the women as though they were friends. Hostage Kristin Ehnmark phoned the prime minister and during the forty-five-minute conversation showed a surprising antagonism toward her would-be rescuers.

> KRISTIN: I am very disappointed. I think you are sitting there playing checkers with our lives. I fully trust Clark and the robber. . . . [They] have been very nice. But, you know, Olof, what I am scared of is that the police will attack and cause us to die.
> PRIME MINISTER: But the police will not do that.
> KRISTIN: I want you to let us go away with the robber. Give them the foreign currency and two guns and let us drive off. . . . Dearest Olof, sweetheart, it may sound stupid, but . . . I trust them. I know they would let us go as long as the police don't chase us. . . .
> PRIME MINISTER: The police will not harm you. Can you believe that?
> KRISTIN: You must forgive me, but in this situation I do not believe it.
> PRIME MINISTER: I think that's terribly unfair. Here are a great many policemen risking their lives, who have not moved aggressively in all this time. The purpose, of course, is to protect you.
> KRISTIN: . . . If the police come in here, he will shoot and then they will shoot, and then nobody has a chance to survive.[5]

Jan Olsson reassured Kristin, holding her hands. Caressing her, he explained that he had not slept with a woman for almost two years. She allowed him to touch her breasts and hips but refused to have intercourse. He turned away and, lying next to her, masturbated on the carpet of the bank vault. So Olsson did not torture, shoot, or rape the hostages. Furthermore, sometimes he was quite solicitous of them, offering them food and stroking them comfortingly. As another hostage put it, "When he treated us well, we could think of him as . . . God."[6]

The hostages began to fear the police more than the bank robbers. From the vault, they phoned their families, the press, and the government, complaining about the police even as the robbers held them at gunpoint. Meanwhile, the robbers feared that the police would pump tear gas into the vault. They forced the hostages to stand, strung nooses around their necks, and warned the police that if gas was used, the hostages would collapse, hang, and die before the police could get to them.

The tear gas came anyway. Miraculously, the robbers surrendered, and there were no further casualties. To everyone's surprise, the hostages kissed their captors and shook hands in farewell. As the two were led off to jail, one hostage called out, "Clark, I'll see you again!"[7] Even during their debriefing in the days following their liberation, the hostages continued to regard the police as the enemy and felt that they owed their lives to the robbers. Some even visited them in prison. But the former hostages themselves were puzzled by their responses, asking their doctors, "Why don't I hate them?"

In the face of sudden unexpected life-threatening captivity lasting for days, it is striking that the hostages became unaccountably fond of their captors and distrustful of the people who were trying to rescue them. They were in an extremely chaotic environment, isolated from their families and in constant fear of sudden death. The hostages were totally dependent upon their captors, who controlled every aspect of their lives—where they could go, what they could eat, when they could use the bathroom. One explanation might be that the captors did not live up to their worst capabilities. While they wounded some policemen, they did not kill them. Nor did they shoot their captives or sadistically torment them. As the hours stretched into days of captivity in close proximity, both captors and captives started seeing some humanity in one another, and the robbers made repeated small gestures to comfort their hostages.

The hostages became convinced they had more to fear from the police than from the hostage takers. On some level, they were right; law enforcement classifies these kinds of cases as HOBAS (hostage and barricade situations). In a study of seventy-seven HOBAS involving 348 hostages, researchers reported that four times as many hostages died in the crossfire of assault by security forces than were executed by terrorists.[8]

★★★

Stockholm syndrome was not some unique Scandinavian liberal aberration; it has resurfaced in starkly different social contexts. In 2002, Chechen terrorists seized more than 800 hostages in a Moscow theater. Armed with bombs and guns, the terrorists held their hostages for three days until Russian Special Forces used a soporific gas to subdue everyone and stormed the theater. Of the 130 hostages who were killed, only 5 were victims of the terrorists; the rest died at the hands of the Special Forces, further substantiating the HOBAS study of risks in such settings.

During debriefing, the Russian hostages reported initial disbelief, shock, and terror. Many thought the Chechen terrorists were part of the evening's entertainment or a joke, but the Chechens promptly corrected that misimpression by savagely beating some of the hostages and murdering others. Unlike Stockholm's Jan Olsson and Clark Olofsson, the Chechens were prepared to murder every hostage and die themselves. As the siege went on, the hostages lost their sense of time and reported emotional numbing because they were exhausted from lack of sleep.

Despite the brutality of the Chechens, some hostages felt sorry for them. One reported, "When I came to [from the gas] I felt very sorry that they were all killed."[9] Some spoke of the Chechens' kindness to the children. Others commented on their manners and seriousness of purpose. In yet another Chechen kidnapping, hostages remarked, "The Chechens were good to us. We should free Grozny [the capital of Chechnya]." The Russians were flabbergasted by these sympathetic responses. One woman snapped at her liberated neighbors, "Have you become Chechens or what?"[10]

In December 1975, a group from the South Moluccan Youth movement seized a Dutch train and held hostages for twelve days, shooting some and keeping the rest in constant terror. One of the passengers, Gerard Vaders, was a prominent Dutch news editor who kept careful notes during his imprisonment: "You had to fight a certain feeling of compassion for the Moluccans. I know this is not natural, but in some way they came over human. . . . They gave us blankets. But we also realized that they were killers. You try to suppress that in your consciousness. . . . I also knew that they were victims, too. . . . You saw their morale crumbling. You experienced the disintegration of their personalities. The growing of despair. Things dripping through their fingers. You couldn't help but feel a certain pity."[11]

In 1976, five Croatian terrorists hijacked a TWA flight scheduled to fly from New York to Chicago. The hijackers were courteous but terrified the passengers and crew. As negotiations proceeded, the plane was diverted to Montreal. The hijackers released some of the passengers, but to show that they meant business, they informed authorities they had left a bomb in Grand Central Station in New York and more bombs had been placed elsewhere. The police found the bomb at Grand Central; when they attempted to disarm it, one officer was killed, and two others were seriously wounded.[12] Meanwhile, the plane proceeded to Gander, Newfoundland; Keflavik, Iceland; and finally to Paris, where the hijackers surrendered.

Richard Brockman, a psychiatry resident who was a passenger on the plane, described his astonishment at the behavior of passengers and crew when the surrender was finalized. "We are all relieved. I see smiles. Some tears. Some of the passengers thank the hijackers. For what? One of the passengers puts his arm around . . . [a hijacker], saying ' . . . Have you and the others thought about going back to New York with us? You could get a fairer trial in America than from the French.' What is he saying? Do I hear right?" Brockman continued, reporting the surprising announcement of the plane's captain to the passengers: "This is the captain speaking. . . . We have all been through an incredible experience. But it is over for us. . . . However, it is not over for our hijackers. Their ordeal is just beginning. . . . They are brave, committed people. . . . Like the people who helped to shape our country. They are trying to do the same for theirs. I think we should all give them a hand."[13]

Not all hostage situations involve politics, extremism, or kidnapping for profit. Some are carried out to satisfy the captor's fantasies about sex and domination. Yet even here, one sees some attributes of Stockholm syndrome.

In 1991, eleven-year-old Jaycee Dugard was kidnapped by Phillip Garrido, who had a previous conviction for kidnapping and rape. Garrido locked her up in a small shed, raped her repeatedly, and told her that she would be killed by attack dogs if she left the shed. After three years of this, the restraints were lessened, but the assaults and victimization lasted until her rescue in 2009.

Stunningly, Dugard avoided detection and rescue despite repeated visits by Garrido's parole agent. When the agent eventually became suspicious of her presence in Garrido's house, Jaycee did not ask for help and did not reveal her true identity—she claimed her name was Alyssa. When the parole agent asked if she was aware that Garrido was a sex offender, she replied that "Garrido was a changed man and a great person who was good with her kids." She then said she didn't want to provide any more information. The agent persisted, asking for identification or the phone number of a relative or friend who could identify her, and Alyssa replied that she carried no personal information and wanted a lawyer. She then concocted a story that she was from Minnesota and was hiding from an abusive husband. Her abductor Garrido, in the meantime, was being questioned separately and he admitted to kidnapping and raping Alyssa. That's right: he confessed first; it took subsequent interviews before Alyssa revealed she was actually Jaycee Dugard.[14]

Years later, when asked about her experiences living with Garrido, she replied she was still mystified about the whole interlude. "I can't fathom how I kept it together. . . . [How] did I even do that?"[15] She emphatically denied having any affection for Garrido and repudiated the suggestion that she had Stockholm syndrome, saying instead that her behavior did not reflect affection for her abductor but was a way to survive: "Well it's, really, it's degrading, you know, having my family believe that I was in love with this captor and wanted to stay with him. I mean, that is so far from the truth that it makes me want to throw up. . . . I adapted to survive my circumstances. There is just no other way to put it."[16]

In 2002, fourteen-year-old Elizabeth Smart was kidnapped and subjected to months of captivity and sexual assault. Her experience reprised some of the themes of Ms. Dugard's experience. For nine months she traveled with her abductors, making no effort to escape. She had been warned that if she ever tried to get away, her abductors would come after her and then kill her and her entire family. When they were at last stopped by the police, "I did as I was told. . . . I initially held to the cover story that I had been told to tell—that I was their daughter."[17] She lied to the police about her birth date and said, "I know who you think I am. . . . You think I'm that Elizabeth Smart girl that ran away, but I'm not."[18]

There is a stigma associated with Stockholm syndrome partly because of the lurid sadomasochistic fantasies that are emphasized in the newspapers and partly because the behavior is so bizarre that people think the hostage must have been "crazy." The hostage survivor (or the survivor of rape, sexual trafficking, and abuse, for that matter) is often confronted by cruel questions: "Why didn't you run, scream, fight back? Did you develop unseemly bonds with your captors?" Survivors rightfully bristle at the tactless insinuation of blame by the police, media, and acquaintances. Elizabeth Smart comments: "Nobody should ever question why you didn't do something. They have no idea what they would have done, and they certainly have no right to judge you. Everything I did I did to survive. And I did. Maybe there were times that, had I done more, I would have been rescued. But maybe I wouldn't have. So do I regret anything I did? No."[19]

★★★

Terrorism marks people—young and old, naïve and educated, passersby, prison guards, abused wives and children. Victims are grateful their experiences were not worse than they were. They appreciate their captor "because he could have killed me and didn't."[20] Sometimes this appreciation transforms into affection. One survivor concluded: "I was alive because they had let me live. You know only a few people . . . who hold your life in their hands and then give it back to you. After it was over, and we were safe and they were in handcuffs, I walked over to them and kissed each one of them and said thank you for giving me my life back."[21]

While victims feel some appreciation for the perpetrator, many feel the world has abandoned them and that in some way their interests and their captors' interests coincide. Diane Cole, a survivor of the 1977 Hanafi terrorism in Washington, described this well: "Terrorists are like pirates. They hold their prisoners for ransom, while they barter with the world and the world's conscience. Make no mistake about it—they trade in lives. . . . Isolated from the world, you wonder if the world cares."[22]

The hostage thus decides to get along with the abductor and make the best of a bad situation. I use the word *decides* with reservations because there isn't a word that captures the complex intermingling of conscious intention and unconscious action. Under continuing exposure to life-threatening stress, some people paradoxically develop more trust and affection for their captors than their rescuers. This constitutes the essence of the Stockholm syndrome.

It is difficult to assess what factors make people more susceptible to the syndrome because most of the literature is based on case reports or small case series, or else reflect highly specific situations that may not generalize to all the variants of hostage scenarios.[23] For instance, Italian investigators studied twenty-four different Sardinian kidnappings in which people were held for ransom. They found that 50 percent of the survivors reported some form of positive bond with their captors. Those who had been exposed to more humiliating experiences during their captivity and those who were held captive for longer amounts of time were more likely to develop such feelings. Neither the victim's age nor the presence of psychiatric diagnoses were associated with vulnerability to such feelings.[24]

Another study reviewed U.S. federal data on 447 hijackers and twenty thousand hostages to learn which situations foster positive feelings between hijacker and hostage. The sample size is dispiritingly large (who knew there were so many?). Captivity experiences of longer duration that featured extensive social interactions with the hijacker seemed to foster the development of Stockholm-like feelings. Interestingly, the development of such feelings was not affected by the amount of the perpetrator's abuse of the victim.[25]

There are wildly different estimates about how often Stockholm syndrome occurs. One FBI agent reported that full-blown Stockholm syndrome occurs "only in a very few victims."[26] On the other hand, in one hostage incident involving schoolchildren, eighty-four of eighty-seven hostages related that "they experienced negative feelings toward law enforcement and positive feelings toward the hostage-taker."[27]

If the incidence ranges from "rarely encountered" to being found in over 95 percent of captives (in the school situation above), it is impossible to characterize how often the phenomenon occurs, other than to state that "it happens sometimes." The literature does suggest that it is more likely to develop in prolonged hostage or kidnapping situations. There is also a whiff of a suggestion that children and people who have relatively little experience out of their home environment are more vulnerable. A RAND report noted: "Surprisingly few hostages bear any grudge against their captors for turning them into human pawns. Indeed, they frequently develop positive relationships with them. Upon release, they often part company amiably, wish each other well. Some former kidnap victims recall their 'hosts' almost fondly—'They were exceptionally polite—especially for terrorists.'"[28]

Psychiatric explanations reflecting older theoretical frameworks ("identification with the aggressor") are typically rejected by today's survivors. On the other hand, when framed from the perspective of life stress and coping, the syndrome is readily understandable, viewed less as a mark of psychopathology and more as an instance of coping under extraordinary stress.

Getting close to the abductor is actually lifesaving. Psychiatrist Frank Ochberg, former associate director of the National Institute of Mental Health and a consultant to the FBI, called Stockholm syndrome an "unholy alliance between terrorist and captive, involving fear, distrust, or anger toward authorities on the outside."[29] The captive focuses attention on the captors' occasional kindnesses rather than their brutality. This can be lifesaving because a positive bond affects both captive and captor. Surrounded and threatened by assault from the police, both captor and captive recognize their joint vulnerability. Captives want to survive but are totally dependent upon their captors. The power differential between the two is enormous, and to survive, captives must do all in their power to turn aside the lethal anger of their captors.

It may be uncommon for FBI agents to speak about child development and regression, but Agent Thomas Strentz described the situation masterfully: "The five-year-old is able to feed himself, speak for himself, and has locomotion. The hostage is more like the infant who must cry for food, cannot speak, and may be bound. . . . The hostage is in a state of extreme dependence and fright. He is terrified of the outside world."[30]

Strentz developed and directed the FBI hostage/crisis negotiations program from 1976 to 1985. That corner of the FBI was extremely aware of the complexities of hostage behavior and Stockholm syndrome. Other corners of the FBI were less understanding when Patricia Hearst was abducted, as we will see in the next chapter.

Frank Ochberg observed that "brainwashing is deliberate, but Stockholm just happens."[31] It's a shrewd observation. In these sorts of situations, the abductor is not intending to indoctrinate the victim. Persuasion just happens, and it is largely transitory. To see what happens when deliberate indoctrination efforts are combined with Stockholm syndrome, one needs to look at another bank robbery that took place six months after the Kreditbanken robbery, half a world away, when the Symbionese Liberation Army kidnapped Patricia Hearst. If the Kreditbanken robbery introduced the concept of Stockholm syndrome in 1973, the Hibernia Bank robbery in San Francisco the following year propelled the concept of flash conversion, Stockholm syndrome, and brainwashing into the tabloids, the courts, and ultimately the White House.

CHAPTER NINE

Patricia Hearst
Where Stockholm Met Indoctrination

I grew up in an atmosphere of clear blue skies, bright sunshine, rambling open spaces, long green lawns, large comfortable houses, country clubs with swimming pool and tennis courts and riding horses, and I took it all for granted. . . . I live now on a private, protected street . . . in a . . . house equipped with the best electronic security system available. . . . I do not live in fear. It is just that I feel older and wiser now. . . . I am aware of the stark reality that I am vulnerable, that there are forces out there . . . which are ever threatening and which are stronger than any single individual.

—PATRICIA HEARST, 1982

ROUGHLY TWENTY-FIVE YEARS after the Korean War POWs were repatriated, the courts deliberated about a new case of brainwashing and criminal responsibility—*U.S. v. Hearst*. The case involved another bank robbery and sudden conversion. Courtroom arguments swirled around whether brainwashing existed, how it differed from a change in beliefs, and whether brainwashing could absolve an individual from criminal responsibility.

Patricia Hearst was a nineteen-year-old Berkeley undergraduate living in an off-campus apartment with her fiancé Steven Weed. On the evening of February 4, 1974, Ms. Hearst was violently kidnapped from her Berkeley apartment at gunpoint, struck in the face with the butt of a gun, and stuffed into the trunk of a car. Her kidnappers were members of a small vicious group known as the Symbionese Liberation Army (SLA).

The SLA had no clearly articulated program. Its leader was an African American ex-con named Donald DeFreeze who read revolutionary literature while he was in prison and who longed for the glamorous life of a professional revolutionary. Proclaiming himself General Field Marshal Cinque Mtume of the SLA, he attracted a handful of followers — principally white, middle-class, educated youth. They played with guns and, deciding they needed more drama, designed a special emblem, a banner with a seven-headed cobra. They were just one of many odd revolutionary groups active in the San Francisco Bay area in the early 1970s (a "flyspeck underground group" in the memorable words of one commentator).[1] As an icon of the hippie community reflected at the time, "Let's face it, this country is weird right now."[2]

The SLA members gave one another revolutionary-sounding names, drilled with weapons, and spun grandiose fantasies about how they would avenge themselves on "racism, sexism, ageism, capitalism, fascism, individualism, possessiveness, competitiveness and . . . capitalism."[3] They issued chilling communiqués that inevitably ended with their trademark slogan, "Death to the fascist insect that preys upon the people." According to one of DeFreeze's typical statements:

> You . . . know me. You have always known me. I'm that nigger you have hunted and feared night and day. I'm that nigger that is no longer just hunted, robbed and murdered. I'm the nigger that hunts you now.
>
> Yes, you know me . . . and we know you — the oppressor, murderer and robber. . . . Now — we are the hunters that will give you no rest. . . .
>
> Death to the fascist insect that preys upon the people.[4]

When the SLA ultimately got the attention it craved, the press was not exactly supportive. The *Richmond News Leader* called their communiqués the "childish imaginings of a make-believe world."[5] That may have been true, but the SLA members were armed and murderous. For unclear reasons, they assassinated Oakland's popular African American school super-intendent Marcus Foster, shooting him down with cyanide-laced bullets on November 6, 1973, and issuing incoherent communiqués about the coming revolution.

Then the SLA decided to kidnap Patricia Hearst, the granddaughter of William Randolph Hearst and the daughter of Randolph Hearst (chairman of the board of the Hearst publishing empire) and Catherine Campbell Hearst (regent of the University of California). *That* target should get some attention. Furthermore, by extracting a sufficient ransom from the Hearst family and donating it to the poor, the SLA thought it could achieve a kind of Robin Hood stature in the revolutionary community.

★★★

As Patricia Hearst describes it, the kidnapping was incredibly brutal. She was crying in the trunk of the car when the group's leader ("Cinque") threatened her, "Shut your mouth, bitch, or I'm going to blow your fuckin head off."[6] When she arrived at the first apartment where the SLA hid out, she was manacled, gagged, blindfolded, and thrown in a closet, where she was left for almost two months.

> I was put into a closet that was padded. I . . . though[t] they would kill me. I was told that I had been "arrested" because I was the daughter of Randolph A. Hearst whom "Cin" called a corporate enemy of the people. . . . I was completely cut off from my environment. . . . Hourly interrogations started on the third day of my captivity. . . . I learned to agree with what my captors said about my family as "enemies of the people" and gave answers I began to know were desired by my captors. . . . [I] became weak, feverish, depressed, and increasingly confused. . . . I felt I was dying. William Wolfe and Donald DeFreeze [SLA members Cujo and Cinque] raped me while I was in the closet.[7]

The group mocked her as an entitled heiress when she requested to leave the closet because "I have to go to the bathroom." Cinque replied: "Look at her, the fancy, la-di-da lady, a real Marie Antoinette. Listen, if you gotta go pee, say, 'I gotta go pee'; if you gotta take a shit, say, 'I gotta take a shit.'"[8]

Hearst later said she was most frightened of SLA members Bill and Emily Harris, asserting that Bill had a volcanic temper and struck her, and that Emily was a terrifyingly committed ideologue of the SLA. According to Hearst, Emily Harris had murdered a bank customer in a robbery and then dismissed it: "Oh, she's dead, but it doesn't really matter. She was a bourgeois pig anyway. Her husband is a doctor." Sadly for Hearst, she was fated to spend the most time with the Harrises before her eventual capture by the police. It was never easy with Bill Harris constantly attacking her. "Stop sniveling around, for Christ's sake. What's the matter with you? . . . You goddam bourgeois bitch!"[9]

Some SLA members showed her occasional acts of kindness, letting her out of the closet for bathroom breaks and telling her when she was panicking, "It's only a closet, for Christ's sake."[10] Patricia accommodated to the group. She learned that if she agreed with everything they said and became a model prisoner, her captors would be friendlier—and the closet door would be opened.[11]

During Hearst's captivity the SLA released various tapes and communiqués from her. The first tape came four days after she was seized. It was straightforward enough—a frightened-sounding message to her parents begging that they rescue her by paying her ransom and stating that she was seized "because I am a member of a ruling class family."[12]

Her kidnappers demanded that the Hearst family distribute millions of dollars' worth of food to California's poor. There were back-and-forth negotiations regarding the amount of the ransom and how to distribute the food.[13] When the food distributions began, it was sheer chaos. People mobbed the distribution trucks and some were struck and injured by frozen turkeys flung from trucks.

Subsequent tapes from Patricia sounded like she was reading from some propagandistic revolutionary script. She angrily called for freedom for oppressed people, referred to her family as the "pig Hearsts," and spoke of herself as "a soldier in the People's Army."

Eight weeks after she was kidnapped, the SLA gave her a choice of joining the group or leaving. Cinque told her: "You're kinda like the pet chicken people have on a farm—when it comes time to kill it for Sunday dinner, no one really wants to do it. . . . You know, we've kind of gotten to like you, so we don't really want to kill you, if we don't have to. Think about it."[14]

Patricia joined the group and changed her name to Tania. Two weeks later, when the gang robbed the Hibernia Bank in San Francisco, Tania was seen on the bank's surveillance videos.

More tapes emerged from an increasingly radicalized Patricia Hearst. Her parents speculated that she must have been brainwashed to say and do

Bank surveillance video of Patricia Hearst and Donald DeFreeze
robbing the Hibernia Bank, April 1974. (Courtesy of the FBI.)

such things, but Patricia fired back over the ensuing months, vehemently
denying that she had been brainwashed.

The attorney general commented that he thought Hearst had voluntarily joined the group and was therefore a criminal who would be hunted
down with the other bank robbers. Thus, like the Stockholm hostages, and
with good reason, Hearst began to question whom she had to fear more—
her captors or the police.

In May 1974, the gang was hiding out in Los Angeles when Tania and
gang members Bill and Emily Harris converged on Mel's Sporting Goods
Store. Bill was caught shoplifting, and Tania fired bursts from her machine
gun to free him. Reflecting about this years later, Hearst wrote: "I acted
instinctively, because I had been trained and drilled to do just that. . . .
I had, in fact, learned . . . to act and to react instinctively—like Pavlov's
salivating dog."[15]

After that shoplifting escapade, rather than join the rest of the gang in
its Los Angeles safe house, Tania, Bill, and Emily hid out in Disneyland.
The next day, the other six gang members were killed and incinerated in
an apocalyptic shootout with the Los Angeles police.

Wanted poster for Symbionese Liberation Army members
William Harris, Emily Harris, and Patricia Hearst, signed by
FBI director Clarence Kelley. (Courtesy of the FBI.)

Tania and the Harrises disappeared for eighteen months, traveling to
the East Coast and working with a writer who wanted to tell their story.
Tania confided that she hadn't trusted the SLA in the beginning but over
time started to feel sympathetic with their goals. She decried the allegations that she had been brainwashed as "bullshit" and said that brainwashing should refer "to the process which begins in the school system . . .
whereby the people are conditioned to passively take their place in society
as slaves of the ruling class."16

The gang eventually returned to the West Coast, attracted a few new followers, and committed more crimes. They planned to assassinate former secretary of defense Robert McNamara and physicist Edward Teller but never got around to it. They did, however, bomb a Bank of America branch in Oakland, a building on the University of California–Santa Cruz campus, the Marin County Civic Center, and various police cars. They also conducted another bank robbery near Sacramento during which they killed a pregnant woman.[17]

Patricia was finally arrested on September 18, 1975. When she was jailed, she stated her occupation was "urban guerrilla" and waved a "power to the people" fist salute. Her jailer surreptitiously recorded a conversation between Hearst and her best friend Trish Tobin in which Patricia made some damaging statements that came back to haunt her at trial.

> HEARST: I'm not making any statements until I know that I can get out. . . . Then I'll issue a statement, . . . and it'll be a, uhm, revolutionary feminist perspective totally and, uh, uhm, you know, . . . I'll just tell you, like my politics are real different from, uh, way back when. . . .
> TOBIN: Right.
> HEARST: (laughter) Obviously. . . . And so this creates all kinds of problems for me in terms of a defense. . . . And, uh, . . . it really kinda pisses me off. . . . Once I get out of here I'll be able to tell you like all kinds of stories that you just wouldn't even believe, man (laughter).[18]

There are so many competing narratives about Hearst's kidnapping that it has a Rashomon-like quality. It is helpful to recall the highly compressed sequence of events that took her from being a carefree heiress to kidnapping victim to gang member to bank robber.

★★★

Patricia claimed that Bill and Emily Harris dominated her and terrified her. She stated she could never have run away from them because they would follow and kill her eventually. Moreover, she thought if she tried to turn herself in, the FBI would likely kill her.

When they were eventually arrested, Patricia and Emily Harris were in adjacent cells; Patricia claimed that because she was terrified of Emily, she made sure to make radical-sounding statements because she thought Emily could hear her. After Patricia signed an affidavit stating she had

February 4, 1974
Kidnapped

April 15, 1974
Robs Hibernia
Bank

September 18,
1975
Hearst
captured

April 3, 1974
Joins SLA as
Tania

May 6, 1974
Fires gun to
rescue SLA
members in
Los Angeles

February 4,
1976
Trial begins

Time line of Patricia Hearst's experience.

been kidnapped and threatened by the SLA, she said Emily Harris passed her a note in jail saying, "I was right. I knew we should have killed you way back when."[19]

As one legal commentator reports, Bill Harris disputed many of these allegations, stating he had never terrorized Patricia but tried to comfort her, even during the earliest days after her kidnapping.[20] He also denied that Cinque raped her. When Bill and Emily Harris were eventually tried for her kidnapping, they denied that Hearst had suffered bodily harm. They suggested that it was her word against theirs.[21] In a long interview Bill and Emily Harris gave their version of her captivity.

> QUESTION: Were there any disagreements or discussions between the members regarding how to interact with the prisoner?
> ANSWER: The intention was to calm and comfort her so that she would not be a security problem. . . .
> Q: Were her communications edited in any way?
> A: Yes, they were edited. We had to tone her statements down. Her statements . . . were too harsh at first. . . . We were worried that no one would believe some of the things she was saying. . . . We certainly didn't expect Tania to be the kind of person she was. . . . We'd psyched ourselves into expecting a typical bourgeois, a Scarlett O'Hara, someone truly despicable.[22]

Emily Harris also dismissed the severity of Patricia's captivity, saying that the closet was, after all, carpeted and that they did let her out from time to time. She also scoffed at Patricia's claims of injury, asserting she sustained only minor scratches during the kidnapping. Harris told her probation officer: "The entire time she was held as a kidnap victim she was not harmed or abused in any way. I am sure she suffered fear and discomfort. . . . [But we] attempted to insure that . . . she was comfortable and we assured her that there was no intention to harm her."[23]

There were inconsistent reports about Hearst's relationship with SLA member William Wolfe (aka Cujo). The Harrises asserted that far from being raped by Wolfe, Patricia was sexually attracted to him and sought him out. Hearst's relationship with him became a crucial matter at her trial. Cujo had given her a small inexpensive Mexican figurine, which she was seen wearing in photographs while she was with the gang. When she was arrested, the figurine was in her purse. If she had been raped by Wolfe and detested him, why would she carry this love token from him? Moreover, after he was killed in the SLA shootout in Los Angeles, she called him "the gentlest, most beautiful man I've ever known. . . . We loved each other so much. . . . Neither Cujo or I has ever loved an individual the way we loved each other, probably because our relationship wasn't based on bourgeois fucked up values, attitude, and goals. Our relationship's foundation was our commitment to the struggle, and our love for the people."[24]

Hearst would later say that she was just reading a script authored by Emily Harris and that she had held onto the figurine because, naïvely, she believed Wolfe when he told her it was valuable. During her psychiatric examination and trial, there was a prurient fascination with her relationship with Wolfe. One of the psychiatric examiners brought her to tears with his aggressive questions. "Tell me about the seduction. Did you kiss him? Was he circumcised? . . . Tell me about your *lover*."[25]

Her former fiancé, Steven Weed, went to great lengths to try to understand Patricia's radicalization, consulting with French Marxist philosopher Régis Debray about her new radical beliefs. Debray, a former associate of Che Guevara, reviewed all her communiqués and concluded, "No one is made a revolutionary in two months. This is more religious than political." Was her change in behavior more akin to a religious conversion? Weed commented: "It was absurd to think of her 'joining' the SLA the way one 'joins' the Republican party, but . . . it was hard to believe, listening to her voice, that she had . . . participated in the Hibernia bank robbery out of simple fear for her life. It was 'something in between.' . . . She had to accommodate somehow to survive."[26]

★★★

In reviewing a trial record, it is important to remember that trials are dialectical struggles. If there is truth to be extracted from a verdict, it is found at the intersection of the existing laws, the arguments of the prosecution and defense, the evidence presented, the judge's guidance, and the jury's deliberation. The Hearst trial featured remarkably colorful and articulate protagonists, and thus the legal issues regarding a brainwashing defense remain vivid even decades later.

Unlike homicide, where there are gradations (for example, murder, manslaughter, justifiable homicide), there are no gradations for bank robbery in federal law. It is hard to argue, "I stumbled and accidentally robbed the bank while I was trying to make a deposit." Similarly, the argument "That bank needed robbing" wouldn't get very far no matter how despicably the bank had acted. Likewise, the degree of impulsivity versus premeditation doesn't affect the verdict either, although it may influence the severity of the sentence.

There is one area that might constitute a defense against the charge of bank robbery. If someone threatened to kill you unless you robbed a bank, that extreme duress would be mitigating. In Hearst's trial, the judge emphasized that the duress must be immediate and personal. A vague indefinite threat is not exculpatory. Thus, the duress defense would not be valid if someone threatened, "Trust me, I will come after you or your family someday when you least expect it." Even if the person threatening you was very believable and had a connection to the Mafia or some other violent organized crime network, it didn't count, according to the judge's instructions.

The SLA members told Hearst they were part of a huge terrorist organization with units in Ireland, Puerto Rico, and the Philippines. They clearly had demonstrated their murderous violence. Hearst claimed she didn't turn herself in during those many months with the group because she was sure the SLA would come after her or her family. Indeed, throughout her long trial, there were constant public threats by sinister radical groups and demands that the Hearst family fund the legal defense of other SLA members. There were also retaliatory bombings of the Hearst castle in San Simeon and another Hearst family mansion. A shadowy radical underground called the New World Liberation Front made bomb threats against the courthouse and death threats against the judge, the prosecution, and various witnesses. According to the judge's instructions to the jury, none of this counted as "duress." Randolph Hearst observed in exasperation, "These people, they're just a bunch of maniacs."[27]

Many have criticized Hearst's flamboyant defense attorney F. Lee Bailey, claiming that he needlessly subjected her to a prison sentence when he could have made a plea deal. They have asserted he had a conflict of interest because he needed a long trial for publicity about his book on the trial. But most of all, people criticize his decision to put Hearst on the stand. Her former attorney Vincent Hallinan denounced Bailey's defense: "No amount of mischance, negligence, stupidity, or idiocy could have loused up the case worse than the way it was loused up."[28] Years after her guilty verdict, Hearst appealed (unsuccessfully), claiming, among other things, that she had been poorly represented by Bailey.

Patricia testified movingly about her kidnapping and terrorization, but on the stand she also faced numerous questions concerning her activities after the Hibernia robbery: what other crimes had she committed? Why didn't she run away? No fewer than forty-two times she refused to answer such questions, lest her testimony incriminate her in other crimes or result in danger to herself or to her family. It was a conundrum: how could she claim duress while refusing to testify about her other crimes with the SLA and explain why she had never run away?

Bailey was active and passionate in her defense throughout the trial. He reminisced about his first meeting with Hearst on September 26, 1975, describing her as a tiny numb person who spoke in a monotone as if she had been partially anesthetized. He came away wondering if "she was retarded, one with a diminished capacity."[29]

On the other side was James Browning, the lead prosecutor, and his assistant David Bancroft. Browning's remarks were enormously effective:

> Ladies and gentlemen, we ask you to reject the defendant's entire testimony as not credible. She asks us to believe that she didn't mean what she said on the tapes. She didn't mean what she wrote in the documents. She didn't mean it when she gave this power salute, this clenched-fist salute after her arrest. . . . She didn't mean it when she told the San Mateo County Deputy Sheriff that she was an urban guerrilla. . . . She says the Tobin conversation wasn't the real Patricia Hearst. The Mel's shooting incident was simply a reflex. . . . She was in such fear she couldn't escape in nineteen months while crisscrossing the country. . . . She couldn't stand Willy Wolfe, yet she carried that stone face with her until the day she was arrested. It's too big a pill to swallow, ladies and gentlemen, it just does not wash.[30]

There was no doubt that Patricia Hearst had participated in the Hibernia bank robbery. The question was why did she do so, or, more precisely, what was her "intent." For this, both sides relied on extensive psychiatric testimony. Indeed, half of the trial was consumed with expert witnesses called by both the prosecution and the defense.

Whatever his other limitations, Bailey did his homework on brainwashing. He sought out four expert witnesses. At first, he considered engaging British psychiatrist William Sargant (who seems to pop up whenever brainwashing is considered—Pavlov, drugs, the Korean War, Frank Olson, and Ewen Cameron), but apparently decided Sargant would be less convincing to an American jury. Also, Sargant had been indiscreet, giving television interviews and writing newspaper articles about his interviews with Hearst even before the trial started. In the *Times* of London, he wrote: "There will never be any doubt in my mind that Patty Hearst was 'brainwashed,' . . . or whatever other expression one chooses to use for the same thing. . . . The last war showed that around 30 days . . . was the maximum period of tension and stress a normal person could endure before breakdown. Then increased states of suggestibility supervene. . . . One's behavior and ideas become the opposite of those normally held, just as the exhausted rabbit finally turns and runs into the mouth of the stoat."[31]

Sargant described his first meeting with Hearst. "I came away horrified. She's pathetic now. She resembles a person during a war who has just come back from battle." Hearkening back to Pavlov, he commented that a nervous system under constant pressure can exhibit paradoxical brain activity.[32] Elsewhere, Sargant commented that had he testified at the trial he would have emphasized Hearst had been converted rather than brainwashed.[33]

Instead of Sargant, Bailey selected three American psychiatrists and one psychologist who had worked extensively with the U.S. military on questions of brainwashing. They were renowned scholars: UCLA chair of psychiatry Jolly West, whom we last met in his MKUltra and LSD days; Yale professor Robert Lifton, an eminent scholar of Chinese brainwashing techniques; University of Pennsylvania professor Martin Orne, who was noted for his work on hypnosis and dissembling (also supported by MKUltra); and Berkeley psychologist Margaret Singer, who specialized in psychological testing and speech characteristics.

Singer (1921–2003) pointed out that when Hearst was arrested, her psychological testing showed such profound impairment that her IQ had dropped by over twenty points. Singer also analyzed Hearst's speaking and writing characteristics, and testified that many of the communiqués and tapes Hearst had released during her SLA days were not at all in her writing style. The prosecution picked away at this by suggesting Hearst had faked her psychological testing to make her look more impaired than she was. Furthermore, prosecutors argued that perhaps Hearst started emulating the writing style of her SLA captors, particularly since, at least in the early days of her captivity, Hearst was told what to say by the SLA.

The question of Hearst's psychological impairment did not go in the anticipated direction of an argument about her competency to stand trial. Rather, the defense argued that the degree of her impairment demonstrated the lingering effects of her harsh treatment during her SLA captivity. Although this wasn't stated outright, the defense implied that such treatment had compromised her decision making such that she collaborated with the group.

Jolly West provided a magnificent overview of brainwashing and coercive persuasion during the Korean War. West recommended that the word *brainwashing* be avoided because it "is a term that has become a sort of a grab bag to describe any kind of influence exerted by a captor over a captive, but that isn't very accurate from the scientific or the medical point of view."[34] He referred to his Korean War studies, where he had observed that captives were readily influenced when they were in a state of debility, dependency, and dread ("DDD," as he termed it). When the prisoner is worn out from malnutrition, sleep deprivation, and medical issues, debility ensues. When the prisoner is forced to rely on his or her captor for every little thing of daily life (going to the bathroom, standing up, walking), the prisoner develops a profound dependency on the captor. Finally, dread follows when the prisoner is constantly threatened with death.

West compared Hearst's experience with DDD to the situation faced by POWs in Korean and Chinese prison camps. When soldiers were released from these prisons, they commonly reported feeling numb, depressed, anxious, and fearful. He noted that Hearst manifested similar symptoms when she was arrested. He also pointed out that very few POWs escaped from Korean custody and attributed this to their DDD, an inference that was not lost on the court regarding the puzzling question of Hearst's lack of attempts to escape from the SLA.

West reported POWs were liable to dissociation—splitting off aspects of memory and feeling as a reaction to massive stress. In Hearst's case, when she assumed the persona of Tania, it gave her "a chance to dissociate more, to put out of her mind the old Patricia Hearst, her feelings about her family, to cut herself off as much as she could from the past . . . and just day by day learn the things she was supposed to learn. . . . It was like putting on a kind of psychological armor so that she couldn't think about the unbearable thoughts."[35]

West's testimony was powerful and damaging to the prosecution, so it attacked him ferociously. Because West had made a point of saying he did very little forensic work, the prosecutor pigeonholed him as an ivory tower academic. While West had enormous experience with prisoners of war, the prosecutor suggested his experience was dated and perhaps not so relevant anymore. The prosecutor continued his attack. While some U.S. officers did in fact defect to China, was there *ever* an instance in which the defector joined the Chinese army and actually attacked the United States? If not, how could West attribute Patricia's participation in the bank robbery to brainwashing?

West was hounded to back up every statement. For instance, the prosecution asked how he could say Hearst suffered sensory isolation when there was a radio playing that was audible in the closet. The prosecution argued that no matter what Hearst said, West fit it into his preconceived conceptual mold of brainwashing. If she reported a symptom, he believed her; if she denied a symptom, it meant she was dissociating. His diagnosis was all too neat and could not be disproved no matter what the evidence showed.

Furthermore, West was confusing his role. Was he objectively evaluating Hearst to form his expert opinion or was he acting like her therapist? Was he inadvertently coaching her on how to portray her symptoms, thereby bolstering her defense of being under constant duress?

The prosecution suggested that West had prejudged the matter, citing the fact that he had written to Patricia's parents during her SLA captivity saying they should have hope and that if Patricia were treated appropriately, she would recover. How could he know that even before examining her? The prosecution also implied that he was too cozy with the Hearst family (he had dined with them), and suggested that as a University of California employee, he was somehow beholden to Catherine Hearst (Patricia's mother), who was a regent of the university.

Martin Orne (1927–2000) discussed why he thought Hearst was telling the truth. He based his testimony on his research about detecting dissembling. It was a rather hard-to-follow argument and the prosecution didn't waste too much time rebutting. Like Jolly West, Orne believed that Hearst was telling the truth about how she was treated by the SLA because she did not try to magnify her symptoms in an effort to win sympathy the way a malingerer might.

Orne also suggested Hearst must have dissociated under the trauma, which might explain why she couldn't remember things or felt in a daze during the bank robbery. Furthermore, as "Tania," she was playing a role just as the isolated POWs in China did. Such role-playing can become real, Orne testified. "I believe . . . she continued to rehearse the role . . . , because she had no opportunity for getting out of it. . . . We sometimes play roles. . . . The man who hates his boss may play the role of . . . liking the boss. But then he can come home and tell his wife how he really feels. . . . If you isolated somebody totally and you make him play a role on the threat of death and you don't allow him to have . . . [someone] with whom he can ever validate himself, that's when the role becomes more and more real."[36]

The prosecution retorted by repeating many of Hearst's statements when she was captured—she "was pissed" about being caught, she had become a radical feminist and an urban guerrilla. How could Orne be sure this wasn't the truth? Maybe she had merely changed her mind and viewed things differently? Why did one need to invoke things like "dissociation" to explain what happened?

Wasn't it self-serving for her to assert she did all these things because she had become accustomed to role-playing the part? After all, Hearst had written: "My decision to struggle to become a guerrilla fighter wasn't one that was pried off the wall. What some people refer to as my sudden conversion was actually a process of development, much the same way that a photograph was developed onto paper. . . . All you have to do after is put the paper into the bath and the picture comes out."[37]

In response, Orne pointed out this wasn't the way Hearst normally spoke or wrote and someone else must have written it. The prosecutor scoffed at this echo of Margaret Singer's earlier testimony. Orne rebutted by saying that in fact the government was very interested in verbal content analysis and had funded wide-ranging studies on the topic.[38]

Orne and West kept referring to "dissociation" and the prosecution asked for a definition. Dissociation refers to a break in the normal continuity of thinking, feeling, remembering, and sometimes even the sense of identity itself. We all dissociate to a certain extent every day. When we drive to work, we hardly notice or remember anything on our commute unless it was somehow remarkable. Attending a good movie or concert, we can "lose ourselves." Sometimes, however, this dissociation is so severe that it becomes a problem. Criminals frequently complain they cannot recall details of their crimes, and it is not always just a convenient way to dodge questions.[39] Hearst repeatedly stated she felt detached or in a fog while she was with the SLA, that there was an unreal quality to her life experience in captivity. The defense experts claimed that these sorts of complaints are common in trauma and abuse and that they reflect trauma-related dissociation; the prosecutors scorned the premise as nonsense.

In the 1970s, there was no entry in the *Diagnostic and Statistical Manual of Mental Disorders* (*DSM*), psychiatry's standard reference book, for a disorder resulting from brainwashing. In *DSM5*, the most recent edition, trauma-related symptoms are in a category called "other specified disso-ciative disorder," described thus: "Identity disturbance due to prolonged and intense coercive persuasion: Individuals who have been subjected to intense coercive persuasion (e.g., brainwashing, thought reform, indoc-trination while captive, torture . . . recruitment by sects/cults or by terror organizations) may present with prolonged changes in, or conscious ques-tions of, their identity."[40] If Hearst had been tried after the appearance of *DSM5*, such arguments would certainly have been introduced, but *DSM5* was forty years away.

The final defense expert, Robert Lifton (1926–), provided a magnifi-cent overview of his early work with Chinese thought reform prisoners. He pointed out that the extensive group interrogation and confession used by the Chinese were potent vehicles for changing thoughts and behaviors. Lifton emphasized that thought reform is facilitated when the prisoner is made to feel guilty and referred to Hearst's lancinating sessions in which the SLA critiqued her background. In China, he said, prisoners became desperate to figure out what their interrogators wanted from them. What-ever they said or confessed to was never enough, and so they experimented with ever more elaborate confessions until their interrogator finally ac-cepted them.

Lifton was measured in his responses, acknowledging that while it was relatively easy to tear people's thinking down, it was more difficult to con-vert them to new beliefs. Expanding on West's discussion of dependency, he pointed out that in situations like POWs had faced in Korea and China, survival itself was called into question daily. Any leniency showed by the guards loomed large in the prisoner's mind and through that leniency pris-oners could be manipulated more easily. He suggested Hearst's participa-tion in the Hibernia bank robbery and her firing the machine gun in Los Angeles reflected "the original terror she experienced in kidnapping and in the closet. You cannot understand what's happened in this young woman unless you appreciate that terror in that early period."[41]

He told the court that the Korean POWs and Chinese thought reform victims were frequently quite confused upon repatriation. It was not unusual for them to parrot back what their former captors had told them in their first few days of freedom. This testimony suggested a potential explanation for some of Hearst's radical statements when she was arrested.

This was again damaging testimony for the prosecution, so it asked Lifton to prove that people had been brainwashed, citing one of his former subjects who said that rather than being brainwashed, she had truly come to believe what her captors had been telling her. The prosecution challenged Lifton about his writings emphasizing the importance of subjectivity and empathy in research and pointed out that he lacked experience in determining criminal responsibility.

The prosecution also argued that most of Lifton's thought reform subjects had been imprisoned by the Chinese for over two years, whereas Hearst was shut in the closet for less than two months. It suggested that his explanations of Hearst's behavior were baroque in their complexity and that the simplest, most logical explanation was she had participated in all the various crimes voluntarily.

Lifton retorted: "For . . . [your] explanation to be true, three things would have had to be true, none of which I think has any possibility of being so, and they are the following: One is that this young woman had a textbook knowledge of traumatic neurosis, and therefore could simulate it or imitate it, which I very much doubt. A second is that she had an equally textbook knowledge of some of the major features of coercive persuasion and I very much doubt that as well. And a third necessity would be that she has some specific also textbook knowledge of how to deceive the psychological tests with their careful objective findings, and I very much doubt that, too."[42]

There was one other theme common to the defense psychiatric experts. Rather than confine themselves to forensic issues, they saw their role as advocating for Hearst and helping the court understand how her criminal acts were a consequence of her exposure to massive stress. Their testimony implied that when Hearst became Tania, it was a result of her violent kidnapping and treatment. She had acted under duress and was coercively persuaded; therefore, she should not be held responsible for her illegal actions. In essence, they focused on exculpation and compassion for Hearst rather than responsibility and retribution.

Enter the two psychiatric experts for the prosecution, who were strikingly different in background and temperament from the defense experts.

Neither were experts in massive trauma, PTSD, or brainwashing, but both had extensive forensic experience. The prosecution psychiatrists held a black-and-white view of the world and used a simpler vocabulary. Personal characteristics aside, they articulated the belief that people are responsible for the decisions they make except under very narrow circumstances. They ridiculed the idea of brainwashing and dismissed the argument that Hearst was under duress for eighteen months, emphasizing instead that she had plenty of opportunities to escape but simply chose not to.

San Francisco's Joel Fort (1929–2015) was trained in psychiatry but called himself a "specialist in social and health problems." He distributed self-promoting press releases in advance of the trial that were in some respects puff pieces, but he also made some good points. He argued that academic psychiatrists with little forensic experience did not have much to offer in court; forensic experts, on the other hand, must be neutral and not confuse the "defendant" with the "patient."[43] Fort told the court he regarded the idea of brainwashing as unsubstantiated and vague—but he was caught short when the defense attorney revealed that Fort had relied on precisely such concepts when he testified for the defense in another case.

The prosecution asked Fort if Hearst had any mental disease or defect that affected her capacity to follow the law or to appreciate the wrongfulness of participating in the bank robbery. Fort replied in the negative.[44] He indicated that he had carefully considered forces that can contribute to attitude change, including religious conversion, group pressures, and kidnapping. He also based his judgment on Hearst's pre-kidnap personality and the background and attitudes of SLA members. Fort concluded simply: "She did not perform the bank robbery because she was in fear of her life. She did it as a voluntary member of the SLA."[45]

Fort thought that terms like *coercive persuasion* and *thought reform* were useful but vague and that the issue boiled down simply to attitude change. Hearst had merely been converted by the SLA, fallen in with a bad crowd at a vulnerable time in her life, and developed strong ties to, even affection for, some of the SLA members. Not only that, but it was exciting for her to get all the international media attention. "My findings . . . were that she was an extremely independent, strong-willed, rebellious, intelligent, well-educated but not particularly intellectually inclined . . . [person. She was] an amoral person who thought . . . laws . . . she didn't agree with should be violated."[46]

He dismissed Hearst's concern that she would be shot by the FBI and commented that the closet where she was held for two months was not really so bad. He found no evidence that she had been sleep deprived and pointed to numerous instances in the Tania communiqués where she explicitly dismissed the suggestion that she had been brainwashed.

Fort was exceedingly sure of himself in providing his testimony. In response, the defense pointed out that he had misrepresented countless elements of his CV; it didn't exactly say he had lied repeatedly, but that was a clear takeaway. He claimed more forensic experience than he really had. He kept referring to a book of his—which had never even been written. He was not board certified and had a checkered employment history. Further, the defense unearthed reports from his supervisors stating that they regarded him as such a weak psychiatric resident they advised him not to perform psychotherapy. All in all, the defense painted a pretty unsavory picture of Fort. But did that invalidate what he said about Patricia Hearst?

Boston psychiatrist Harry Kozol (1906–2008) ran a center for the diagnosis and treatment of criminally dangerous sex offenders. Unlike Joel Fort, Kozol was a forensic psychiatrist who also treated patients, and he had considerable clinical legitimacy. He had no animus against psychiatry and was very respectful of the defense psychiatrists. He had experience with patients trying to con him in legal cases. On the stand he radiated confidence and was maddeningly long-winded in his testimony, but he eventually came to the point and answered questions.

There was something different and difficult about Kozol's interactions with Hearst. Although Kozol asked many questions obliquely, trying to put her at ease and tiptoe into hot topics, she repeatedly ran out of his interviews in tears.

In court he repeatedly referred to her as "this girl," and Hearst was offended by his condescension. Kozol argued that her actions with the SLA were undertaken of her own free will. How did this come to pass? Patricia had become increasingly disillusioned and disenchanted with her life before her kidnapping.

> This girl was disappointed and frustrated. A very proud girl, with a great deal of dignity. . . . But the girl who got kidnapped was a bitter, angry, confused person. . . . Angry at authority, angry at power, angry at hypocrisy, angry at . . . [her fiancé]. . . . So this is the girl who was picked up, in a sense with no place to go.
>
> This girl was a rebel. Whatever developed in the subtle interplay of a million experiences in her life, . . . she had gotten into a state where she was ripe for the plucking. . . . I don't think she

was in a clear frame of mind, but she was in a receptive frame of mind. She was ready for something, she was a rebel in search of a cause. . . .

And the cause found her, in the sense that she was kidnapped by the cause, a terrible, terrible, terrible misfortune for her.[47]

Kozol traced the rapid change in Hearst's behavior and scrutinized the series of tapes released after she was kidnapped. Like others, he noted her fear in the initial propagandistic communiqués, which were obviously not of her writing. Kozol then sketched her increasing anger at not being rescued until, on April 3, she stated, "I have joined them" and then participated in the bank robbery on April 15. Kozol noted: "I think she was a spiritual sister to the SLA. . . . That she was ready for it. . . . For a long, long time preceding [her kidnap]."[48]

Kozol was a very effective witness. The defense tried to paint him as a dirty old man who leeringly asked Hearst questions about her sex life. It also pointed out that despite all his statements about Hearst's unhappy family life, he never obtained collateral information and never even interviewed the Hearst family. Bailey attacked Kozol for saying Patricia caved in under captivity because she was *predisposed to* by her anger and disillusionment.

> BAILEY: Listen to this, Doctor, and tell me if you recognize it.
> "My powers of resistance gradually faded. Apathy and indifference grew. More and more the boundaries between true and false, reality and unreality, seemed blurred to me. . . . I was left with only one certainty, that there was no longer any way out of this situation. My shaken nervous system weakened the resistance of my mind, clouded my memory, undermined my self-confidence, unhinged my will."
> BAILEY: Do you recognize that description?

When Kozol said he did not recognize that description, Bailey triumphantly revealed it had been written by Cardinal Mindszenty, implying that Kozol would also have found some "predisposition" in the cardinal's case because he also caved in during his captivity in Hungary.[49]

The defense tried to impugn Kozol's integrity and called to the stand a former colleague. The colleague suggested that Kozol was hardly objective in his assessment of Hearst. Months before he had even interviewed

Patricia, Kozol had described the Hearst family as "venal and disgusting people. . . . If I had grown up in a family like Patricia, you would understand what she is rebelling against. They are pigs."[50] Bailey characterized Kozol's examination as "deplorable, inquisitorial . . . he was more like an interrogator than a psychiatrist or a doctor sent to examine."[51]

In his memoir, written years after the trial, Lifton vividly described the trial as relentlessly adversarial and wrote how shocked he was that the prosecution psychiatrists could assert "with straight faces that Hearst had voluntarily joined the SLA out of deep rebellion against her parents, that she was 'a rebel in search of a cause.'" He went on to criticize both the prosecution and defense attorneys: "Browning was young, nasty, legally effective, and politically ambitious. Bailey, perhaps the country's most famous criminal lawyer, was extremely intelligent but had something of the style of a con man, drank too many martinis at lunch, and turned out to be commuting back and forth from legal seminars he was giving in Las Vegas."[52]

Judge Oliver Carter handled the attorneys firmly and respectfully, often cooling the tense atmosphere with humor. He explained his rulings carefully and gave clear directions to the jury. Although Carter tried to move the trial along, it still required two months, and the trial transcript runs to thousands of pages. In Carter's final instructions, he reminded the jury:

> There is no way of . . . scrutinizing the operations of the human mind. You may infer the defendant's intent from the surrounding circumstances. You may consider any statements made and done or omitted by the defendant, and all other facts and circumstances . . . which indicate her state of mind. . . .
>
> Intent and motive should never be confused. Motive is what prompts a person to act, or fail to act. Intent refers only to the state of mind with which the act is done or omitted. . . . Good motive alone is never a defense where an act is done or omitted as a crime. . . .
>
> Coercion or duress may provide a legal excuse for the crime charged in the indictment. . . . [But] the compulsion must be present, and immediate, and of such a nature as to induce a well-founded fear of impending death or serious bodily injury; and there must be no reasonable opportunity to escape the compulsion without committing the crime.[53]

Prosecutor Browning focused his closing comments on the question of mental intent, psychiatric opinion, and Hearst's credibility. He reminded the jury "we can't . . . unscrew the top of their head and peer over the rim and say, 'You say that right there, that was their intent on April 15, 1974 [the date of the Hibernia robbery].'" Then he commented that any defendant's testimony would likely be self-serving and unreliable, but one could draw inferences from other data. For instance, Hearst's behavior in Los Angeles (firing a gun to help her SLA companions escape) suggested that she was working with the SLA. She had been totally alone in the car at that point and could have escaped. Furthermore, there had been numerous times when she had stood guard in the apartment while the other SLA members slept.[54]

Browning characterized the defense strategy as a duress defense and said all the talk about psychological coercion "was injected by the defense in the hope that if duress does not stick to the ceiling, maybe something else will." He disparaged the defense psychiatrists as academics who were inexperienced in forensic matters and who were basically gullible in accepting whatever Patricia said. Finally, Browning reminded the jury of Hearst's many inaccuracies and false statements as well as the fact that despite her repeated allegations of suffering and fear of the SLA, she had said she was "pissed off, goddammit" to be arrested.[55]

In his closing, defense attorney Bailey reminded the jury that kidnap victims survive when they cooperate with their captors and that the FBI had threatened Hearst while she was at large. He tried to refocus the trial: "This is not a case about a bank robbery. . . . It is a case about dying or surviving—that is all Patricia Campbell Hearst thought about. . . . A young girl, who absolutely had no political motivations or history of activity of any kind, was rudely snatched from her home, clouted on the side of the face with a gun butt, and taken as a political prisoner. . . . You are not here to answer [whether she robbed that bank]. . . . The question you are here to answer is why? And would you have done the same thing to survive? Or was it her duty to die, to avoid committing a felony?"[56]

After a surprisingly brief deliberation, the jury found Patricia Hearst guilty. It was not an easy decision for the jurors—some wept and even vomited because of the stress of the deliberations. They had been sequestered for months as the trial dragged on. "Every one of us wanted to believe she was innocent because of the . . . kidnapping. And when she was first on the witness stand, every one's heart went out to her."[57]

They recalled the Trish Tobin tape recording in which Patricia revealed how pissed she was at being arrested. Her credibility was destroyed when the testimony surfaced about the monkey charm figurine that William Wolfe had given her. How could they believe her description of him as a rapist whom she despised when she held onto this small love token months after his death?

The jury listened to all her taped communiqués and concluded that she had been converted, rather than coerced, to join the SLA. Hearst's repeated pleading of the Fifth Amendment persuaded many of the jurors that she wasn't telling the truth. All those months in captivity without trying to escape just didn't ring true. On the other hand, the alternate juror, who had sat through the entire trial except the jury deliberations, said she would never have voted guilty because "if they had never kidnapped her, she would never have been in that bank."[58]

Patricia Hearst was sentenced to seven years in prison. The world wasn't ready to consider the implications of dark persuasion when it came to her case, and she was tarred with accusations of being an entitled heiress, a child of privilege, the product of too much leniency. Nonetheless, many people advocated for her release, including odd political bedfellows like Senator S. I. Hayakawa, Ronald Reagan, and César Chávez. Her congressman Leo Ryan was one of her greatest champions. Writing to her in prison just before leaving for Jonestown, he said, "Off to Guyana. See you when I return. Hang in there."[59] He would never return.

The Jonestown connection struck others. As Jeffrey Toobin perceptively observed, the murders in Jonestown in 1978 showed a skeptical world that perhaps brainwashing was not such a bogus concept after all.[60] Speaking up for Hearst, John Wayne drew the logical connection between Hearst's experience and Jonestown: "It seems quite odd to me that the American people have immediately accepted the fact that one man can brainwash nine hundred human beings into mass suicide but will not accept the fact that a ruthless group, the Symbionese Liberation Army, could brainwash a little girl by torture, degradation and confinement."[61]

When President Carter was considering clemency for Hearst, an astonishingly large number of supporters lobbied the president. Indeed, during the week ending February 2, 1979, the Hearst clemency matter was the seventh most common reason for writing the president, just ahead of support for his position on the Middle East and his programs to deal with inflation. The Hearst matter stayed in the top ten for the rest of the month.[62]

Thanks to Patricia's diverse and powerful supporters and a newer zeitgeist that was more accepting of coercive persuasion, President Carter commuted (shortened) her sentence in 1979 and she was released after serving twenty-two months in prison. The Department of Justice supported reducing the length of her sentence because of the unique features of her case.[63] In other words, even the Department of Justice was willing to go along with brainwashing as a *mitigating* factor to be considered in sentencing. But could brainwashing *exonerate* her?

Years later, many people lobbied President Clinton to pardon Hearst, that is, to absolve her from blame. For instance, the retired mayor of West Covina, California, wrote: "She was taken against her will, kept in closet, . . . subject to a continuous barrage of fanatic rhetoric. . . . I recall vividly her tired, monotone voice . . . which bespoke of one who is broken, tired, and will say anything to relieve her suffering. . . . [She was] a sad, beaten young woman, not a defiant bank robber. I believe it was a miscarriage of justice to convict her given the circumstances."[64]

The Department of Justice firmly opposed a pardon. To its way of thinking, President Carter's shortening of Hearst's prison time was acceptable; that she should retroactively be declared innocent was not. Robert S. Mueller III, then U.S. attorney, strongly opposed the pardon, saying her request "repeats her false and self-serving version of events after her kidnapping and her unsupported claim that she was not a willing participant in the Hibernia Bank robbery." He reminded the Department of Justice that Hearst's behavior at Hibernia was not an anomaly. She had also shot at a store clerk at Mel's Sporting Goods, kidnapped a young man while trying to escape, participated in a robbery a year later during which one of her confederates murdered a pregnant woman, and had been involved in various bombing incidents in San Francisco.[65]

Hours before he left office in 2001, President Clinton pardoned her.

★★★

Given the twists and turns of this case, was Patricia Hearst brainwashed or had she fallen in with a bad crowd and made bad choices?

In the space of one year, the Stockholm and Hibernia banks were robbed. Criminals demonstrated they could readily persuade hostages to support them, even after relatively brief imprisonment. The extent of that coercive persuasion was not lethal to their hostages in those instances. It would be up to religious groups to demonstrate those fatal possibilities.

CHAPTER TEN

From Racial Harmony to
Death in the Jungle

The devil can cite Scripture for his purpose.
An evil soul producing holy witness
Is like a villain with a smiling cheek.

—WILLIAM SHAKESPEARE,
The Merchant of Venice

We didn't commit suicide. We committed an act of revolutionary
suicide protesting the conditions of an inhumane world.

—JIM JONES, 1978

O N NOVEMBER 19, 1978, I had never heard of Jim Jones or Jonestown and, regrettably, was also pretty unsure where Guyana
was. I was just finishing up an exhausting meeting in Washington and had been too busy to read the newspapers, but Washington is a city of flagpoles, and on my taxi to the airport, I couldn't help
noticing that all the flags were at half mast. I asked the driver what had
happened, and he said Congressman Leo Ryan and others had been shot

in the jungles of Latin America. That was also the first time I had heard of Congressman Ryan.

On November 18 at 5:25 p.m., the congressman and four others were killed and eleven more wounded at an airstrip at Port Kaituma, Guyana. That evening, 909 members of the Peoples Temple died in an act of "revolutionary suicide" in Jonestown and another 5 died in the capital city of Guyana.[1] Eighty-seven people from Jonestown survived because they had been away from Jonestown on that day, had left Jonestown with Congressman Ryan's group, or had fled into the surrounding jungle.[2]

Who were these people and how were they persuaded to kill themselves and their children? How could a church, of all things, be involved in such gruesome actions? Could this be a variant of brainwashing? The questions haunted me as I flew home from my meeting.

★★★

The group was led by the Reverend Jim Jones, who had started his ministry in Indianapolis in the 1950s, moved to California, and then took his congregation with him to Guyana. Jones was committed to social justice and fighting racism. He was eloquent, charismatic, and shrewd, but those strengths were more than offset by his other characteristics. He was self-aggrandizing, exceedingly manipulative, and pathologically suspicious. Throughout his career, he lied so often that I wonder if he even knew when he was lying and when he was telling the truth. In the end, he led almost one thousand people to their deaths. How was the Peoples Temple subjugated to Jones's lethal influence?

Jones was affiliated with various Protestant denominations and eventually became an impassioned socialist who rejected God and encouraged his congregation to idolize him. "You prayed to your sky God and he never heard your prayers. You asked and begged and pleaded in your suffering, and he never gave you any food. He never gave you a bed, and He never provided a home. But I, Your socialist worker God, have given you all these things. . . . Because I am freedom. I am peace. I am justice. . . . I AM GOD!!!"[3]

He preached his social gospel to thousands of people. It is difficult to estimate the size of the church; one spokesperson claimed, improbably, that there were 250,000 members but, more realistically, there were about 7,500 members in California.[4] All the parishioners shared his commitment to a church where social class and race were unimportant, where congregants were committed to the social welfare of their fellows and were politically active in their communities. The church provided food, clothing, shelter, job counseling, and legal advice. It supported the elderly and schooled the young, established licensed care homes, and used the revenue from the homes to help support the church's broad social missions.

Along the way, Jones dabbled in faith healing, staged fraudulent cancer cures, and claimed that he had resurrected forty-three people.[5] These counterfeit miracles were abetted by some members of his congregation who obligingly "died" or coughed up "cancers" upon his command. After multihour religious services and fiery sermons, supplemented by organ music and choir hymns, members of the congregation were swept away in ecstatic belief. Many truly believed Jones performed miracles—including even the Jonestown nurse.[6] Others dismissed the fake healing, acknowledging that Jones liked to indulge in theatrics and drama, but nonetheless believing that his intentions were good.[7]

The congregation was committed to a communal form of apostolic socialism dating from the New Testament book of Acts. In a sermon in February 1977, Jones explained: "We all live as it was on the day of Pentecost, we all share and have all things common. If somebody only has fifty dollars and somebody else makes four hundred, we share . . . [as] was revealed in the church on the Apostolic day."[8]

In that same sermon and subsequently, Jones drifted into his recurring fears that the government was readying concentration camps for the poor. Ironically, in a sermon in the summer of 1973, Jones warned the congregation about government experiments in mind control with brain surgery and drugs that would induce passivity and make slaves out of African Americans. He cautioned the congregation: "They're trying to get a whole breed of automatons. . . . They [will] put a monitoring device inside the brain, and from a central office, give them signals, or relay signals of what their behavior is."[9]

Back in 1962, Jones had become increasingly fearful of nuclear war and concluded that Redwood Valley—a small town near Ukiah, California— was one of the few relatively safe spots in America. Jones and some of his Indianapolis followers relocated there. The church flourished, attracting a diverse crowd that included elderly and primarily poor African Americans as well as young, idealistic, educated white people who wanted change. He had all sorts of followers, from Pentecostal believers to Unitarians, atheists, ex-convicts, drug addicts, residents of California's ghettoes, and even descendants of a Nobel Prize winner.

Peoples Temple invested in Redwood Valley, buying properties, starting a food truck, selling grapes to neighboring wineries. While members

Jim Jones speaking in a Peoples Temple church service, 1976.
(Courtesy, California Historical Society, Peoples Temple Publications
Department Records, MS 3791; California Historical Society.)

of the Temple lived crowded together in group homes, many worked in
various county welfare offices and helped people obtain their social services benefits. As they had done in Indianapolis, they set up residential care
facilities for the elderly, foster homes for children, and a ranch for mentally disabled adults. All of these enterprises produced income to support
the church, and as it grew, it attracted more and more people: the poor
and dispossessed, professionals, teachers, lawyers, civil servants, laborers,
and ex-convicts.

    While the church allied itself with local conservative politicians and
appeared to fit into the community well, there were conflicts with locals

who didn't care for the racial polyglot congregation in their midst. Mysterious "attacks" on the church began (for example, gunshots from the woods), similar to those that had bedeviled the congregation in Indianapolis. Back then, Jones, a member of the Indianapolis Human Rights Commission, had reported receiving many threats, although none of the other members received any.[10] Several of these attacks were staged by Jones himself to foster the community's cohesiveness in the face of victimization. It was a ruse he used in Indianapolis, California, and Guyana.

Long before and after Jim Jones, people have been vandalizing their own homes or cars with racist messages in an attempt to gain sympathy, attention, or support for their political beliefs.[11] The Reverend Jones was thus not original in his pseudo-victimization, but he resorted to it repeatedly. Once he claimed that he had been shot in the chest, pointed to his bloody shirt with a bullet hole in it, and collapsed. But then, standing up as if resurrected, he declared, "I'm not ready [to die]." He changed into a new shirt, held up a bullet and the bloody shirt, and proclaimed that he had healed himself so there was no bullet hole, no blood, not even a scratch on his body.[12]

In the face of these purported threats and attacks, the church began retreating from its early openness. Gone were the days in Indianapolis with advertisements inviting all comers to join with Peoples Temple in an interracial fellowship and to enjoy its free meals and miracle healing services.[13]

In California, newspaper articles began to appear reporting former members' accusations of fraud and violence. The Peoples Temple adamantly denied the reports, calling them lies spread by defectors and apostates. In Redwood Valley, guards started patrolling the entrance to the Temple and screening strangers, and Jones was shadowed by bodyguards.

Tales of violence emerged about the group confessions held in the Temple. Confrontation groups, ostensibly dedicated to the well-being of the attendees and modeled on encounter groups from the 1960s and 1970s, spiraled into vicious destructive sessions that lasted up to twelve hours. Members were told to write down all their faults and offenses against community rules and to inform on others. In Guyana, after being publicly berated for their faults, they were then assigned to a "learning crew," which was in reality a punishment brigade. If their dissent continued despite beatings and learning crew assignments, they were sent to the "extended care unit," where they were drugged heavily.

It is not surprising that Jonestown used phrases like "learning crews" and "extended care units"—such distortions of language are commonly found in totalitarian regimes. New arrivals were welcomed by a "greet-ing committee" whose sinister function was to inspect and confiscate be-longings, censor any mail or printed material that people were bringing into the colony, and confiscate passports. Another group, the "diversions committee," was charged with tracking down former members and playing dirty tricks to intimidate them. The "counseling committee" paid home visits to congregants, and while "counseling" was part of their job, other parts involved enforcing tithes of 25 percent, spying on members, and ap-proving all member purchases.

Unusual financial arrangements were also imposed. In addition to pay-ing heavy tithes, congregation members gave the Temple power of attor-ney. In return for signing such documents and deeding over their homes, the Peoples Temple promised that it would take care of its members in the future—a kind of continuing care commitment.

The community discouraged members from having deep personal at-tachments with anyone other than Jones. Romantic love was regarded as selfish and egotistical. Parents were not supposed to insist on close re-lationships with their children because the children belonged to the com-munity. Couples who wanted to live together needed to obtain clearance from a special committee.

In addition to the group confessions, members were forced to write affidavits admitting to terrible acts—molesting a child, murdering some-one and throwing the body into the sea. Some were asked to sign a blank document with a typed statement at the bottom of the page declaring, "Everything on this page is true and correct to my knowledge."[14] These documents were locked in the Temple vaults, to be used to discredit mem-bers if they strayed.

Accusations by former members and their concerned relatives sur-faced in negative press reports about Jones and the Temple. In response, a letter-writing crew from the Temple besieged magazines and newspapers with complaints about their "one-sided and biased distortions." The *New West* magazine reported receiving fifty phoned-in complaints and seventy letters *daily* in response to its articles criticizing Jones and the Temple.[15]

Despite these problems, the Peoples Temple expanded its presence to Los Angeles and San Francisco. Members also made road trips across the United States to perform faith healings and support their political aims. They were tightly disciplined, with a "hostess" assigned to each bus to ensure proper behavior so others would have a good impression of the church.[16]

Because of its strong social conscience and racial tolerance, the Peoples Temple was supported by liberal politicians and cultural figures. Although it supported conservative causes in rural Redwood Valley, in urban areas, the church made political alliances with liberal causes and helped turn out the vote for liberal candidates. Members sat in the church social hall churning out hundreds of letters in a factory-like process, lobbying for the people and causes they supported, and vehemently criticizing those they opposed. They created an illusion of mass support by posting the letters from multiple mail drops around town. They were the darlings of the Left—Angela Davis, California legislator Willie Brown, Native American activist Dennis Banks all admired them. In appreciation for his election support, Mayor George Moscone appointed Jones to the San Francisco Housing Commission, saying, "Your contributions to the spiritual health and well-being of our community have been truly inestimable, and I'm heartened by the fact that we can continue to expect such vigorous and creative leadership from the Peoples Temple in the future."[17]

Educators like Philip Lee, chancellor of the University of California–San Francisco, lauded Jones: "Many of the world's problems would be solved if others participated as fully and with as much concern as you have shown." Law enforcement was similarly enthusiastic about the Temple. The chief of the Los Angeles Police Department wrote: "The Peoples Temple has done a fantastic job for us. . . . We are deeply indebted to you for your hard work." The Temple shrewdly donated to support freedom of the press, and as a result had many friends in the media. Katharine Graham (president of the *Washington Post*) wrote, "I am very touched that your church has been so dedicated to issues of press freedom." Politicians like Bella Abzug, Ron Dellums, Phillip Burton, and Hubert Humphrey added their tributes to Jones and the Peoples Temple.[18]

In other words, Jones and his followers were not "out there" dressed in saffron robes like the Hare Krishnas or engaged in public mass weddings like the Moonies. Nor did they advocate violent revolution like the Black Panthers. They were a politically powerful and tightly disciplined communal group.

Jones made himself into an idol to be worshiped. He believed that he was the Promised One because he was so good at healing people. He preached in 1973: "All these people I've healed, given jobs, homes . . . , healed them from blindness, saved them from cancer. . . . I'm doing more good than anybody on earth today. . . . I've set people free all over this world. I've healed. . . . I'm the savior."[19]

In other sermons one can see his increasing grandiosity and his transformation from what he called a "sky God" to a "socialist God."[20] He pretended to be omniscient, famously sending his confidants to the houses of potential parishioners to spy out hidden details of their lives. Then he would pounce during a sermon, saying things like "I'm having a revelation! There is a woman here today who lives on Adams Street who is troubled by diabetes and is in arrears on a loan from Crocker Bank." Such remarkably detailed knowledge was regarded as a manifestation of his gifts of prophecy.

Along with such tricks and his rhetoric, he fostered a childlike dependency. Most Temple members called him "Dad" or "Father." The dependency went so far that one congregant, a prominent lawyer, wrote Jones asking what kind of car he should drive. "What factors should one employ in purchasing a car—new vs. old, big vs. small, American vs. foreign?"[21] Not yet satisfied, he went on to ask Jones for advice about selecting clothes.

The dependency extended into sexual matters. Jones at various times encouraged free love or celibacy, but he made sure to satisfy his own sexual needs with his congregants. He broke up marriages so he could have another sexual partner, rationalizing that he was the one being victimized by his congregants' sexual needs, or complaining how exhausting it was for him to satisfy the sexual needs of the men and women of his congregation. On occasion, he told women that he was having a heart attack and that the only thing that would save him was sex.[22] Jones wasn't just another minister surreptitiously sexually abusing his flock. His sexual affairs were in no way clandestine—they were openly acknowledged. He rationalized the behavior as giving of himself, raising the self-esteem of his congregants, or proving that all men (except himself) had latent homosexual longings.[23] It was clear that he was to be the focus of everyone in the Temple and that members' other attachments were to be cut.

★★★

Increasingly angered by attacks on the Temple, Jones decided to relocate out of the United States where he could not be harassed by the "fascist racists" who attacked him so relentlessly. He settled on Guyana because it had a multiracial legacy and a socialist government. For the bargain rate of 25 cents per acre for the first five years the Temple leased about four thousand acres of isolated land in the jungles of north Guyana, close to the border of Venezuela. The agricultural commune was named Jonestown.[24]

By September 1977, about a thousand Peoples Temple members had moved to Guyana. Fifty to one hundred remained in Guyana's capital

Georgetown to maintain amicable relations with the government and to handle banking and shipping to the commune. They maintained constant ham radio contact with the jungle settlement and also with the church in California. The Georgetown contingent also kept a lookout for the arrival of potential critics of the church—former members, families trying to reach their loved ones, and reporters.

It is important to emphasize the dedication and deliberateness of the operation, given how it ended. This was no impulsive decision carried out by Jones and a few addled followers. It was, rather, an entire town constructed in the wilderness. The group carried out the arduous work of clearing three hundred acres: chopping down trees; pushing back the jungle; laying out roads; building dormitories, a school, a library, a medical clinic, and a town square with an open-air pavilion. The work consumed more and more of the members' time, beginning initially with a commitment of twelve hours of labor a day, increasing to sixteen hours a day when it became evident that the land was not as productive as they had hoped. However, even after a day of exhausting work, the residents had to attend long evening "catharsis" sessions or listen to Jones preaching for hours. As a result, they rarely got more than a couple hours of sleep.

They built an impressive library stocked with thousands of children's books, medical texts, books on education, agriculture, and socialism, unusual books like *Psychic Discoveries behind the Iron Curtain*, and an extensive collection of Kim Il Sung's writings from North Korea.[25] Jones admired the North Korean model of socialism. Its reliance on an infallible father figure resembled Jones's own position in the Temple. Both controlled their communities by requiring hard physical labor, broadcasting ideological material over loudspeakers, and using harsh mass meetings for self-criticism.[26]

The settlement was carefully planned, with roughly forty cottages, named in honor of revered heroines like Harriet Tubman and Sojourner Truth. It functioned like a small town ruled by an autocratic mayor (Jones) with all the departments necessary for efficiency. A finance office handled wired funds and used residents' Social Security checks to sustain the community. It also procured supplies and machinery that were necessary for this improbable settlement in the wilderness of the Guyanese jungle.

A quasi-foreign affairs department handled relations with Guyana, the United States, and various Communist nations. Given the arduous problems of building a settlement in this difficult environment, Jones considered moving to some other sympathetic country, perhaps Cuba, Russia, or

North Korea. At one point, Jones's staff grandiosely suggested that Fidel Castro should invite Jones for a state visit to Cuba, claiming that Jones had 250,000 followers.[27] This wasn't just duplicity and political chicanery. By the time the Peoples Temple had moved to Guyana, the members were true believers who had come to believe their own misrepresentations. These illusions were certainly easier to maintain once they were isolated in their jungle settlement remote from the outside world.

The medical clinic was staffed by a physician and a nurse who handled primary care medical problems. The doctor, Larry Schacht, had been rescued by Jones from drug addiction and was staunchly committed to him. When Jones started considering revolutionary suicide, he asked Dr. Schacht for advice on how this could be done. Schacht initially suggested sedating people and then giving them an injection in the heart. Jones countered that shooting people would be easier. "It's better for us all to die together, proud, than have them discredit us and . . . make us look like a bunch of crazy people."[28]

Schacht ultimately settled on cyanide as the best suicide method. He wrote Jones proposing "to give about two grams to a large pig to see how effective our batch is to be sure we don't get stuck with a disaster like would occur if we used thousands of pills to sedate the people and then the cyanide was not good enough to do the job." He also wrote that he wanted a recent medical article on cyanide poisoning but proposed covering his tracks by reporting "that a child was brought in to our free medical clinic who had ingested rat poison containing cyanide and [that is why] we want this article on the subject."[29]

As in any community of a thousand citizens, there was sometimes unruly behavior that necessitated a police department. People were spanked or beaten if they misbehaved. Armed guards detained and drugged dissenters and those with psychiatric disorders. They guarded the boundary of the settlement and blocked unauthorized entry or exit—with devastating effectiveness when the end came. Jones warned the community that the jungles were dangerous—filled with Guyanese mercenaries, snakes, tigers, and crocodiles. The guards, he said, were there to protect them.

When investigators sorted through the debris in Guyana, they found roughly a thousand tapes, some featuring Jones and his enforcers interrogating—he would say *correcting*—bad behaviors. He tolerated no dissent. A woman was placed in a sensory isolation box for disciplinary reasons because of hostility. Listening to the tape, one wonders who has the problem with hostility.

TOM GRUBBS: I'm concerned about your hostility level, 'cause I think you're still *hostile as hell*. As long as you're hostile as *hell*, and haven't come to *grips* with this, . . . I don't think you're safe outside that box.

BARBARA WALKER: (muffled, almost unintelligible) I'm not hostile.

GRUBBS: . . . You have *masked* it quite well. . . . You try to come off as the passive, quiet, almost meek child. But sister, it's *there*, a lot of it, and I'm *not* deceived by it. In fact, the only way I'm gonna be convinced . . . that this thing is *dealt* with, is that you can come out with it, . . . and come up with some responsible alternatives as a way of handling it.[30]

The tapes include a public criticism session replete with beatings for things like talking too much, being bossy, being late to socialism class, not working hard enough. People were terrorized by threats that they would be tied to stakes in the jungle where the tigers would eat them. The continual screams and moans from the howler monkeys in the jungle added to the sense of danger. One woman, afraid of snakes, was told that she would have to endure having a snake slither over her body in punishment for some misdeed.[31] Another tape features Jones threatening one of the residents with a box filled with poisonous frogs.[32] If people fell asleep during the long required community meetings, they were severely punished. Once the guards were told to put a ten-foot boa constrictor around the neck of a screaming Temple member who, exhausted by his work in the fields, had fallen asleep during a meeting.[33]

The historical records from Jonestown are extensive. The public affairs office was led by a member who wrote with verve. Many residents kept detailed diaries. Jones's sermons were not only broadcast through the Jonestown loudspeakers but also tape-recorded and archived. Radio transmissions from Jonestown were secretly recorded by the Federal Communications Commission, which suspected that something was amiss in the jungle. Finally, we have many letters to and from family members desperate to communicate with loved ones who had left to join Jones in this utopian settlement. The nurse Annie Moore wrote her sister Rebecca before moving to Guyana: "You obviously think that the Peoples Temple is just another cult or religious fanatic place or something like that. Well, I'm kind of offended that you would think I would stoop so low as to join some weirdo group. . . . The reason that the Temple is great is . . . because there is the largest group of people I have ever seen who are concerned about the world and are fighting for truth and justice for the world. . . . So anyway it's the only place I have seen real true Christianity being practiced."[34]

Families panicked about what might be going on in the Peoples Temple. Visits were discouraged or curtailed. Mail was censored. Phone calls somehow didn't go through. Families had heard from defectors that armed guards were stationed around Jonestown, that passports and money were confiscated, that Jones alone made all decisions. They had also heard that residents were told that if they tried to leave the Peoples Temple, they would be killed, their bodies left to rot in the jungle. Most disturbing, they had learned that Jones held mock "mass suicide" sessions to train the congregation to die for "the cause."[35]

To represent the Peoples Temple in its inevitable legal difficulties, Jones engaged the prominent liberal attorney Charles Garry. In response to the concerned relatives' press releases, Garry fired back: "This is an organized, orchestrated, premeditated government campaign to destroy a politically progressive church."[36] Garry visited the settlement in November 1977 and reported back: "I had been in paradise. I saw it. . . . The society that is being built in Jonestown is a credit to humanity. . . . This is not propaganda. . . . I'm a hard-hitting, factual-analysis lawyer. I saw this with my own eyes. I felt it."[37] He would later regret his enthusiastic support of the Temple.

Desperate family members kept writing to their loved ones in Jonestown begging them to return, and the Temple struck back. Jones encouraged members of the congregation to accuse their families of child abuse and molestation, thereby discrediting the families' pleas to investigate Jonestown. In public criticism sessions, the congregants competed with one another in describing the vengeance they would take on their families for defaming the Temple—how they would burn them up and chop them into little pieces.

Jones's increasing paranoia was infectious. In September 1977, Temple members armed with farm implements patrolled the perimeter of Jonestown looking for Guyanese invaders (who were not there). They radioed their suspicions to the world, and from a distance Angela Davis, ever sure of herself, broadcast her message of support back to the community: "This is Angela Davis. I'd like to say to the Rev. Jim Jones and to all my sisters and brothers from Peoples Temple to know that there are people here . . . across the country who are supporting you, who are with you. . . . I know that you're in a very difficult situation right now and there is a conspiracy

. . . designed to destroy the contributions which you have made to the struggle. . . . We will do everything in our power to ensure your safety and your ability to keep on struggling."[38]

As part of his intoxication with martyrdom, Jones became enamored with Huey Newton's concept of "revolutionary suicide." Newton distinguished between reactive suicide, triggered by despair, and revolutionary suicide, which he saw as an act of defiance. As more and more people raised allegations against the Peoples Temple, Jones and his followers felt unfairly victimized by the larger society, which they considered fascist. Even in their jungle stronghold they felt hostile forces closing in around them.

Jones repeatedly called crisis meetings of the community, blaring out threats and worries over the public address system. He read news accounts over the loudspeakers, droning on and giving his view of world events. No other news was available. The community members were told that they were being targeted by the fascist American government and mercenary armies in the jungles.

Such pronouncements kept the community, already exhausted, awake all night long. Misinformed and sleep deprived, residents continued the brutal work clearing the jungle, but were also required to attend socialism classes two nights a week and take weekly exams, every Sunday, about their knowledge. People literally had no time to themselves for that precious and dangerous commodity—individual thought.

There were a few nights when Jones's tirades brought people out with pitchforks and machetes to patrol the perimeter of the settlement looking for invading enemies. These were instances of what Jones called his "White Night" drills. In September 1977, Jones added a suicide drill. As one escapee from Jonestown recalled: "During one 'white night' we were informed that our situation had become hopeless and that the only course of action open to us was a mass suicide for the glory of socialism. We were told that we would be tortured by mercenaries if we were taken alive. Everyone, including the children, was told to line up. . . . We were given a small glass of red liquid to drink. We were told that the liquid contained poison and that we would die within 45 minutes. We all did as we were told. When the time came when we should have dropped dead, Rev. Jones explained that the poison was not real and that we had just been through a loyalty test."[39]

Jones was enraged by defections from the Peoples Temple. He was furious when anyone left but particularly wounded when senior members of the Temple left. The worst betrayal was by his former consigliere, the lawyer Tim Stoen. Grace and Tim Stoen had joined the Temple in Redwood Valley; both were prominent in the leadership. Grace, the head counselor, functioned like a chief of staff, controlling Jones's calendar and schedule. Jones had an affair with Grace and then encouraged Tim to sleep with other women in the temple. Grace and Tim had a child, John Victor Stoen, born in January 1972. The Stoen marriage ended in divorce and both Grace and Tim drifted away from the Temple, with Tim becoming active in Concerned Relatives—a group of defectors and their families. Meanwhile Jones claimed that *he*, not Tim, was John's father. The predictable custody battle went through the courts, but Jones defied the legal system by taking the boy to Guyana. The Temple ignored rulings that John Stoen be returned to the United States and panicked when the Guyana court supported the California rulings. This child stealing was the last straw for the previously sympathetic media.

★★★

Congressman Leo Ryan decided to take a fact-finding mission to Jonestown to see if people were being held against their will and if they were being defrauded of their Social Security checks. On November 14, 1978, he, his aide Jackie Speier, and a half dozen reporters flew to Guyana, where they were joined by several relatives of Temple members as well as critics of the Temple. Also present were Temple attorneys and a diplomat from the U.S. mission. Jones at first refused the visitors admittance into Jonestown. Meanwhile, he drilled the community on how to respond to the outsiders' questions and put the visitors off track. "If asked why you came here? Because I wanted to . . . I didn't like the racism. I don't have anything against the United States—my family soon will be coming here. However, we didn't visit that much when we were there, so am not really lonely for them. I just love it here too much to be back."[40]

Eventually, permission to enter was granted. Some of the group flew to a rural landing strip near the town of Port Kaituma. From there, they journeyed on a rusty dump truck down a muddy road into the jungle until they reached the gates of the compound ninety minutes later.

The meeting started out awkwardly, but it was civil. The visitors met Jones, took a tour, and interviewed many members of the community. Congressman Ryan even praised the community for its achievements: "From what I've seen, there are a lot of people here who think this is the best thing that happened in their whole life."[41] Then Vernon Gosney, a young Jonestown resident, surreptitiously passed a note to a reporter saying that he wanted to leave. Eventually, fifteen people asked to leave and

Jones became enraged. To lose that number of members out of a community of a thousand was not a catastrophe, but Jones viewed it so.

By that point Jones had a severe addiction to barbiturates and amphetamines and was abusing so many other drugs that his speech was noticeably slurred and his logic tenuous. He took opiates for pain, amphetamines to keep him alert, and barbiturates and other sedatives so that he could sleep. He may also have been struggling with other medical issues. After a lifetime of pretending that he was dying whenever he needed attention (or sex), it is hard to assess his true medical condition. He let it be known that he had cancer, hypertension, prostatitis, and recurrent severe fevers. He may well have made the same appalling decision to kill the community even if he had not been ill, but his medical situation certainly did not help his decision making.

As the Ryan contingent and the defectors prepared to leave, a Temple member lunged at the congressman with a knife. Ryan was uninjured but demanded that the Guyanese police follow up on the assault. Then the group left Jonestown and made its way to the Port Kaituma landing strip. Jones instructed longtime Temple loyalist Larry Layton to shoot defectors on the plane and Layton ran to join the Ryan group, posing as another defector.

At the landing strip, Layton smuggled a gun onto one of the planes and wounded two of the defectors. Meanwhile, a Peoples Temple tractor pulled up alongside the congressman and the others as they waited on the landing strip. They killed Ryan and three others and severely wounded many more, including Ryan's aide, the future congresswoman Jackie Speier.[42] Then they drove slowly back along the mud track to the settlement to report their mission's success. While they were driving back to Jonestown, the airstrip radioed for help.

When Jones learned what had happened, he screamed out, "White Night!" over the PA system. We know many details about the last hours of Jonestown because of the tapes recorded in the pavilion and the testimony of the few survivors. The FBI acquired the tapes when it investigated Jonestown. They are known as the "Rymur" tapes (short for "Ryan murder"). Filled with static and extraneous noises, they are hard to follow but have been meticulously transcribed and are readily available.[43]

Dr. Schacht mixed cyanide into a barrel full of Flavor-Aid fruit punch and sedative drugs. He set up a table, lined with rows of paper cups and syringes, to efficiently administer the poison. One could easily have mistaken this for a mass immunization program. The syringes were for squirting the solution down the throats of people not willing or able to swallow it from the cups. Some syringes had needles to inject those who resisted. The guards had guns and crossbows to enforce compliance.

Jones convened an emergency meeting of the community in the pavilion.

> How very much I've tried my best to give you the good life. But in spite of all of my trying, a handful of our people, with their lies, have made our life impossible. . . . We've been so betrayed. We have been so terribly betrayed. . . .
>
> So my opinion is that we be kind to children and be kind to seniors [that is, kill them first] and take the potion like they used to take in ancient Greece, . . . because we are not committing suicide. It's a revolutionary act. We can't go back. They won't leave us alone.[44]

Jones then invited comments from the community. One brave member, Christine Miller, remonstrated that killing the whole community of over nine hundred people including the children couldn't be proportionate to the loss of fifteen deserters. Jones countered: "I can't live that way. . . . Death is not a fearful thing. It's living that cuts ya. . . . It's just not worth living like this. . . . I'm tired of being tormented to hell, that's what I'm tired of. Tired of it. (Applause) Twelve hundred people's lives in my hands. . . . I'm going to I tell you, Christine, without me, life has no meaning. (Applause) I'm the best thing you'll ever have. . . . We have no other road."[45]

Christine continued to resist, arguing that the babies deserved to live, and people have a right to their own destiny. The community shouted her down. Others proclaimed their commitment to Jones and the struggle. "My name is Dianne Wilkinson. I am twenty-eight years old. And first of all, I would like to let the world know that to live in America is a curse and especially if you're black. And the only place that I have found that freedom and opportunity to become somebody in my life is in Peoples Temple. . . . Yes, we love our children, we love our seniors, but everybody here has made up their own individual decision. . . . I'd rather have my dignity, than have to be on my knees begging for my freedom. And I'd rather take my own life. Thank you."[46]

Bill Oliver testified that he was a committed Marxist-Leninist and that his decision to commit revolutionary suicide was well thought out, that he had been a member of the Temple for seven years and knew its goodness. He hoped that his death "would be used as an instrument to further liberation."[47]

Others passed notes to Jones, supporting his decision. One wrote: "I see no way out—I agree with your decisions—I fear only that without you the world may not make it to communism. . . . For my part—I am more than tired of this wretched, merciless planet & the hell it holds for so many masses of beautiful people—Thank you for the *only* life I've known."[48]

★★★

Was it murder or suicide? Certainly, for the hundreds of children and frail elderly, it was murder. For the rest, possibly suicide, but postmortem exams performed on dozens of bodies and other reports suggest that many of the victims had been injected with the poison. This implies that some individuals did not voluntarily drink it.[49]

Throughout the three-hour massacre, the tape continued, recording shouts of joy and of despair, directions to move along, and intermittent hymns on the organ.[50]

> JONES: Please get us some medication [poison]. It's simple. It's simple. There's no convulsions with it. It's just simple. Just please get it. Before it's too late. . . . Get movin', get movin', get movin'. . . . Don't be afraid to die. . . . They'll torture some of our children here. They'll torture our people. . . .
> NURSE: There's nothing to worry about. Every—everybody keep calm and try to keep your children calm. . . . They're not crying from pain. It's just a little bitter tasting. It's not—they're not crying out of any pain. . . .
> JONES: All right, it's hard but only at first—only at first is it hard. . . . Living . . . is much, much more difficult. Raising up every morning and not knowing what's going to be the night's bringing. It's much more difficult. . . . Please. For God's sake, let's get on with it. . . . They'll pay for it. This is a revolutionary suicide. This is not a self-destructive suicide. . . . They brought this upon us. And they'll pay for that. . . . I don't want to see you go through this hell no more. . . . The best thing you do is to relax, and you will have no problem. . . . Lay down your life with dignity. Don't lay down with tears and agony. There's nothing to death. . . . It's just stepping over into another plane. Don't be this way. Stop this

Bodies inside the pavilion, Jonestown, 1978. (Peoples Temple photographs from the San Francisco Examiner Archive, BANC PIC 2006.088–AX, The Bancroft Library, University of California, Berkeley.)

hysterics. . . . Adults, adults, adults. I call on you to stop this nonsense. I call on you to quit exciting your children, when all they're doing is going to a quiet rest. I call on you to stop this now, if you have any respect at all. Are we black, proud, and socialist, or what are we?. . . Hurry, hurry, my children. Hurry. . . . There are seniors out here that I'm concerned about. Hurry. I don't want to leave my seniors to this mess. . . . Where's the vat, the vat, the vat? . . . Bring it here so the adults can begin.[51]

As the tape suggests, the end was *not* peaceful. Dr. Schacht had been sloppy in his preparation of the cyanide drink. He had mixed it with sedatives, assuming that the sedatives would act before the cyanide. But there was no time for the sedatives to be absorbed. Instead, people writhed, screamed, and vomited, with death ensuing neither quietly nor instantaneously but only after four minutes of agony long before the sedatives had the remotest chance of acting.

It took the Guyanese army a couple days to enter Jonestown. In the meantime, the bodies—sometimes four deep—baked and bloated in the jungle's heat. They identified many of the corpses, tying labels around the toes, but in many instances the ink washed away in the jungle rain. In addition to the tape recordings, the army found diaries and farewell letters. The community historian Richard Tropp wrote:

> Collect all the tapes, all the writing, all the history. The story of this movement, this action, must be examined over and over. . . . We hope that the world will someday realize the ideals of brotherhood, justice and equality that Jim Jones has lived and died for. We have all chosen to die for this cause. . . . The world was not ready to let us live. . . .
>
> Look at Jonestown, see what we have tried to do—This was a monument to life. . . . Look at all that was built by a beleaguered people. We did not want this kind of ending—we wanted to live, to shine, to bring light to a world that is dying for a little bit of love. . . . We are grateful for this opportunity to bear witness. . . .
>
> There is quiet as we leave this world. The sky is gray. People file [by] us slowly and take the somewhat bitter drink. Many more must drink. . . .
>
> People hugging each other, embracing, we are hurrying—we do not want to be captured. . . . We have chosen. It is finished. . . .
>
> I am ready to die now. Darkness settles over Jonestown on its last day on earth.[52]

As the end approached, Jones radioed the Temple communities in Georgetown (Guyana's capital) and in California, ordering their members to kill themselves. Fortunately, most disobeyed, except Jonestown representative Sharon Amos and her children in Georgetown. Temple loyalists described the Amos family deaths, resorting to their typical stance of aggrieved innocence. James Reston captured the event vividly, describing Catholic Father Morrison's anxious phone calls to learn what had happened. As rumors of what had happened at Jonestown swirled around Georgetown, Morrison called the Peoples Temple house in Georgetown asking to speak with Sharon Amos. Instead, he reached another representative (Paula Adams) who told him that Amos wasn't available. Reston writes:

> "Paula, what happened?" an astonished Father Morrison asked.
> "We have a lot of police here," she replied. "They think we're

going to do some craziness, but you know me, Father. Do you think I'd do that? Do you think I'd do that? Do you think we'd do the sort of craziness they did up there? I just can't understand it. We're not that sort of people."

"Well, what happened to Sharon?" Morrison asked.

"She slit her children's throats and then her own," Adams replied.[53]

Jonestown's mass suicide has been compared to that in Masada, the fortress in the Judean desert where Jewish zealots made their last stand against the Roman Empire in AD 73–74. Nine hundred and sixty men, women, and children killed themselves rather than surrender. The historian Josephus (AD 37–93) recounts the speech made by their leader Elazer ben Yair where he proposed mass suicide. It is eerie to see some of the same themes echoed by Jones nineteen hundred years later in Guyana.

My loyal followers, long ago we resolved to serve neither the Romans nor anyone else but only God. . . . Now the time has come that bids us prove our determination by our deeds. . . . We must not disgrace ourselves: hitherto we have never submitted to slavery . . . : we must not choose slavery now. . . . [It] will mean the end of everything if we fall alive in the hands of the Romans. . . . I think it is God who has given us this privilege, that we can die nobly and as free men. . . . Life is the calamity for man, not death. Death gives freedom to our souls and lets them depart to their own pure home. . . . Let us die unenslaved by our enemies, and leave this world as free men in company with our wives and children.[54]

The comparisons to Masada may be right in terms of the body count, but the settings were very different. At Masada, the Romans would certainly have killed or enslaved the zealots upon capture. Furthermore, the fortress had been literally besieged for three months by a force of some fifteen thousand soldiers, comprised of the legendary Tenth Legion and auxiliary units. In Jonestown, on the contrary, the peril was in the minds of Jones and the Temple members. Despite Jonestown protestations like "We died because you would not let us live in peace," there was no besieging Guyanese or American army.[55] Undoubtedly, the Jonestown critics would have continued condemning the community, and perhaps more members of the Temple would have abandoned the settlement, but there is no reason to believe the settlement was in the kind of life-threatening peril the people of Masada faced.

★★★

The media described the Reverend Jim Jones as a depraved monster and his parishioners as addled, uneducated, credulous people who had been brainwashed. While I would not quibble with the description of Jones, there are problems with describing the congregation that way. Many of the families of the Jonestown victims took great umbrage with such a characterization of their loved ones. First off, many congregants were educated, idealistic, and articulate. Second, there were many laudable aspects of the Peoples Temple.

But what about the "brainwashing" allegation? There is that awful word again that explains so much and so little simultaneously. I prefer to say—"They were persuaded." The persuasion was coercive. It was surreptitious. It was accompanied by extreme stress and sleep deprivation. It wasn't in the interest of the congregation; instead, it was lethal. Call it brainwashing; call it coercive persuasion; call it a crime; call it a tragedy.

An event like Jonestown leaves many casualties behind even among survivors. I am not referring so much to the depression, PTSD, suicide, or drug abuse that emerged in survivors haunted by their losses, but to more immediate casualties.

Temple spokesman Michael Prokes survived Jonestown because Jones instructed him to deliver a suitcase of money to the Russian embassy in Georgetown.[56] Four months later, Prokes was back in California contacting former supporters of the Temple, trying to explain what had happened. He wrote to San Francisco columnist Herb Caen: "No matter what view one takes of the Temple, perhaps the most relevant truth is that it was filled with outcasts and the poor who were looking for something they could not find in our society." He held a press conference blaming the U.S. government's persecution of Jonestown for the deaths. Then he went into the bathroom and shot himself.[57]

Some survivors painfully rebuilt their lives, learning to live with the ghosts of the past while sculpting a new identity far away from the Temple. Laura Kohl, for instance, taught for years in the public school system until her retirement. She has written a beautiful autobiography about her years in the movement and speaks widely to civic groups about life in Jonestown.[58] Vern Gosney, one of the defectors shot by Larry Layton, moved to Hawaii and became a policeman. Years later he would settle up with Layton in a remarkable fashion.

Larry Layton was tried in Guyana and the United States. Testimony circled around the issues of cults, brainwashing, and criminal responsibility—in many ways, a reprise of the trial of Patricia Hearst. Layton had wounded two Temple defectors on the plane at Kaituma, but he was not a part of the crew in the tractor who shot Congressman Ryan and the others. When questioned by a Guyanese constable at the scene, he admitted, "Yes, I shot the motherfuckers."[59] He added later, while in Guyanese custody: "I Larry Layton take full responsibility for all the deaths and injuries that took place at the Port Kaituma airstrip. . . . I felt that these people were working in conjunction with C.I.A. to smear the Peoples Temple and to smear Guyana. . . . When the shooting started, I also started shooting . . . I don't know why I did it."[60]

Layton initially expressed no remorse and stated that he regretted not dying with Jim Jones, "the most evolved person in the universe."[61] Charged with wounding two defectors, Layton spent two years in a Guyanese jail before being acquitted.[62] He was then extradited to the United States and charged with conspiracy to assassinate a congressman. The first trial ended in a hung jury. The second convicted Layton and sentenced him to life imprisonment. During both trials and his unsuccessful appeal, there was considerable discussion about Layton's testimony in Guyana.

A psychiatrist who treated Layton in Guyana commented that Layton had lost his memory of many of the events at the airstrip and that his "hysterical personality, combined with hypochondriacal tendencies, his fear, and the fact that [he] had taken several Elavil tablets, could have caused him to lose his memory."[63] That information was not introduced into court testimony.

Layton claimed that in Guyana he had been subjected to coercive conditions prior to signing the statement. He stated that he "had been shackled, threatened with a knife and a gun, deprived of food and drink, deprived of light, ventilation and bedding, subjected to interrogation by Guyanese officials throughout the day and night, subjected to mental and physical abuse, and confined in cells that were filthy, infested with insects, and foul smelling."[64] The Guyanese, of course, disputed these allegations. At Layton's trial in the United States, the judge declined to rule that Layton's Guyanese confession resulted from coercion and allowed it to be introduced into evidence.

Should psychiatric testimony have been considered by the jury? Layton adamantly rejected this idea. In fact, he was examined by psychiatrists two to three years after the shootout, but his lawyers doubted that examinations obtained so late after the event would be persuasive to the jury regarding his mental state at the time of the shootings.

Was the jury biased by the notion that Layton was a member of a cult? During voir dire, potential jurors were asked if membership in a cult should affect a person's legal responsibility. The jurors believed that membership in a cult didn't mean that one should be absolved of blame, guilt, or responsibility. Maybe *absolution* was the wrong word. To my way of thinking, the better question is: "Should membership in a cult influence a sentence?" Viewed that way, I believe there was ample reason for mitigating Layton's sentence.

Layton's first wife, Carolyn Moore Layton, was taken from him by Jones. Carolyn divorced Larry in 1970 and informed her family that she was actually the reincarnation of Lenin's mistress and that Jones was Lenin's reincarnation.[65] She became one of the leaders in the Peoples Temple. Not satisfied with Carolyn, Jones cuckolded Larry Layton with his second wife as well, yet Layton didn't protest.[66] Layton was loyal beyond belief. He had brought his mother and sister into the Temple. When his sister Debbie, the Temple's de facto treasurer, defected in March 1978, Jones constantly accused Larry of disloyalty. His mother died of cancer ten days prior to the Jonestown massacre and his second wife Karen, five months pregnant, died in Jonestown. With all these stresses, Layton "fell apart," according to his lawyer, who added that it was Jones who was responsible, not Layton: "Look at the poor diet, the loss of weight, the physical exhaustion, the desperation, the lingering illness and death of his mother and the fear of punishment and humiliation. . . . The story of Jonestown is really the story of a world gone mad."[67]

Charles Garry was called as a witness. Garry described Layton as a "pacifist. . . . I don't believe what Larry Layton did or didn't do was of free volition on his part. . . . I would call him a kind of zombie who did exactly what he was told. . . . It's unfortunate they're picking out Layton as a sacrificial lamb. The real son-of-a-bitch [Jones] got away with it by dying."[68]

The judge, although sentencing Layton to life, recommended that he be considered for parole after four years, "taking into consideration the bizarre psychological atmosphere in which Layton . . . [operated] and numerous letters from family, friends and jurors."[69] The judge commented: "Although Larry Layton must be held responsible for his actions, a just sentence requires consideration of the environment in which Layton and other members were virtually imprisoned."[70]

When Layton came up for parole, many supporters provided letters.

One wrote: "I see him as a totally basically destroyed person. . . . I don't feel he is a threat to anyone." Another wrote, "In my mind [Layton] is no different than any other victim of Jim Jones. I cannot separate him from those who were found dead in the jungle."[71] Vern Gosney, the defector shot by Layton in 1978, flew in from Hawaii to attend Layton's parole hearing and made an impassioned plea for his release, which finally occurred in 2002.[72]

John Moore, the father of Jonestown nurse Annie Moore and Jones's companion Carolyn Moore, gave a sermon one week after the tragedy at Jonestown:

> During these past days, we have been asked frequently: . . . "What went wrong?" What happened to turn the dream into a nightmare? I shall mention two things that were wrong from the beginning. These are idolatry and paranoia. . . .
>
> The adulation and worship Jim Jones' followers gave him was idolatrous. . . .
>
> The second thing that was wrong was paranoia. . . . There's a thin line separating sensitivity to realities from fantasies of persecution. . . . [Jones] saw conspiracies in the opposition. . . . [In Jonestown] the air was heavy with fears of conspiracy. . . . They fed each other's fears. There was no voice to question the reality of those fears. As their fears increased, they increased their control over the members. Finally, their fears overwhelmed them.[73]

Was Jim Jones a lethal anomaly in his demonstration of the power of religion in brainwashing? To answer that question, the world would need to wait a few years.

CHAPTER ELEVEN

Heaven's Gate
Beliefs or Delusions?

Desires are tortures, aren't they? It is clear, therefore, that
happiness is when there are no longer any desires, not a single
desire any more.

—EUGENE ZAMIATIN, 1924

TWENTY YEARS AFTER JONESTOWN, the world had grown
complacent about cults. Certainly Jonestown was an anomaly,
right? The problem was that cults kept cropping up, but as
long as they weren't close by, they were easy to ignore.[1] It became impossible for me to ignore lethal cults when my neighbors killed
themselves in 1997 in the largest mass suicide in American history. The
preface to this book recounts the story of the last days of Heaven's Gate,
but how did the movement start? How did the members structure their
day-to-day life? What was the nature of their beliefs? How do we understand those beliefs? What is the boundary between belief and delusion?

We know a great deal about the group from interviews with former
members, press accounts, and the group's still-active internet site. In
addition, there are research reports by a number of scholars who covertly
observed the group in its early days and religion professors who studied

their beliefs and social practices.[2] As you might expect, different perspectives are offered from scholars, an unsympathetic press, and the bereaved friends and families of the Heaven's Gate members. Were the Heaven's Gate adherents religious seekers, California wackos, or cruelly ensnared? One needs to study their origins and practices to grapple with such questions.

The group was founded by Marshall Applewhite and Bonnie Nettles, later known as Do and Ti (pronounced Dō and Tē).[3] Marshall, the son of a Presbyterian minister, grew up in a religiously observant home. He aspired to the ministry, got his BA in philosophy but shifted emphasis and graduated with a master's degree in music. Then he moved to Houston, where he was choral director of an Episcopal church, performed with the Houston Grand Opera, and taught at Houston's University of St. Thomas. Marshall was described as a charismatic man with a powerful baritone voice. He married and had two children, but the marriage ended when his homosexual affairs came to light. In the early 1970s he left his job at the University of St. Thomas because of "health problems of an emotional nature."[4] His friends described him as depressed and so disorganized that he was admitted to a psychiatric hospital.[5]

Bonnie Nettles was raised in an observant Baptist family in Houston. She became a nurse, married, and had four children. Along the way she developed an all-consuming interest in astrology, theosophy, and contacting spirits through séances. She was particularly close to the ghost of Brother Francis, a nineteenth-century monk. Her increasing preoccupation with these matters led to the slow unraveling of her marriage, and she was divorced in 1973.

When these two met in Houston in March 1972, they came to believe that they had known each other in former lives. They had a platonic love affair, studied Christian asceticism, diverse mystic traditions, and science fiction, and then wandered together across the United States. By 1975, they had crafted a mission statement and sent it to ministers far and wide. Over the next year, they drifted from town to town, giving over one hundred lectures and posting notices about their workshops. Gradually people started to notice them. Bonnie was the brains of the couple, Marshall the voice—and what a resonant voice it was. In audiotapes he sounds like Mr. Rogers—reasonable, calm, self-deprecatory. With his gentle sense of humor, he seemed eminently trustworthy.

Like many New Age religious groups, Do and Ti preached that people needed to give up their cravings, make peace with one another, and con-

Marshall Herff Applewhite and Bonnie Lu Nettles, 1975.
(Bettmann / Getty Images.)

template the universe. But there was a bit *more* to their beliefs. Do taught group members that they came from outer space; they were merely part of "the away team" from the heavens. Their bodies were just "vehicles" that were rusted by sexual desire. Newer and better vehicles solved that flaw because they featured asceticism, and when that did not suffice, there was always the option of castration. As one of the members explained, castration ended the influence of "hormones that keep the body intoxicated, stupid, empty-headed and 'blind.'"[6] Like Pied Pipers, Do and Ti persuaded their followers not only to join them, but to sell their possessions, say good-bye to their families, drop their old names, and assume new identities.

Do and Ti achieved national prominence in Waldport, Oregon, after posting a notice that they would be speaking about "UFOs, why they are here, who they have come for and when will they leave."[7] Two hundred people attended the lecture at a small Waldport hotel. Many were seeking enlightenment, had previous experiences with drugs, and held various New Age beliefs, including a conviction in the existence of UFOs.

Do and Ti told the attendees that they had come to teach and gather followers who were ready to be transformed to a new destiny, the Next Level, where they would be free from suffering and corruption. Christ had come to Earth two thousand years ago but found people too depraved for heaven. Now it was time to try again. Heaven was a place—a real planet—and you get there via a UFO. The attendees were told to abandon their possessions and families and to follow them *now*.

In response to their message, twenty attendees, constituting 3 percent of the town's population, disappeared. As Walter Cronkite described it on a broadcast (October 8, 1975) on *CBS Evening News*, "A score of persons . . . have disappeared. It's a mystery whether they've been taken on a so-called trip to eternity—or simply been taken." Melvin Gibson, an Oregon state trooper who investigated the disappearances, described the attendees: "Most of these people were hippie types, guess you'd call them. Some of them had lived around here for several years, but they're not what you'd call, prominent citizens. There's no question there's something funny going on. It's hard to say, but I kind of feel some of them will be drifting back."[8]

The group faded out of prominence for the next twenty years, popping up now and then in various locations, holding meetings about space aliens and the Christian tradition. Do and Ti taught that the reason people felt disconnected with society is that we are all space aliens stuck in a lower world. Heaven's Gate rescued people, taught them about the new representatives of the kingdom of heaven, and prepared them to leave Earth. Do and Ti helped new members to surmount their addictions to drugs, cigarettes, junk food, and coffee; transcend their childlike interests in sexuality; and extricate themselves from the swamp of human relationships.

In the meantime, they wandered and studied. Some members became skilled at internet communication and marketing, using those talents to support the group and to maintain a communication network for their followers and potential recruits. Their studies told them that to get to heaven, each follower had to forsake human ties, thinking, and sexuality. To triumph over the distractions of sexuality, "some . . . [chose] on their own to have their vehicles neutered in order to sustain a more genderless and objective consciousness."[9]

Ti died of cancer in 1985, leaving Do bereft and ruminating about mainstream society's rejection of the movement. In May 1993, Do resumed proselytizing with a large advertisement in *USA Today* advising people to heed his message and join him. The next year, he preached coast to coast and, although membership increased, the group was repeatedly ridiculed. Slowly, he and his followers came to the belief that the world was filled with weeds. "The weeds have taken over the garden and truly disturbed its usefulness beyond repair—it is time for the civilization to be recycled—'spaded under.'"[10] In other words, the End of Days was coming, and Earth was doomed to be recycled.[11] Do believed he and his group would be saved because, by dying, they would get a new vehicle and be picked up by a passing spacecraft. He had the key, Do told his followers, to help them board that spaceship and leave behind human ignorance and misinformation.

Communal living arrangements gave members a powerful sense of belonging. Like any cloistered group, the residents had rules of behavior regulating external interactions as well as internal thoughts and responses (see table 3). They were prohibited from having any contact with their families and friends. All their finances were shared, including the trust fund of one wealthy young member. They purged themselves with lemonade, cayenne pepper, and maple syrup for a month. Bathing was precisely limited: six minutes and one gallon of water.[12] All the rules emphasized following instructions and being considerate, modest, gentle, sensitive, and clean. Members were warned against "polluting the ears of others," procrastinating, and being pushy, aggressive, or demanding. Each person was assigned a "check partner" to be a constant companion and watcher.

If there was a golden rule for the group, it was succinct and clear: "You've got to get your mind into your vehicle and get control of it."[13] Members learned they could control their vehicles by focusing on chores, work, and study but they were never to trust their own judgment, take any action without checking with their partner, or permit private thoughts and distracting emotions.

Not surprisingly, many followers abandoned the movement. From its peak of several hundred members, the Heaven's Gate community dwindled to a small group of about forty believers, most of whom had lived together

Table 3. Selections from Heaven's Gate's *Additional Guidelines for Learning Control and Restraint*

MAJOR OFFENSES

- Deceit: Doing an act "on the sly." Lying to my teachers or any of my classmates. Keeping an offense to myself, not exposing it the same day.
- Sensuality — permitting arousal in thought or in action (not nipping it in the bud).
- Breaking any instruction or procedure knowingly.

LESSER OFFENSES

- Taking any action without using my check partner.
- Trusting my own judgment — or using my own mind.
- Twisting procedures for my own benefit.
- Responding defensively to my classmates or teachers.
- Criticizing or finding fault with my classmates or teachers.
- Allowing blatant or lingering negativity, accepting the position of "I can't."
- Permitting physical or verbal abuse (outbursts, harsh words, sarcasm, swearing, anger, hurtful teasing, loss of temper) toward classmates.
- Allowing jealousy towards any classmates or comparing myself to others.
- Staying in my own head, having private thoughts, not staying open with my partner — separateness.
- Putting myself first, wanting my own way, rebelliousness — selfishness. Having likes or dislikes.
- Permitting lack of control over emotions to the point that it interferes with my work or rest or is a distraction to others.
- Engaging in familiarity, casualness, gossip, lack of restraint with others.
- Being too aggressive or pushy.
- Exercising poor control of thoughts running through my head, being easily distracted.
- Permitting impatience or intolerance.
- Being vain about my appearance, vibrating femininity or masculinity in any way.
- Having inappropriate curiosity.

Source: Additional Guidelines for Learning Control and Restraint: A Self-Examination Exercise, Spring 1988, http://heavensgate.com/book/2-6.htm.

sequestered in their community for twenty years, having little interaction with anyone on the outside.

Were they all misfits? Many of them were seekers, but some joined just to escape the tedium of life's hassles. "You wouldn't believe what a relief it was to have that off my shoulders. Even if we didn't leave [the planet], I would never go back to my past life." Others joined at a time of loss. "I got into this . . . not so much from wanting to get to heaven as wanting to get out of the Hell I'm in."[14]

They came from diverse backgrounds from all over America and were evenly split in terms of gender. Most were white and most were in their forties at the time of their deaths, but ages ranged from members in their twenties to those in their seventies. Many had dabbled in New Age ideas before joining the group, but there were outliers as well. A Colorado real estate developer who ran on the Republican ticket for state assembly left his family to join the group. In the end, Heaven's Gate included former pilots and nurses, computer programmers, students, a grandmother, the daughter of a federal judge, a massage therapist, a computer whiz, and a postal worker.

★★★

Heaven's Gate incorporated bits and pieces of Christian tradition into its theories of the world. "[Two thousand years ago] a member of the Kingdom of Heaven . . . left behind His body . . . came to Earth, and moved into . . . an adult human body (or 'vehicle') that had been 'prepped' for this particular task. The body that was chosen was called Jesus."[15]

The movement had gnostic beliefs that the body and soul were separate entities, that matter was evil, and that the only good was in the spirit world. Like early Christians, the Heaven's Gate believers encountered opposition. To their way of thinking, they offered a path to the gate of heaven, but lower forces (followers of Lucifer) opposed them, using "sexual behavior to keep humans 'drugged' and ignorant, . . . [and] preoccupied with their addictions."[16] The "Luciferans" encouraged people to follow the safe and socially acceptable path—get a job, pay your mortgage, be "reasonable"—rather than join the Heaven's Gate movement.

Do and Ti cautioned adherents that they would be rejected by the rest of the world, which would regard them as "duped, crazy, a cult member, a drifter, a loner, a drop-out."[17] Furthermore, Do warned, apostates who had fallen away from the movement would end up working closely with government and industry to oppose them. After the apocalyptic end of the Branch Davidians in 1993, Do worried constantly that members would be kidnapped and deprogrammed by outsiders.

The group meditated together, supported one another, and provided a tremendous sense of belonging, structure, and hope. Life in the group was tightly regulated in terms of what television channels they could watch, which books they could read, where they could sit, and what they could eat. All of this was methodically detailed in a "Procedures" book. The movement did not encourage individualism. For their last meal at Marie Callender's restaurant in Carlsbad, they ordered thirty-nine chicken pot pies, thirty-nine salads, and thirty-nine pieces of cheesecake.[18] The comet was coming for them.

The members loved science fiction, believing passionately that their destiny was in the heavens, but as Do grappled with his loneliness after Ti's death, he started to believe that the only way to heaven was through suicide. He discussed this extensively with the group. Some left because they would not consider such a step. The remaining members maintained they would merely be shedding a worthless husk and that they would emerge like a caterpillar out of the chrysalis.

At first it was not clear when this ritual suicide might take place, but then an extraordinarily bright and totally unexpected comet was discovered on July 23, 1995. It was visible to the naked eye from May 1996 until December 1997. The Hale-Bopp comet was so bright that it was visible even at twilight. I well remember my shock at first seeing it, high in the heavens above Santa Fe.

Throughout history, comets have frequently been viewed as a sign from the heavens, some kind of cosmic emissary signifying momentous events like the birth and death of Julius Caesar, the fall of Jerusalem, or the Norman invasion of England.[19] Heaven's Gate was already atwitter about the new comet even before Houston astronomer Chuck Shramek claimed he had seen an object trailing it. No one else saw this purported companion to the comet, but Shramek informed radio talk host Art Bell, a notorious purveyor of conspiracy theories and believer in the paranormal. Bell trumpeted the news that a large spaceship was hiding in the shadow of the comet. Devouring all the information about this he could find, Do became convinced that the hidden spaceship was his way home to eternity. He calculated what day the comet would be closest to Earth, reasoning that would be the easiest time to teleport to the ship. The group members joyfully planned for their voyage to eternity.

During the disciples' long years of retreat and study, their families were desperate to contact them. They set up internet groups to share information about where the group was living, how to persuade loved ones to come home, even how to talk to them at all. The father of one of the victims confessed sadly, "There was nothing we could say or do to get her back. We tried everything. It was like they kidnapped her mind."[20]

★★★

As their last day on Earth approached, some members posted farewells on the internet. One wrote: "I have been so lucky to have . . . my Teachers

Hale-Bopp comet. (Photograph by Geoff Chester.)

and Older Members, and I thank the Next Level many times for sending them to help me. They have been so patient and caring. They have shown me through their high standards what an orderly and wonderful place the Next Level will be. . . . The most exciting thing is that the wait is almost over."[21]

Another wrote about frustration with the culture at large—Madison Avenue, computer technology, and an intrusive, corrupt government. The student felt that the body is merely a vehicle or suit of clothes to hold the soul. Living cloistered was one way of minimizing conflict with outsiders. Explicitly addressing the question "why I want to leave at this time," the devotee wrote: "I know my . . . [Leader] is going. Once He is gone, there is nothing left here on the face of the Earth for me, no reason to stay a moment longer. . . . Choosing to exit this borrowed human vehicle or body and go home to the Next Level is an opportunity for me to demonstrate my loyalty, commitment, love, trust, and faith. . . . There is nothing here in this world that I want. . . . [I am] not this biological outer garment that I am currently occupying."[22]

In addition to these written farewells posted on the internet, the group videotaped exit interviews to explain their beliefs about death and the future.[23] Their names on the tape deserve some comment. Bestowing a new name at the time of conversion is a common religious practice, but at Heaven's Gate, the chosen names were decidedly unusual, typically comprised of six letters and ending in "ody" (a reference to Ti and Do).

Filmed on the lovely grounds of the group's Rancho Santa Fe mansion, the farewell statements are replete with belief and belonging. Dressed in loose-fitting casual clothes and with their short-cropped hair, each member looked into the camera and explained what the movement had meant to him or her and why each was leaving Earth. These parting videos provide an unusually vivid window into their thinking. They are not the stuff of a traditional suicide note—no revelations of depression, anger, or feeling trapped. Instead, the films have an evangelical quality, testifying to the joys of Heaven's Gate. They are beautifully crafted farewell notes to explain the adherents' actions. I found it difficult to select which interviews to include in these pages. They are all unique and poignant—ghosts' voices clamoring for attention.

Strody testified: "This is the answer to all of our prayers. I could not have had a better life these many years and I know it's going to be twice as good when I get up there [points with her hand to the sky]." Lggody echoed her sentiments, "This is something that I am doing of my free will, that I know deep inside is important for me. I can hardly wait and I am ready to go."

Some chose to talk about the limitations of their flesh, regarding their bodies as primitive vehicles. Alxody explained: "I don't identify with this flesh vehicle. . . . I look forward to this next step when we will be shedding these primitive creatures which we have used for our testing ground and that we will be moving to the next evolutionary level." On a similar note, Trsody talked about his relief at being able to put aside his sensual longings and have himself neutered. "Laying down this vehicle is going to be *great* for me."

Some sounded weary of the world. Nrrody confided to the camera, "I'm very glad that I am leaving this vehicle. I'm tired of this world. I feel no bitterness. . . . I feel excited that we all will be able to leave as a class together" before breaking into tears.

All spoke of their joy as they anticipated their pending departure. Some even cracked jokes and expressed relief that they were no longer stuck in the world. They were thrilled about the promise of inheriting new and more refined vehicles in their next life. One member declared that going to the Next Level made him the happiest person on Earth.

Some members worried about how outsiders, particularly their families, might view their deaths. They fretted about how the media would describe their deaths and went to great lengths to deny that the movement had brainwashed them. As Stmody put it: "We know that the spin doctors, the people who make a profession out of debunking everybody and putting down everybody are going to attack what we're doing. . . . They're going to say these people were crazy, they were mesmerized, whatever. We know it isn't true. . . . For us, this step of laying down these human bodies . . . is like going on a holiday. . . . We are all looking forward to it."

These healthy men and women stared into the camera, shared a moment of intimacy with us, and said farewell. They bore witness. Most had been members of the group for over twenty years and regarded it as their salvation. Tddody gazed into the camera and said: "I have tried it all and there is nothing on this planet that is of any interest to me. I have made the conscious choice to exit this vehicle." They had been preparing for years to move to the kingdom of God and were happy to do so.

It is an eerie experience to view the tape—a brief glimpse into the lives of thirty-nine people on the brink of suicide. I couldn't help but wonder whether the tears expressed anxiety, depression, or joy.

★★★

Heaven's Gate and Jonestown both ended in mass death, but as communal movements they were profoundly different.

Both leaders were suspicious of the outside world, but there were overpowering dissimilarities. Applewhite did not forbid members from leaving the commune; they worked in the outside world, shopped, took out library books, and went to movies. In contrast, Jones built his commune secluded in a jungle and stringently limited who could interact with the outside. He formed an armed security service to police his borders.

The leaders handled apostates differently as well. Whereas Jones refused to let dissident members leave Jonestown, even locking them up for punishment, Applewhite gave members a choice of staying or leaving. He regarded departed members with sadness, compared to Jones, who threatened apostates with murder.

Their belief structures were different, too. Applewhite went through a period of evangelizing but stopped engaging with the world in his final twenty years. He founded a cloistered community that more or less turned its back on the world. There was some degree of disdain for the outside, but it was flavored with pity for the benighted majority who would never reach the Next Level. Jones was enraged with the world, particularly its all-pervasive racism, which shattered so many people's lives. For Jones, outsiders were to be controlled and manipulated in any manner possible.

The two groups also differed in terms of drug use and personal privileges. In his later days, Applewhite's special privileges as leader consisted only of having a private bedroom. He preached against drugs and followed what he preached. Jones chronically abused stimulants and sedatives, lived in a separate house equipped with luxuries, and surrounded himself with guards.

Finally, of course, there was a difference in the manner of dying. Applewhite persuaded his followers to kill themselves in a manner as free of violence as possible—barbiturate overdose. Jones forced members to kill themselves with cyanide and if they refused, he had them shot.

Jonestown and Heaven's Gate differed primarily in the presence or absence of fear and rage. There was little rage at Heaven's Gate; rather, there was joy in fellowship and a conviction among members that they would be reborn. In Jonestown, however, rage against a hostile world was palpable and fear tactics were used to control behavior.

★★★

Religion is inherently about a community's belief, faith, and ritual. It is a mistake to think that new religious groups are rare—there are hundreds of them. A Gallup study estimated that half of American teenagers were at some point interested in cults, although considerably fewer had actually joined one.[24] The abundance and heterogeneity of new religious beliefs led one scholar to observe wryly that "a cult is any religion more bizarre than your own."[25]

What are typical beliefs? A Gallup poll conducted in 2004 found that 90 percent of Americans believe in God, 70 percent believe in the devil, 78 percent believe in angels, 81 percent believe in heaven, and 70 percent believe in hell.[26] But nontraditional beliefs are also common. A 2018 poll by the Pew Religious Center found that 60 percent of Americans accept at least one New Age belief. For example, 40 percent believe in psychics and think that spiritual energy can be found in physical objects, 33 percent believe in reincarnation, and 29 percent believe in astrology.[27]

These sorts of observations are foundational to a sociological or anthropological point of view. After all, "strange" beliefs are not even statistically rare.[28] More important, social scientists are disinclined to make value judgments about religion because each has its own way of viewing reality, and it is a rare religion that doesn't at times employ cruel practices.

Most social scientists who study new religions are uncomfortable labeling them as pathological just because they do not conform to traditional religious beliefs and practices. Some scholars bridle at any suggestion that adherents of a new religion like Heaven's Gate might have been brainwashed into joining the movement. Instead, they argue that members experienced a religious conversion and the term *brainwashing* is merely a label to justify repression. As one hotly contended, "Brainwashing has lost all academic credibility."[29] Others charge that brainwashing "provides a dangerous, pseudo-scientific rationale for the violation of First Amendment rights."[30] There are nasty arguments on this topic, ones that dispassionate social scientists have accurately labeled "fruitless culture wars."[31]

It is foolish to label all new religions as cults that brainwash their congregants. But it is legitimate to ask if and how individuals "become swept away by commitments to charismatic social movements."[32] Such analyses must consider how people are recruited into a movement, how their beliefs are changed, and—perhaps unique to brainwashing—how they are restrained from leaving the movement.

Some feel that the social relativist perspective heartlessly ignores the risks in new religions. There are cults that prohibit their members from leaving. The important question, though, is *how* they restrict exit from the community. If they use a fence and guards, I can see the point of those who believe it necessary to seize loved ones and help them escape. But what if it is an invisible fence? What if the cult member can no longer conceive of a life outside the cult? If her sole interactions are within that community, is it possible for her to live and have an identity outside that community? That question could pertain to a new religion or an established one.

In the old Hindu practice of sati, for instance, the bereaved widow kills herself because she has no social function after the death of her husband. It is interesting to note that after the thirty-nine Heaven's Gate members died, some former members killed themselves as well. In some instances, they felt there was a chance they could "catch up" with their peers and board the spaceship. In others, the survivors felt no connection with the rest of the world; they killed themselves out of guilt for not being on site at the time of their friends' deaths and because they could not imagine a life for themselves away from the group—whether or not they caught the spaceship—a sati-like despair.

I don't think there are villains in these vocal disagreements about new religions and coercive persuasion. I think both sides have lost their perspective. While I agree that *brainwashing* is a silly term, that doesn't mean one should ignore how charismatic leaders can attract members, shape their thoughts and behavior, transform their beliefs, and restrict them from leaving.

It may be useful to consider two questions in the context of Heaven's Gate; the answers to these questions may be unsettling. First, to what extent were Heaven's Gate views or practices startlingly different or at odds with the prevailing culture? Second, to what extent did the leaders and/ or followers of Heaven's Gate have a mental disorder that would account for their behavior?

We've already established that "unusual" religious beliefs are in no way rare. Even some of the more peculiar aspects of Heaven's Gate have deep roots in history. Asceticism, for instance, is hardly unique to Heaven's Gate. Cloistered communities with carefully prescribed hairstyles, clothing, and diet are so common that they do not even raise an eyebrow. Even the castrations at Heaven's Gate were hardly new. Early Catholic Church fathers had themselves castrated to deal with sexual temptation. Revered Church leader Origen of Alexandria (AD 185–254), perhaps the most notable example, believed that he would assure himself a place in heaven by so definitively cutting off his sexual temptation.[33] Church leaders cited Matthew 19:12 as their justification: "There are eunuchs who have made themselves eunuchs for the sake of the kingdom of heaven." Indeed, the self-castration craze was so troublingly common that the Council of Nicea in the fourth century banned castrated men from joining the clergy.[34]

Horrible things were done with biblical encouragement two thousand years ago: slavery, chopping off the hand of a thief, and death by stoning would be regarded as barbaric and illegal in today's civilized world, despite their religious lineage. Ordering people to kill themselves, as Jim Jones did, can be considered religiously inspired homicide or perhaps assisted suicide. At Heaven's Gate, there was no "commandment" to kill yourself; the persuasion was softer but no less lethal. In the twentieth century, religious leaders could order their congregants to kill themselves in face-to-face conversations and sermons. In the twenty-first century, we are learning that such lethal directives do not even have to be conducted in person, thanks to the internet.

So how do we evaluate religiously encouraged suicides? These acts must be viewed in the context of society's broader definitions and values concerning suicide. If all the Heaven's Gate acolytes had a terminal illness, some of us might conclude that situation justified suicide. If all of the members were severely depressed, some might find that an acceptable reason. If the members fully understood the consequences of their actions, they would probably be judged competent, even if their actions were criticized. Certainly, the Heaven's Gate members knew what they were doing, but they were convinced their suicide would gain them immortality on a spaceship, not a coffin. Were they competent to make that fatal decision based on their leader's powerful persuasion? I suspect most of us would have doubts about their judgment.

Some individuals hate the word *cult* because it sounds judgmental and biased in favor of the religious status quo or else because it conveys a certain amount of disdain for religion. I believe the crux of the issue isn't a group's theology but rather how its leader dominates and controls its members. Columnist Frank Rich said it perfectly: "What makes a cult a cult is not its religion, whatever it is, but the practice of mind-control techniques, usually by a charismatic leader, that robs its members of their independence of thoughts."[35] Cults use group pressures, isolation, and sensory deprivation in ways resembling the reeducation camps of Korea and China. Unlike those camps, Heaven's Gate employed no torture or severe physical hardship; however, there were aspects of the movement that were coercive.

Were the beliefs delusions? Did Heaven's Gate rely on some form of coercive persuasion or did its members share a delusion? The press regarded the Heaven's Gate believers as "Southern California deluded wackos." It is seductive to label people we disagree with as "deluded"; political commentators frequently use this term to dismiss their opponents. It's a form of name-calling like describing an adversary as an "idiot." But people can disagree passionately about all kinds of things without being idiots, and people can have false beliefs without being deluded. One might regard such beliefs as "mistaken," but it is dodgy to consider them "delusional."

This matter of delusions is surprisingly complex. Psychiatrists and psychologists use the term in a very specific sense and are uneasy applying it to beliefs that are shared by a group or culture. Most religions teach doctrines that are nonfalsifiable; that is, after all, another way of defining "faith." Does that mean that believers are deluded? It is tempting to use that term with new religious groups with few followers, but certainly the size of the religious community shouldn't determine whether its beliefs should be regarded as delusional. In fact, the current edition of the *DSM*, psychiatry's diagnostic manual, goes out of its way to caution that "culture and religious background must be taken into account in evaluating the possible presence of delusional disorder."[36]

There are so many bizarre things that people believe in and that cultures espouse. I have treated fire walkers—New Age believers—who retreated to the desert to walk on burning coals to test their religious beliefs. They wound up on the burn unit, where I treated them for their pain and depression, not their atypical beliefs.

I have emphasized what delusions are not, but what are they and how does this apply to Heaven's Gate? Delusions are fixed beliefs that are unchangeable even in the face of conflicting evidence. It is easy to recognize delusions when they are accompanied by other stigmata of major mental illness like deteriorated functioning, impaired cognition, hallucinations, or poor impulse control. Delusions are common in schizophrenia but can occur in other psychiatric disorders, in hostage situations, and instances of sleep deprivation and sensory isolation.

Bizarre delusions that are logically impossible or incomprehensible are easy to recognize. I treated a patient who cut her stomach open "to let the frog babies out." However, many delusions, not quite so bizarre, are still held with rigid intensity. I wish I could say there was a clear distinction between a belief and an inflexibly held opinion. There isn't. We all filter reality through our life experience. Some of us are dogmatic, but that is not the same thing as being delusional.

Unshakable persecutory beliefs are surprisingly common in the general population. Twenty-five percent of patients in a French medical clinic thought they were being persecuted and 10 percent believed there was a conspiracy against them.[37] It's not just the French. Six percent of Swedes also had paranoid ideation, and 7 percent of New Yorkers felt that others were trying to poison them.[38] Thirty-six percent of Americans believe that it was "very likely" or "somewhat likely" that 9/11 happened because governmental officials wanted the United States to go to war in the Middle East.[39]

Some themes of persecutory beliefs are quite common; for example, that government agencies are watching us. It is easier to recognize this as a delusion if people believe that the government has implanted a transmitter in their dental fillings. It is a dicier proposition to disprove the conviction that the NSA is watching us.

Strong beliefs are different from the inflexible beliefs of delusion. Deluded people live in a black-and-white world with no shades of gray. They jump to conclusions and look only for evidence that supports their beliefs; they simply dismiss contradictory evidence.

Delusions tend to be long lasting, but they do vary in intensity.[40] Delusions can be deemed bizarre on objective grounds (for example, that I can fly), cultural grounds (such as a departure from consensually shared views of reality), or individual grounds (for example, a change in belief that is startlingly incompatible with the individual's life course).[41] But studies have shown that even experts have limited reliability in judging whether or not a delusion is bizarre. In one study there was consensus about some delusions ("A man believes that he is pregnant"), but there was an awkward amount of disagreement about rating others ("A woman believes that in the next year she will become a famous rock star, but she has minimal musical skills and can't read music").[42] In other words, in the absence of other signs of serious mental illness, it is difficult to call a belief delusional rather than dogmatically mistaken.

Our beliefs get even stronger if we associate only with people who share those beliefs and if we attend only to media that preach to our biases. In this sense, delusions can be infectious; an extreme example is folie á deux—where two closely associated people can acquire shared delusions.[43] Occasionally, both individuals truly are delusional. More commonly, the dominant individual is delusional and induces the other to adopt that delusion. The most recent version of *DSM* does away with the French terminology, preferring use of "delusional disorder" for the dominant patient and "delusional symptoms in partner of individual with delusional disorder" for the other person. The new terminology acknowledges that the partner may not meet criteria for a delusional disorder and could be construed as having a different disorder, such as dependent personality disorder.[44]

So, how well does "delusion" capture the Heaven's Gate scenario? Given all the caveats about applying such a term to closely knit groups of individuals, one would hesitate to say the group suffered from a delusional disorder. Even if folie á deux were still accepted as a diagnosis, it is hard to say that Do was delusional, given all the caveats about labeling religious beliefs as delusions. Therefore, we are left with a group contagion of belief or conversion as possible explanations. These forty individuals had lived together in a cloistered community for decades. They had no ties with their families or friends outside of the community. While they ventured out to work and shop, their outside interactions were highly circumscribed. They believed that the Earth was all washed up and their destiny was in the stars, and once their leader and companions had departed, there was nothing more for them in this world. They were persuaded to end their lives.

I think most of us come to the conclusion that Heaven's Gate exemplifies not coercive brainwashing but rather a contagion of belief. I suppose it is a relief that it required so many years to reach such a powerful level of persuasion. The twenty-year gestation period leaves open the possibility of deliverance sometime during that long interval. But the experience of the Stockholm hostages suggests that people can also be devastatingly persuaded in a matter of hours or days.

PART III

Into the Twenty-First Century

CHAPTER TWELVE

The Beleaguered Persistence
of Brainwashing

We can, of course, be deceived in many ways. We can be deceived by believing what is untrue, but we certainly are also deceived by not believing what is true.

—SØREN KIERKEGAARD

IT WAS A MISTY overcast morning when my son drove me to the cemetery in Oakland. I wanted to pay my respects to the lost souls who had died in Jonestown. Many had come from the San Francisco Bay area, and it was only fitting that they should return home. After their deaths they had rotted in the jungle sun for days. The Guyanese hesitated to touch them—in addition to the soldiers' fears of contamination, the place seemed haunted by a thousand ghosts.

There were troubled negotiations with the United States about returning the remains. The country did not want them back. There was grumbling about the cost of repatriating the remains, and there was again a fear of contagion—not so much bacterial contagion as another kind. We didn't wish to be reminded that people could be persuaded to do such things. Some families took their loved ones' bodies, but over four hundred waited unclaimed at the Dover Air base in Delaware. The owner of

Jonestown Memorial at Evergreen Cemetery, Oakland, California.
(Photograph by author.)

Oakland's Evergreen Cemetery brought them home and buried them on a hillside in a mass grave. Today, the graves are marked by four flat granite panels listing the names of all who died at Jonestown. It is a simple, respectful memorial in a quiet place. I am pleased for the lost ones that they are home. I am pleased for their families and friends that they have a place to visit and remember them.

The seventeenth-century philosopher Spinoza said, "No man's mind can possibly lie wholly at the disposition of another."[1] I am not sure that he was right. In the hundred years since Lenin and Pavlov met, there have been too many instances of coercive persuasion to dismiss the idea out of hand. It has become an international preoccupation—a theme in movies and books as well as a focus of sponsored research and congressional inquiries.

Lurking like a bogeyman, Pavlov is always referred to in discussions about brainwashing, and it is important to reflect on whether his notoriety is justified.[2] Pavlov stood for two things—materialism and scientific method. What outraged people in the early part of the twentieth century was his materialism. His suggestion that there is nothing unique about human consciousness, emotion, and intellect was anathema. But what frightens us today is his meticulousness in shaping behavior. People look askance at B. F. Skinner for some of the same reasons.[3] In defense of behaviorism, Skinner commented: "My image in some places is of a monster of some kind who wants to pull a string and manipulate people. Nothing could be further from the truth. People are manipulated; I just want them to be manipulated more effectively."[4]

Brainwashing goes beyond behaviorism and is comprised of many elements. As Skinner implied, one element entails manipulation and, in some instances, coercion and isolation. Another element is that the manipulation may be so surreptitious individuals may not even know *how* or even *if* they are being targeted. A third characteristic is that actions are taken at the expense of the targeted individuals; someone else benefits from the manipulation. Finally, some degree of sleep deprivation is often part of the regimen, leaving the victim fatigued, confused, and suggestible.

These characteristics are on a continuum; thus, brainwashing is not crisply defined. Table 4 (next page) reviews how these features were evident in the cases I've discussed in this book. There are countless other examples. I deliberately chose instances that varied extensively, ranging from carefully planned attacks on large numbers of victims to spontaneous assaults on a solitary individual. Some of the orchestrators had benign intentions; most operated with malice.

Some people criticize the concept of brainwashing because it is vague. Others don't like the term because it seems to blame the victims for being gullible and weak, even though the list of victims of brainwashing includes many outstanding and gifted individuals. People lose sight of the fact that this form of dark persuasion occurs in extremis, when people are literally at their wits' end because of the manipulation. Still others don't like the term because it has been used to disparage new movements' beliefs ("Don't pay attention to them; they were brainwashed").

The 1960s witnessed a profusion of new religions, communes, psychedelic drugs, and confrontational encounter groups. Distraught families sought to understand their straying children. Rather than accept that their children had voluntarily chosen a different path, many parents felt ideas had been implanted in their brains. In another era, they might have simply lamented that their children had fallen in with a "bad crowd." We have always known the immense power of social influence in leading people astray, but "influence" does not adequately capture the specter of "brainwashing."

Table 4. Features of brainwashing

	Coercion and manipulation[a]	Intentionally surreptitious[b]	Not in victim's best interest[c]	Sleep manipulation[d]
Stalin show trials	+++	++	+++	+++
Cardinal Mindszenty	+++	++	++	+++
Korean War POWs	+++	+	++	++
MKUltra studies	+++	+++	+++	+++
Stockholm	+++		+	++
Patricia Hearst	+++	+	++	++
Jonestown	+++	+	+++	++
Heaven's Gate	+	+	+++	+

[a] Actions where subjects were physically restrained from fleeing are rated +++. Actions that were grossly manipulative, like forbidding communications with outsiders, are rated ++. Actions that discouraged members from interacting with outsiders are rated +.

[b] Instances where there is clear evidence that subjects were surreptitiously manipulated with drugs are rated +++. Surreptitious manipulations with probable but less well-established evidence of drug manipulation are rated ++. Manipulations such as repeated forced confessions to induce guilt are rated +.

[c] Actions that resulted in the death of the target are rated +++. Actions resulting in imprisonment are rated ++. Actions that endangered subjects' safety are rated +.

[d] Instances of repeated and consistently manipulated sleep are rated +++. Instances of continuing sleep deprivation are rated ++. Instances of occasional sleep deprivation are rated +.

   Some families were so worried they hired people to deprogram their loved ones (that is, used brainwashing to erase the brainwashing).[5] One victim of deprogramming described his experiences, and it is striking how similar the deprogrammers' tools were to those used by brainwashers—isolation, abuse, sleep deprivation: "They took me up to Connecticut, locked me in a basement there and subjected me to brainwashing for almost six days. I was never left alone for more than an hour or two to snatch a nap. They rotated night and day, throwing water on my face to keep me awake and giving me constant verbal abuse. . . . They kept working on me, and I finally just pretended to break down and go along with them. All of a sudden . . . [the lead deprogrammer] became real nice and friendly, saying that he really cared about me and that my parents loved me very much."[6]

   Many have questioned whether brainwashing is even a legitimate topic. The American Psychological Association (APA) famously flip-flopped on this matter. In 1983, the APA formed the Task Force on Deceptive and Indirect Techniques of Persuasion and Control to study cults and large group awareness training (that is, sensitivity groups and encounter groups). The six-member group, chaired by Margaret Singer, also included Jolly West. Its conclusions could have been predicted, given the members' long-standing criticism of many new groups. The report was a strident indictment of cults. It featured a casual, almost informal, writing style, attacking cult leaders as "new gurus, messiahs, mind-manipulators." Yet the report never got around to defining cults or coercive persuasion and seemed to paint all new therapies and religions as exploitative. Despite its flaws, the report's four recommendations were sensible:

> Psychologists should devote more effort toward understanding the mechanisms of action, effects, and ethical implication of social influence techniques, especially those that are deceptive and indirect. . . .
>
> [They should] study . . . how such techniques can be resisted and neutralized, and how those harmed by such techniques can be [helped]. . . .
>
> The American Psychological Association ought to consider how future versions of APA's ethical code . . . should be revised in light of the ethical implications of deceptive and indirect techniques of persuasion. . . .
>
> Psychologists ought to direct more attention to educating the public about such techniques . . . [and should] consider advocating stricter regulations regarding . . . the systematic application of deceptive techniques of persuasion and control.[7]

The APA declined to accept the report. Reviewers worried that the term *cult* would be used promiscuously to stifle new movements. They also criticized the report's lack of even-handedness. One reviewer said the report "reads more like hysterical ramblings than a scientific task force report." Another concluded that "the term 'brainwashing' is . . . just a sensationalist 'explanation' . . . [that] should not be used by psychologists."[8]

The problem was that in repudiating the report, the APA didn't take seriously the concerns about manipulative new groups or their ethical ambiguities. It did not address the dangers of cultic coercion, violence, and restricted civil liberties. Nor did it consider if it was ethical for psy-

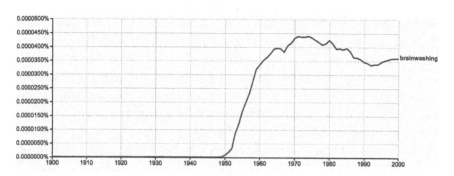

Google Ngram Viewer shows how frequently the term *brainwashing* was used in published books written in English in a given year. The term shows a meteoric rise beginning in 1950, and it continues to be widely used.

chologists to participate in coercive persuasion. Eventually, at the APA's 2002 annual meeting, a panel called on the organization to form a new task force to investigate mind control among destructive cults. The panel commented that while many psychologists regard brainwashing and mind control as science fiction, these techniques continue to be "used by cults to recruit and maintain followers and . . . [could] have dangerous and lasting psychological consequence. . . . Cults that use mind-control techniques have been able to do so with impunity, and the people who are victims of these techniques get no treatment."[9]

In 2015, a scathing report criticized the APA for its vague ethical guidelines concerning psychologists' participation in coercive interrogations of military prisoners. The report accused the APA of colluding with government agencies, thereby allowing psychologists to conduct "enhanced interrogations" of military prisoners in facilities like Abu Ghraib.[10] Note that Singer et al. had specifically warned about the risk of vague ethical guidelines in their report that the APA repudiated in 1987.

★★★

Despite its outlandish name, brainwashing continues to be a focus of concern. It never disappeared from social consciousness or research. I used Google Ngram Viewer to determine how frequently the term *brainwashing* appeared in English-language books published in the twentieth century. It's obvious that the term flourishes in print.

People might say, "Well, you would probably see something similar if you searched for something else that doesn't exist, like unicorns." Just because a word is commonly used it doesn't mean people are taking it

PubMed citations on *brainwashing* from 1948 to 2018.

seriously. For that analysis, I turned to PubMed, the National Library of Medicine's index of biomedical journals. Beginning in 1948, there has been a progressive increase in *brainwashing* research citations, proving that it is still a matter of considerable medical interest.

Formal brainwashing developed in the twentieth century for political purposes and was sustained by science. It also had a parallel track of development in small religious groups and kidnappers. It is easy to dismiss the latter efforts as involving small numbers of people, but it should be remembered that given the right weapon, small groups can have devastating impact. The late David Hamburg used to say, "There is no group too small or too far away that cannot do us grievous harm."[11]

Given brainwashing's volatile history, what are the likely new directions this field will take in the twenty-first century? There are two prime candidates. One encompasses neuroscience; the other involves social psychology, media, and the internet. It is hard to know which is more frightening.

CHAPTER THIRTEEN

The Future of Brainwashing in
Neuroscience and Social Media

And what rough beast, its hour come round at last,
Slouches towards Bethlehem to be born?

—WILLIAM BUTLER YEATS

P AVLOV WAS LYRICAL ABOUT a future when science would finally
alter human nature for the better, although Machiavelli might
smirk at his optimism. One can guess two directions science will
take in exploring brainwashing in the twenty-first century: how
coercion can be intensified by adopting neuroscience insights on memory,
cognition, pleasure, and pain; and how to exploit the capabilities of social
media to intensify coercion.

From a government's perspective, it might be desirable to remove certain memories from an individual's brain. Ewen Cameron demonstrated
that he could do this on a gross level, rendering his subjects practically am-
nestic for huge chunks of their lives—hardly an optimal solution.

Although this sounds like a terrible goal, there are many situations
other than espionage where people might desperately wish to "un-live"
certain memories. Trauma, rape, assault, and abuse all come to mind. Surgical trauma teams have been able to save people with devastating injuries

that would assuredly have been lethal without their care. Unfortunately, long-term follow-up studies reveal that, while these patients survive, their quality of life is poor because of incapacitating depression and PTSD.[1] Could there be a way of "immunizing" such patients when they arrive at the emergency room so that they would not remember their terrifying injury and hospitalization? In other words, could one pry out a little piece of memory that would be devastating to recall?

This is a topic of active clinical investigation, and there are interesting implications for intelligence agencies. A group of us tried to forestall development of PTSD symptoms in patients with severe traumatic injuries.[2] We knew that patients who were severely anxious and had tachycardia in the emergency room were more likely to develop long-term emotional problems. Could we somehow disrupt those memories and sensations? We randomized people to receive propranolol (which blocks a patient's rapid heart rate), gabapentin (a drug that decreases anxiety), or a placebo. It was an impossible study. Out of 569 trauma patients, we could find only 48 who were willing to even try the intervention, far too small a sample to test the treatment. Other investigators have tried similar designs to see if they could block the development of PTSD, with inconclusive results.[3] Such interventions may work, but it is too early to tell.

The flip side of erasing memories is to find a drug that would restore them. Researchers have methodically added a drug, tested its effects on memory, and then added an antagonist to the drug and retested. Recall that scopolamine was used as a sedating drug that might loosen the tongue during interrogation. Whether or not scopolamine makes people more susceptible to interrogation, it does make them more tired and less able to perform well on certain learning tests. The higher the dose of scopolamine, the worse the learning.[4] There are also drugs that reverse scopolamine's actions (for example, physostigmine); if a person is treated with both scopolamine and physostigmine, memory function returns to normal.[5]

Similar studies have been performed with other classes of drugs.[6] Antihistamines, for instance, are typically sedating, but they also impair learning and memory. Investigators started wondering about the memory effects of drugs that *increase* histamine production.[7] There are some fascinating and powerful studies of such effects in animals.

It is known that mice will spend more time exploring a novel object than one they recognize. Given that information, there are intriguing experimental designs for testing memory. For instance, an experimenter shows an object to a mouse and then reexposes the animal to the same object and a new object thirty minutes later. The mouse will spend more time with the new object *if* it remembered its prior encounter with the old object. If it couldn't remember the old object, it would spend equal time exploring both objects because they are both considered "new." Mice typically forget after three days, but when they are given a drug to increase histamine production, they remember the old object and thus spend more time reconnoitering the new one. Similar findings have been observed in humans a week after a memory task. Histamine-enhancing drugs boosted recall on items that were normally difficult to remember and in individuals who scored less well on the original memory challenge.

Thus, there are already pharmacological probes for testing whether memories can be removed or restored. Just as drugs for labor and delivery in childbirth were adopted for use in interrogations, one can anticipate that newer compounds will be similarly exploited in the future. However, these various memory studies focus solely on memory retrieval rather than the willingness to disclose information. To deal with volition, neuroscience has other probes.

Pavlov observed that sleep disruption weakens resistance, but he was hardly the first to make such an observation. Centuries earlier, Shakespeare noted that sleep deprivation enhances persuadability.[8] But Pavlov's model and Shakespeare's as well relied on total sleep deprivation. Studies of total sleep deprivation are expensive and hard to administer; staff must be unbelievably vigilant to prevent even brief bouts of sleep. It turns out that partial chronic sleep disruption or sleep restriction to about four hours a night is also effective in impairing cognition and making subjects more malleable. Future studies will probably test different models of sleep deprivation to learn what dose is most effective and practicable.

Memories are not fixed like computer passwords or a combination lock; instead, they are constantly being reconstructed. During this process, they can become distorted so much that imagined events can be confused with actual memories. Here again, sleep deprivation influences the construction of false memories. One study showed volunteers a series of words (*dog, cat, parrot*) and then a new list containing those words, other words, and a "theme word." The theme in this example would be *pet*. Subsequently, the volunteers were asked to recall the words they had originally seen. The sleep-deprived subjects showed an increase in false reporting; they stated that they had seen the theme word (*pet*) even though it was not on the original list.[9]

Other probes for false memory have tried to mimic real-world experiences. Experimenters showed sleep-deprived subjects news clips. Then they handed the subjects a slightly distorted summary of the video. Afterward, the subjects were asked to recall details based *only* on the film they viewed. People with restricted sleep were more likely to develop false memories; they reported what the experimenter provided in the distorted summary, rather than what the film portrayed.[10]

Sleep-deprived subjects are also more susceptible to social influence. One study presented a task—like estimating the distance between Berlin and Copenhagen—and allowed subjects to modify their estimates after receiving assistance from an "advisor." The advisor swayed the judgment of sleep-deprived subjects more readily than non-sleep-deprived subjects.[11] It is as if sleep deprivation amplifies the persuasiveness of social influence and conformity pressure.

False memories are common.[12] False confessions are thought to account for 15 to 25 percent of wrongful convictions in the United States and are commonly elicited after prolonged late-night interrogation. Might sleep deprivation increase the likelihood that a person will confess to something that never happened? One experimenter enrolled people to perform various computer tasks, cautioning them never to press the "escape" key because it would erase their data. Some subjects were allowed to go to sleep afterward and the others were kept awake all night. The next morning all the subjects were misinformed that they had accidentally pressed the escape key, thereby erasing all their work. They were then asked to sign a statement admitting their error. The odds of signing such a false confession were four and a half times higher in the sleep-deprived subjects.[13]

One of the reasons that sleep disruption is so disturbing is that it interferes with other rhythms in the body. Our bodies are filled with tiny clocks that regulate when we sleep, when we wake, when we go to the bathroom, as well as countless clocks that regulate metabolism, hormone levels, and temperature. These clocks establish circadian rhythms, and when they are disrupted, there are adverse effects on mood, wakefulness, and cognition.[14] Jetlag is the most familiar manifestation of disrupted circadian clocks.

While circadian rhythms can obviously be altered by sleep disruption, there are other ways of disrupting rhythms, like exposing people to bright light at the wrong time of the day. Ongoing work examines the effects of different types of light exposure (such as wavelength, brightness, or timing) on mood and energy. Other research examines how circadian rhythms affect human performance in settings as diverse as space exploration, military activities, diplomacy, and international business. While current work seeks to ameliorate the effects of circadian disruption, it is only logical to assume that individuals interested in coercive persuasion will mull over how circadian disruption can make people more tractable.[15]

★★★

Pavlov anticipated that we would be able to localize and visualize brain activity. In a passage eerily accurate in describing today's neural imaging, he forecast the development of the field. "If we could look through the skull into the brain of a consciously thinking person, and if the place of optimal excitability were luminous, then we should see playing over the cerebral surface a bright spot with fantastic, waving borders, constantly fluctuating in size and form, and surrounded by a darkness, more or less deep, covering the rest of the hemispheres."[16]

That development in neuroscience would have to wait until the waning years of the twentieth century, but it was anticipated by brainwashing research in the 1960s. In addition to the MKUltra studies of LSD and memory, researchers in that decade employed neural probes that were at least as alarming as those used by Ewen Cameron. It is worth recapping some of those studies because they offer a glimpse of what could be done with greater precision in the future. The studies used different techniques for stimulating or ablating (that is, destroying) various parts of the brain. Stimulation could be applied with electrical current or direct infusion of chemicals into the brain. Ablation could be done intraoperatively either through surgical excision or electrical cautery. All of the interventions in the 1960s were quite coarse, making the outcomes less specific than what one could achieve if the studies were done today.[17]

We do not have a precise topography of the brain in terms of specific thoughts or feelings. Thus, it is hard to imagine where one would begin if one wanted to surgically "force" someone to talk about one particular secret or to persuade him or her to vote "Republican" (or "Democrat," for that matter). Penfield stimulated precise areas of the brain and elicited memories, but he had no guarantee that such memories weren't stored as a "backup" in other regions of the brain. Nor could he decide in advance where to stimulate the brain in order to elicit one specific memory.

José Delgado (1915–2011) implanted electrodes in the brains of bulls and demonstrated that he could remotely transmit signals that could halt a raging bull.[18] This was most impressive, particularly if you, like Delgado, stood in the path of the bull's attack. But note that we have no idea what the stimulation "did" to the bull. Did the stimulation make the bull "decide" he wasn't interested in charging Dr. Delgado? Did the bull forget

José Delgado with a bull in a Spanish corral. The bull, with electrodes
implanted in its brain, responded to radio signals from a handheld
transmitter. (Courtesy of Yale Events and Activities Photographs
[RU 690]. Manuscripts and Archives, Yale University Library.)

what he was doing? Did he suddenly "hear" or "feel" a stimulation that
distracted him from the attack? One would have to conclude that while
the intervention obviously changed the bull's behavior, there is no evidence that the bull's "opinions" were in any way modified by the stimulation.

Neurosurgeon Vernon Mark (1925–2014) and psychiatrist Frank Ervin
(1926–2015) collaborated on psychosurgical studies to change human behavior. Moving from larger lesion lobotomies to smaller and more specific surgical procedures, they treated severely ill patients who had failed
conventional treatments for severe pain, obsessive compulsive disorder,
depression, or schizophrenia. When they started treating patients with
uncontrolled aggression and criminal records, there was considerable
pushback, particularly when they asserted that violence is frequently a
neurological disorder needing neurological treatment.[19]

One would have to conclude that these various studies of direct intervention on the brain itself were interesting but not so useful for brainwashing per se. The study of pleasure and pain brings us far closer to effective brainwashing. James Olds (1922–76) was yet another McGill alumnus, having trained with Donald Hebb. Olds implanted electrodes deep in the brains of rats and started observing their responses to electrical stimulation at various sites.

Olds revealed that his key observation resulted from an accident; he had missed the desired anatomical site slightly on one particular rat. After recovering from surgery, the animal was placed in a special chamber. Every time it went to the corner of the chamber, it received a small electrical stimulus to the brain, and each corner of the chamber stimulated a different site in the brain. The rat kept returning to one specific corner. Indeed, the rat would skip eating in order to hang out in the corner and get the brain stimulation. Olds inferred that there was something pleasurable about receiving a shock at that site in the brain. Next, he started training the rat to go to different parts of the box or to turn right or left before it could receive the desired electrical stimulation. Using this technique, Olds could elicit complex behaviors easily. Pavlov would have been envious about this shortcut to behavioral conditioning. As Olds observed: "Left to itself in the apparatus, the animal . . . stimulated its own brain regularly. . . . We found that the test was repeatable as often as we cared to apply it. When the current was turned on and the animal was given one shock as an *hors d'oeuvre*, it would begin stimulating its brain again . . . from 500 to 5,000 times per hour."[20]

If a rat would forgo eating or if it could be "steered" by an investigator giving a shock to its pleasure center, then the training possibilities for this intervention sound almost limitless. Would it work on humans?

Psychiatrist Robert Heath (1915–99) performed studies with implanted electrodes that provided intermittent stimulation to various parts of the human brain. One of his patients, code-named B-7, was a twenty-eight-year-old man with severe narcolepsy. Heath implanted a series of electrodes in various areas of the brain and asked the patient what he felt after each area was stimulated. One area was so aversive that the patient intentionally broke the stimulus button so that he would never have to experience *that* sensation again. However, the feelings evoked by stimulating a different site were intensely pleasurable ("as if he were building up to a sexual orgasm"). Interestingly, the patient learned that he could block an incipient narcoleptic attack by self-stimulating; the sexual thrill woke him

Dr. Robert G. Heath experiments with planting deep-brain electrodes
in a human skull, November 11, 1966. (Courtesy of AP Images.)

up. He was able to control his symptoms so well that he was finally able to
get a job. On the rare occasion that he fell asleep too rapidly to press the
button, his friends knew that they could promptly waken him by pressing
the button on his unit for him.[21]

In a notorious extension of this work, Heath used the self-stimulating
paradigm on patient B-19, a twenty-four-year-old homosexual man with
temporal lobe epilepsy, drug addiction, and depression. The goal was to
convert him to heterosexuality. After recovering from surgery, the patient
learned that if he pressed the button, he would experience feelings of
sexual pleasure, so much so that he pressed the button as often as fifteen

hundred times during a three-hour interval and protested when the device was taken from him. Investigators showed B-19 heterosexual pornographic films, which he thought were repellent, but when they let him use the self-stimulation, he became interested in the films and masturbated while watching them. Then they brought in a female prostitute. He was initially anxious but when the deep brain stimulation began, he relaxed and they had intercourse, "which culminated in a highly satisfactory orgastic response, despite the milieu and the encumbrances of the lead wires to the electrodes."[22] At one point the CIA approached Heath, asking if he would work with the agency to study the brain's pleasure and pain system. Heath spurned the invitation: "Disgusting. If I had wanted to be a spy, I would have been a spy. I wanted to be a doctor and practice medicine."[23]

This kind of work, most of which was conducted in the 1960s and 1970s, has largely been shut down because of ethical concerns. However, the underlying neurosurgical techniques have continued to evolve. Fifty years after Heath's studies, procedures are less invasive, less risky, and can be applied to very specific areas of the brain. Implanted deep-brain stimulators (DBS) are used for diverse reasons at other sites in the brain. Thousands of patients with Parkinson's disease use such stimulators to help control their muscle movements. DBS are also used for other conditions, most notably pain and epilepsy. There is ongoing interest in using such interventions on different sites in the brain to treat patients with psychiatric disorders, particularly patients with treatment-resistant depression.[24]

Given the power of the intervention, one wonders if some latter-day devotee of brainwashing might use deep-brain stimulation (electric or magnetic) to elicit pain or pleasure in order to alter beliefs and behaviors. Would patients acquire new beliefs if that allowed them to continue pleasurable stimulation? In the right location, the stimulation is so pleasurable that it can be addicting, and addicts are not particularly squeamish about what they need to do to obtain their drugs. On the other side of the coin, would patients repudiate old beliefs in order to turn off painful stimulation?

The deep-brain stimulator approach requires painstaking, precise surgery and expensive equipment, suitable for an individual but hardly appropriate for group interventions. Is there some way of stimulating a group of people without implants? Margaret Singer described "love bombing," an indoctrination technique used by some cults. Potential recruits are practically mobbed by established members who praise them with so much flattery and adulation that they feel welcome and safe.[25] There is a neuroendocrine equivalent of love bombing—a hormone called oxytocin that is manufactured deep in the brain.

People release oxytocin when they are bonding with another; it is sometimes nicknamed the feel-good hormone. Early research found that it is increased during breastfeeding and during sexual intimacy. Subsequent research showed that it could be increased in other situations of closeness—prayer and spirituality, team sports, even when dog owners interact with their pets.[26] It's not always warm fuzzy stuff; there is a darker side to oxytocin. Oxytocin stokes ethnocentrism—in-group trust and cooperation at the expense of distrust of the out-group.[27] Currently, the most effective way of administering oxytocin is through a nasal spray, but if it were possible to administer it orally or via aerosol, it could conceivably be used in group settings to increase attachment and thereby recruit new potential members.[28]

When the dystopian movie *A Clockwork Orange* was released in 1971, people were stunned by its violence and its portrayal of the power of aversive conditioning. I would not dismiss such concerns out of hand. When Pavlovian behaviorism meets sophisticated neuroscience, the dark potential of coercive persuasion is clear. That outcome is kept in check only by a sense of professional medical ethics and governmental regulation. Will such self-restraint be sufficient? I doubt it.

Governments always seek new weaponry, and they disagree about the definition and consequences of war crimes. As to professional medical ethics, the experience of the twentieth century suggests that many researchers will close their eyes to the implications of their work or will justify their research as a tool to protect society from looming threats.

★★★

Twenty-first century brainwashing researchers will also exploit the capabilities of a very different area—social media. Recall how governments seized upon pharmaceutical developments in obstetrics and used those drugs to facilitate interrogations. How could countries *not* study social media as a tool for brainwashing in the twenty-first century?

If that sounds too far-fetched, recall that brainwashing is facilitated by limited communication with outsiders and when people are subjected to surreptitious destructive coercion. How well does that describe the capabilities of social media when it is deployed for disinformation, fake news, stoking fundamentalism and extremism? To answer that question, one needs to recall social media's roots in social psychology, advertising, social modeling, and social intoxicants.

In numerous experiments Solomon Asch (1907–96) demonstrated that adult judgments are surprisingly malleable to group pressures. Social factors influence even simple matters like judging the length of a line. If the first few members of a group report that line A is longer than line B, most subsequent people will go along with that judgment even if it is incorrect.[29] Less than one-third of individuals are able to resist conformity pressures in such a simple task. Even more important, the conformity pressures need not be oppressive. Simply being part of a group influences one's judgment, perception, and behavior. As Singer and Lalich observed: "If you say it in front of others, you'll do it. Once you do it, you'll think it. Once you think it, you'll believe that you thought of it yourself."[30] Asch's most famous student, Stanley Milgram, demonstrated darker implications of such conformity pressures. Mentally healthy, normal individuals could be persuaded to administer unconscionably painful electric shocks to another person in a laboratory setting.[31] To what extent can social media stoke conformity pressures?

One of the reasons social media is so powerful is that it can aim its messages so effectively. Around the time when Asch was studying how groups can influence people, Vance Packard described how advertisers target their audience, treating consumers "like Pavlov's conditioned dog."[32] There is indeed a whiff of surreptitious manipulation embedded in product marketing; after all, advertisers employ the term *targeting* the audience.[33]

Marketing is a form of mass persuasion. It may be done with good intentions ("Get a flu shot"), it may be neutral ("Shop at Vons"), or it may be against an individual's best interest ("Smoke Marlboro"). While mass campaigns can be effective, advertisers get a higher response rate by targeting the appropriate audience. Here is where social media excels. When people identify their interests and preferences on platforms like Facebook, shrewd marketers can draw inferences from one "like" to another. An individual's interest in something like Scrabble can suggest how to market another product for that individual to buy.[34] Such approaches allow specific targeting of messages to sell a product, idea, or behavior.[35]

In 1957, Norman Cousins cautioned about targeted advertising and market analysis. His warning seems unnervingly contemporary, given today's concerns about privacy and social media: "[Market researchers] coolly propose to break into the deepest and most private parts of the human mind. . . . Nothing is more difficult in the modern world than to protect the privacy of the human soul. We live in an age where what we don't see and don't know can hurt us."[36]

Social modeling also contributes to social media's influence. We are great imitators, sometimes without being aware of it. Albert Bandura (1925–) staged a series of studies with Bobo, a five-foot balloon clown with weights at its base. The doll was placed in a playroom and children observed adults interacting with Bobo—either ignoring it or socking it. The question was whether the children would imitate the adult. Kids who had witnessed an adult's aggressive play with Bobo were more likely to punch or kick the doll.[37]

Children and adolescents are particularly susceptible to modeling their behaviors on what they see in media. There are heartbreaking incidents where little boys have died while trying to imitate Superman by leaping out of a window.[38] But adults are also sensitive to social modeling. When the actor Robin Williams killed himself, deaths from suicide increased in the following month and calls to the National Suicide Prevention Line nearly tripled during the same interval.[39] The internet likewise evokes imitative behaviors that are sometimes deadly.

The speed and anonymity of the internet are intoxicating, and it is worth recalling that cultures are generally helpless against novel intoxicants. It takes generations before cultural norms begin to shape how we deal with such intoxicants. The Gin Craze of the seventeenth century provides a vivid example. When William of Orange moved from Holland to become king of England in 1689, gin became so popular that the mean per capita consumption rose to a phenomenal 10 liters of gin per year. For comparison, the current annual U.S. per capita consumption is 0.21 liters.[40] The heavy consumption of gin was devastating because it led to public drunkenness, crime, child abandonment, and malnutrition. It took sixty years to control the Gin Craze with a series of taxes and licenses.[41]

Similarly, we have been struggling with drunk driving ever since automobiles were invented. Even after a century of laws, norms, and education, driving under the influence is still a major problem.[42] Given that we have been fighting drunk driving for over one hundred years, how confident can we be that social media will be reined in as an intoxicating tool for fostering coercive persuasion?

Social media is a new "substance" that compels attention, and there is worldwide concern about its addictive nature.[43] Someone can post an inflammatory story, and somewhere out there, another someone believes the post and decides to take action. We don't know whether to call such people gullible or unstable, but they certainly are not uncommon. Studies have shown that 50 to 75 percent of American adults regard fake news headlines as credible.[44] One group of scholars studied some 126,000 Twitter news stories and found that false news spread through social media faster and more broadly than true stories. The fake news was more riveting because it appeared novel and roused feelings of fear, disgust, and/or surprise.[45] Disseminating such news is certainly surreptitious and deceptive, but is it persuasive?

Brainwashing can be recognized by its use of surreptitious harmful manipulation. Regrettably, social media—such a powerful tool for communication and support—can be directed to coercion. During the 2016 presidential campaign, rumors swirled on social media that Democratic Party officials were engaged in a child sex ring centered on the Comet Ping Pong pizzeria in Washington, DC. The restaurant received hundreds of threats, and a twenty-eight-year-old man from North Carolina traveled to DC with his rifle and shot at the restaurant.[46] A poll was taken of American adults two weeks later, asking if they believed the social media postings about pedophilia and satanic ritual abuse among Hillary Clinton's staff: 46 percent of Trump supporters and even 17 percent of Clinton supporters said yes.[47]

These sorts of malevolent rumors are instances of propaganda disseminated to sow discord. Given that so many people are gullible in the face of preposterous rumors, what will happen when propaganda artists increase their use of digitally altered videos and photographs? Given the amount of groupthink on the internet and the tendency of social media to intensify beliefs, there can be incendiary consequences of malicious rumors. Chat rooms offer a restricted social communication network and frequently veer off into conspiracy theories and ideas about the world that are not informed by science or common sense. The chat room participants suffer from confirmation bias, the tendency to look for and remember information that supports their beliefs.[48] As we have seen repeatedly, restricted communication is an accelerant for brainwashing.

Propaganda is merely a variant of advertising. Governments have quickly embraced social media for "white propaganda" (supporting the current regime and promoting morale) and "black propaganda" (fomenting distrust and demoralization). The Chinese government posted 448 million social media comments purporting to be the candid opinions of ordinary Chinese people. While the authenticity of the posts had been suspected, proof was elusive until researchers fell upon a treasure trove of leaked emails to and from the Internet Propaganda Office of one Chinese district. They examined the communication patterns of the commentators, the content of the communication, and the timing of the postings.

For this particular propaganda ministry, the postings were inauthentic. Instead, they were instances of white propaganda, distributed with the intent of distracting the public and praising China.[49]

Nation-states use social media to disseminate black propaganda as well. During the years of the Trump presidency, the United States was riven by concerns that Russia interfered with elections via social media. The Senate Select Committee on Intelligence concluded there was ample evidence of Russian meddling in the 2016 presidential election as well as efforts to undermine confidence in U.S. democratic institutions and voting processes.[50] Russian trolls and hackers implanted some 140 million Facebook advertisements about divisive wedge issues, hoping to increase voting among some groups and dissuade others from doing so.[51] A dispiritingly long report from the Department of Justice details the extent of the social media weaponization.[52] Interfering with another country's elections is not new, nor is it limited to Russia.[53] What is different now is that the interference has become vastly more effective through use of social media.

Social media also facilitates cyber-bullying—sometimes to a lethal extent. Eighteen-year-old Conrad Roy, troubled by anxiety and depression, was persuaded by seventeen-year-old Michelle Carter to kill himself in July 2014. Although Roy was ambivalent about committing suicide, Carter persuaded him to go ahead via numerous text messages and phone calls; she was subsequently convicted of involuntary manslaughter.[54] Roy tried to kill himself with carbon monoxide but got scared and texted Carter, who later told a friend: "His death is my fault like honestly I could have stopped him. I was on the phone with him and he got out of the car because it [the carbon monoxide] was working and he got scared and I fucking told him to get back in. . . . He called me and I heard like muffled sounds and some type of motor running and it was like that for 20 minutes and he wouldn't answer. I think he killed himself."[55]

Another suicide involved twenty-two-year-old Alexander Urtula. In the last two months of his life, his girlfriend sent him over forty-seven thousand text messages urging him to kill himself.[56] According to the prosecution, the girlfriend's constant repetitive demands and threats demonstrated "that she had complete and total control over Mr. Urtula."[57]

If you can use social media to persuade an individual you know well to do something awful, can you persuade a wider circle of friends and acquaintances? Thoughtful studies involving millions of Facebook users have demonstrated a small but discernable amount of influence in such circumstances.[58]

Social media is a powerful, inexpensive technique—and it allows anonymity. Contagious rumors fly over the internet, and when they appear on the computer screen, the rumors seem credible. Shakespeare called rumor "stuffing the ears of men with false reports."[59] With the internet, we can now "stuff" much faster. A RAND Corporation report warned of a "firehose of falsehood" coming from Russia's copious use of disinformation. The sheer volume of messages generated by paid trolls can drown out competing information. When observers receive the same message from multiple sources, they find the messages more believable, even if they are preposterous. To make matters worse, the messages are difficult to counteract. As the RAND authors ruefully observed, "Don't expect to counter the firehose of falsehood with the squirt gun of truth."[60]

Social media has gone from techno-utopianism to dystopic weaponization. Perhaps Timothy Leary was more accurate than he realized when he branded the internet the new LSD (and we saw how well the LSD story worked out in the government's hands). Social media can be so compelling that it verges on being coercive. Furthermore, it is subliminally persuasive in ways that can be profoundly destructive to the user. Tomorrow's brainwashers could not help exploring the possibilities. Experts in cognitive science, communication, and computer science will continue enhancing the capabilities of social media to link people and carry messages. Plato cautioned that storytellers rule the world.[61] Tomorrow's citizens will need to evaluate the storytellers' tales on social media with great care.

Afterword

IN MY STUDIES OF how brainwashing evolved in the twentieth century, I have necessarily been highly selective. Nonetheless, the examples come from around the world — the United States, Canada, Korea, China, Cambodia, Russia, and Hungary are just a few of the countries where coercive persuasion has flourished. Frequently, governmental intelligence services have sponsored the research. Occasionally, new religious movements have proven adept at applying the techniques, and sometimes even criminals have stumbled upon its capabilities.

When I started writing this book, I thought brainwashing was long ago and far away, but everywhere I looked, I saw the shadow of Pavlov. As I delved deeper, I learned that the work has continued to evolve. It surprised me to find that I knew so many of the research protagonists, but they were, after all, leaders in my field. What I had not realized is how much my own research on stress and sleep fits in with the larger conversation about the nature of brainwashing.

I know *brainwashing* is an outlandish term, but we are stuck with it. I also know that for one hundred years we have been scaring ourselves silly with the idea in countless novels and movies, but that does not mean the danger isn't real.[1] Governments and academics have been studying brainwashing for a century. Various religious groups, new and old, continue to attract followers and persuade them to make devastating choices. Hostages continue to be suspicious of their would-be rescuers; prisoners continue making false confessions under interrogation. All of these phenomena are manifestations of coercive persuasion. Given the developments in neuroscience and social media, we have to assume that brainwashing will evolve further and continue to be part of our lives in the future.

George Orwell soberly observed, "If you want a picture of the future, imagine a boot stamping on a human face—for ever."[2] If we ignore the potential developments of brainwashing in the twenty-first century, we will be defenseless against it, and Orwell will have been right. But I do believe we have a choice. We need to look back and consider how brainwashing developed in the twentieth century in order to prepare ourselves for the new century. And we need to listen to H. G. Wells, who warned that "human history becomes more and more a race between education and catastrophe."[3] We are in such a race now. It is up to us to control how dark persuasion shapes our future.

Acknowledgments

People think that writing is solitary; in fact, it is one of the most gregarious activities imaginable. I have so many people to thank for helping me with this book. It would have been impossible without you.

Special thanks to Nancy Dimsdale, who suffered through drafts, commented profusely, questioned, and inspired. My agent Sandy Dijkstra provided continuing encouragement and wisdom. I also thank my editor at Yale University Press, Jennifer Banks, for her enthusiastic backing and advice throughout the whole process. My thanks also to the anonymous reviewers whose comments strengthened the manuscript. My vizsla Molly was always good for distraction when the research grew too oppressive.

Such books are possible only with the assistance of research libraries with their special collections and their archivists. As Jorge Luis Borges once said, "I have always imagined that Paradise will be a kind of library." I have been helped greatly by the following libraries and archivists:

UCSD's Special Collections and interlibrary loan service.

Teresa and Russell Johnson at the UCLA Biomedical Library Special Collections facilitated my access to the Lehmann Papers.

Neil Hodge and Molly Haigh at the Charles E. Young Library, UCLA Special Collections, helped me with the extensive Louis Jolyon West Papers.

Nathan Ponzio of the National Archives helped me locate OSS files on truth drugs.

Lewis Wyman, reference librarian, Library of Congress, unearthed Winfred Overholser files.

Yasmine Legendre, Macy Foundation Program associate, provided access to the Macy archives.

Nicole Milano and Elizabeth Shepherd at the Medical Center Archives of New York-Presbyterian/Weill Cornell helped me delve into the Wolff Papers.

Marisa Shaari, Special Collections librarian, Oskar Diethelm Library, DeWitt Wallace Institute for the History of Psychiatry, helped me with the American Psychosomatic Society papers on Wolff.

LeTisha Stacy, William J. Clinton Presidential Library, located presidential clemency and pardon files on Patricia Hearst.

Edwin Moloy, Harvard Law Library Special Collections, guided me through the Toobin Papers on the Patricia Hearst case.

Jack Eckert, Harvard Countway Library, located the Beecher Papers regarding truth drugs in World War II.

Anna Dysert, Osler Library of the History of Medicine, McGill University, provided access to material related to Ewen Cameron and Wilder Penfield.

Mary Curry, National Security Archive, George Washington University, assisted me with the voluminous MKUltra files.

Bill Landis, Yale University Library, helped me locate the image of Dr. Delgado.

Debra Kaufman, California Historical Society, helped me access Jonestown files.

Lorna Kirwan, UC Berkeley Bancroft Library, helped me access the *San Francisco Examiner* files on Jonestown.

In addition to these institutions, certain individuals have made enormous contributions to scholarship by sharing their own extensive research archives. I thank in particular:

Rebecca Moore, San Diego State University, for her donated collection to the library's Special Collections on Alternative Considerations on Jonestown.

Jeffrey Toobin for sharing his extensive papers on the Patricia Hearst case with the Harvard Law Library.

John Marks for his groundbreaking investigative journalism into MK-Ultra and for sharing his CIA FOIA documents. I also thank the National Security Archive and the Black Vault for making these documents readily accessible.

Daniel Pick for his thoughtfully curated website Hidden Persuaders, http://www.bbk.ac.uk/hiddenpersuaders/.

Eric Olson for his valuable website on Frank Olson, http://frankolson project.org, and his kindness in sharing a photograph of his father.

Many colleagues generously shared their thoughts. I would like to thank:

Will Carpenter and Rajiv Tandon for discussions about delusional disorder.

Frank Biess and Christoph Hermann-Lingen for assistance with translation of SS documents.

Paul Kleinman for translating a document written by Pope Pius XII.
Pey-Yi Chu and Robert Edelman for discussions about Soviet history.
Faye Girsh for discussions concerning assisted suicide.
Jim Holman for locating Heaven's Gate files at the *San Diego Reader.*
Paul Sherman for assistance with Hale-Bopp photograph rights.
Arthur and Helen Dawson for observations on the Allan Institute.
Randy Rieches, San Diego Zoo, regarding discussions about Tusko.
Stephen Stahl and David Braff for discussions about psychopharmacology.
Gregory Vecchi and Frank Ochberg for discussions about Stockholm syndrome and the FBI.
Steve Campman, San Diego County medical examiner, for helping me access the Heaven's Gate autopsies.
Andrea Tone, McGill University, for discussions regarding Ewen Cameron.
Eric van Young and Andrew Devereux for comments on the Inquisition.
Norton Wheeler for references on brainwashing in Chinese history.
Jonathan Dimsdale and Colin Depp for observations on social media.
Jack Fisher for constant cheerleading and helpful edits.
Steve Cox for discussions on religious conversion.
Robert Lifton for his decades of scholarship on thought reform and his comments about the Hearst trial.
Michael Parrish and Mark Evans for discussions about law.
Bill Lovallo for discussions about Jolly West.
Karl Gerth for guidance on the Korean War.
Don Oken for reminiscences on Harold Wolff.
Tom Wise for discussions concerning psychiatry and the Cold War history of psychosomatic medicine.
Muffie Knox for her reminiscences concerning an acquaintance in Heaven's Gate.
Perry Shipman for helping me manipulate over sixteen thousand TIFF documents from the CIA.
Colonel Roger Dimsdale (USA Ret.) for discussions concerning the Korean War and code of conduct.
Kristina Orth-Gomer for her reminiscences about Larry Hinkle.
Sonia Ancoli-Israel for discussions on sleep.
Sheriff Bill Gore for assistance with Heaven's Gate photographs.

The author David Grann observed in *Killers of the Flower Moon:* "History is a merciless judge. It lays bare our tragic blunders and foolish missteps and exposes our most intimate secrets, wielding the power of hindsight like an arrogant detective who seems to know the end of the mystery from the outset." One of my potential blunders is to have forgotten to acknowledge someone. I hope not. If there are blunders in scholarship, attribute them to me rather than to the many people who generously offered advice.

Notes

Preface

1. J. Wolff, "San Diego Polo Club Site Developed by Heaven's Gate," *San Diego Reader*, July 16, 1998.
2. See http://heavensgate.com/ (accessed September 19, 2017).
3. Dwight Reed, Brian Blackbourne, Yvonne Wiliams, John Rodrigues, and Calvin Vine, "Rancho Santa Fe Mass Suicide Discovered March 26, 1997," County of San Diego Medical Examiner's Office, 1997.
4. Reed et al., "Rancho Santa Fe Mass Suicide."
5. For a thoughtful reconstruction of the royal inquiry on mesmerism in 1784, see *Report of the Commissioners Charged by the King with the Examination of Animal Magnetism*, republished in *International Journal of Clinical and Experimental Hypnosis* 50 (2002): 332–63.
6. J. Dimsdale, *Anatomy of Malice: The Enigma of the Nazi War Criminals* (New Haven: Yale University Press, 2016).

Chapter One. Before Pavlov

Epigraphs: Aesop, "The Wind and the Sun," in *Fables*; William Sargant, *Battle for the Mind: A Physiology of Conversion and Brain-washing* (1957; repr., Cambridge, MA: Malor Books, 1997).

1. George Ryley Scott, *The History of Torture throughout the Ages* (London: Kegan Paul, 2004), 172; Edward Peters, *Torture*, rev. ed. (Philadelphia: University of Pennsylvania Press, 1996), 170. Interestingly, in Argentina, it was called "the Asian torture."
2. Senator Lott, quoted in Deborah Solomon, "Questions for Trent Lott," *New York Times Magazine*, June 20, 2004, 15.
3. Ulpian, quoted in Alfred McCoy, *A Question of Torture: CIA Interrogation, from the Cold War to the War on Terror* (New York: Metropolitan Books, 2006).

4. Peters, *Torture*, 71.
5. McCoy, *A Question of Torture*, 204.
6. Peters, *Torture*, 129–30.
7. Peters, *Torture*, 124.
8. Peters, *Torture*, 71, 69.
9. R. L. Kagan and A. Dyer, *Inquisitorial Inquiries: Brief Lives of Secret Jews & Other Heretics*, 2nd ed. (Baltimore: Johns Hopkins University Press, 2011).
10. Henry Kamen, *Inquisition and Society in Spain in the Sixteenth and Seventeenth Centuries* (Bloomington: Indiana University Press, 1985).
11. Carlo Ginzburg, *The Cheese and the Worms: The Cosmos of a Sixteenth Century Miller*, trans. John Tedeschi and Anne Tedeschi (Baltimore: John Hopkins University Press, 1980), 5.
12. Ginzburg, *The Cheese and the Worms*, 87.
13. Ginzburg, *The Cheese and the Worms*, 70.
14. L. E. Hinkle and H. G. Wolff, "Communist Interrogation and Indoctrination of 'Enemies of the State': Analysis of Methods Used by the Communist State Police (A Special Report)," *AMA Archives of Neurology & Psychiatry* 76 (August 1956): 115–71.
15. Sargant, *Battle for the Mind*, 201.
16. Kagan and Dyer, *Inquisitorial Inquiries*, 17.
17. David Hawk, "Tuol Sleng Extermination Centre," *Index on Censorship* 1 (1986): 27.
18. See Susan Jacoby's fine book *Strange Gods: A Secular History of Conversion* (New York: Pantheon Books, 2016).
19. Duane Windemiller, "The Psychodynamics of Change in Religious Conversion and Communist Brainwashing: With Particular Reference to the 18th Century Evangelical Revival and the Chinese Thought Control Movement" (PhD diss., Boston University, 1960).
20. Windemiller, "The Psychodynamics of Change in Religious Conversion and Communist Brainwashing," 130.
21. Jonathan Edwards, quoted in Tanya Luhrmann, *When God Talks Back* (New York: Knopf, 2012), 103.
22. For an interesting discussion concerning these changes in the nature of churches and their membership, see Stephen Cox, *American Christianity: The Continuing Revolution* (Austin: University of Texas Press, 2014).
23. Reverend George Salmon, quoted in Sargant, *Battle for the Mind*, 135.
24. Edwin Diller Starbuck, "A Study of Conversion," *American Journal of Psychology* 8, no. 2 (1897): 283.
25. Starbuck, "A Study of Conversion," 298.
26. Douglas Cowan, "Conversions to New Religious Movements," in *Oxford Handbook of Religious Conversion*, ed. L. H. Rambo and C. E. Farhadian (New York: Oxford University Press, 2014), 695.
27. James H. Leuba, "A Study in the Psychology of Religious Phenomena," *American Journal of Psychology* 7, no. 3 (1896): 322, 366.

28. J. T. Richardson and M. Stewart, "Conversion Process Models and the Jesus Movement," *American Behavioral Scientist* 20, no. 6 (1977): 819–38.

29. John Wesley journal, quoted in Windemiller, "The Psychodynamics of Change in Religious Conversion and Communist Brainwashing," 63.

30. Long after Wesley, diaries and confessions have been obtained to coerce people into self-destructive acts. Japanese kamikaze pilots were instructed to attend to their spiritual training and to keep diaries focusing on self-reflection and dedication to the emperor. Importantly, they were obliged to share the diaries with their flight leaders every week. One pilot trainee confessed: "My spiritual training is still deficient. I believe one must . . . work at spiritual cultivation for the goal of body crashing" (crashing his plane into a ship). For an extensive discussion of the Japanese pilots' confessional requirements, see Samuel Yamashita's fine book *Daily Life in Wartime Japan, 1940–1945* (Lawrence: University Press of Kansas, 2015), 140.

31. Windemiller, "The Psychodynamics of Change in Religious Conversion and Communist Brainwashing," 71.

32. Hugh Freeman, "In Conversation with William Sargant," *Bulletin of the Royal College of Psychiatrists* 11 (September 1987): 290.

33. Malcolm Lader, quoted in F. R. Tallis, "A London Landmark: The Workplace of Al-Qaeda's Favourite Psychiatrist," *Huffpost*, June 20, 2013.

34. Sargant, *Battle for the Mind*, xvii, 81.

35. William James, cited in Sargant, *Battle for the Mind*, 148; my emphasis.

36. William James, *The Varieties of Religious Experience: A Study of Human Nature* (New York: Longmans, Green, 1920), "Lecture I: Religion and Neurology," 13.

37. Sargant, *Battle for the Mind*, 155.

38. Luhrmann, *When God Talks Back*, xxiv.

39. John G. Clark, "Cults," *Journal of the American Medical Association* 242, no. 3 (1979): 279–81.

Chapter Two. Pavlov's Dogs and the Soviet Show Trials

Epigraph: Central Intelligence Agency, *Communist Control Methods*, appendix 1: "The Use of Scientific Design and Guidance, Drugs and Hypnosis in Communist Interrogation and Indoctrination Procedures, Declassified from Secret and Released May 17, 2000" (CIA-RDP78-03362A000800170002-1).

1. Ivan Pavlov, *Conditioned Reflexes: An Investigation of the Physiological Activity of the Cerebral Cortex*, lecture 18, trans. G. V. Anrep (London: Oxford University Press, 1927), http://psychclassics.yorku.ca/Pavlov/lecture18.htm.

2. See Daniel Todes's magnificent biography *Ivan Pavlov* (New York: Oxford University Press, 2014), 372.

3. Todes, *Ivan Pavlov*, 481.

4. Boris Sokoloff, *The White Nights: Pages from a Russian Doctor's Notebook* (New York: Devin Adair, 1956), 67–68.

5. Sokoloff, *The White Nights*, 71.
6. Ivan Petrovitch Pavlov, *Lectures on Conditioned Reflexes*, vol. 2, *Conditioned Reflexes and Psychiatry*, trans. W. Horsley Gantt (New York: International, 1941), 144.
7. Ivan P. Pavlov, *Psychopathology and Psychiatry*, trans. D. Myshne and S. Belky (New Brunswick, NJ: Transaction, 1994), 225. Originally published in Moscow in 1961.
8. Pavlov, *Conditioned Reflexes*, lecture XVIII.
9. William Sargant, *Battle for the Mind: A Physiology of Conversion and Brainwashing* (1957; repr., Cambridge, MA: Malor Books, 1997), 17–18.
10. Todes, *Ivan Pavlov*, 572.
11. Stalin supported Trofim Lysenko's ideas about inheritance and removed Soviet geneticists who didn't share the party line. Pavlov was influenced by one of his colleagues, who claimed that the learned responses of mice could be inherited. A colony of mice required 298 training sessions before they learned a task. Their progeny learned the task after 114 repetitions, and *their* progeny mastered the task after 29 repetitions. Pavlov was convinced that these observations demonstrated inheritance of acquired characteristics until a colleague pointed out that perhaps it wasn't that the mice were learning faster but that his research staff members were becoming better animal trainers. (See Todes, *Ivan Pavlov*, 451.)
12. Robert Conquest, *The Great Terror: Stalin's Purge of the Thirties* (London: Macmillan, 1968), 77.
13. W. Horsley Gantt, introduction to Pavlov, *Lectures on Conditioned Reflexes*, vol. 2, *Conditioned Reflexes and Psychiatry*, 31.
14. Pavlov, *Lectures on Conditioned Reflexes*, vol. 2, *Conditioned Reflexes and Psychiatry*, 191.
15. *Pravda*, September 27, 1949, quoted in R. C. Tucker, "Stalin and the Uses of Psychology," U.S. Air Force Project RAND Research Memorandum, March 10, 1955, 29.
16. Conquest, *The Great Terror*, 538–39.
17. N. Khrushchev, quoted in Joel Carmichael, *Stalin's Masterpiece: The Show Trials and Purges of the Thirties—The Consolidation of the Bolshevik Dictation* (London: Weidenfeld and Nicolson, 1976), 71.
18. V. Rogovin, *Political Genocide in the USSR: Stalin's Terror of 1937–1938*, trans. F. S. Choate (Oak Park, MI: Mehring Books, 2009), 199.
19. J. Stalin, quoted in Hiroaki Kuromiya, *Stalin's Great Terror and Espionage*, National Council for Eurasian and East European Research, contract 824-09 (Seattle: University of Washington, 2009).
20. Arch Getty and Oleg V. Naumov, *The Road to Terror: Stalin and the Self-Destruction of the Bolsheviks, 1932–1939* (New Haven: Yale University Press, 1999), 527.
21. Arkady Vaksberg, *Prosecutor and the Prey: Vyshinsky and the 1930s Moscow Show Trials*, trans. Jan Butler (London: Weidenfeld and Nicolson, 1990), 81.

22. Marc Jansen and Nikita Petrov, *Stalin's Loyal Executioner: People's Commissar Nikolai Ezhov* (Stanford, CA: Hoover Institution Press, 2002), ix.

23. The quotas are meticulously described in Getty and Naumov, *The Road to Terror.*

24. Karl Schlogel, *Moscow 1937*, trans. Rodney Livingstone (Cambridge: Polity, 2012), 162.

25. Robert Gellately, *Lenin, Stalin, and Hitler: The Age of Social Catastrophe* (New York: Knopf, 2007), 269.

26. Carmichael, *Stalin's Masterpiece*, 118. Ironically, Vyshinsky completed his career as the Soviet ambassador to the United Nations, where there was less call for his invectives.

27. Vaksberg, *Prosecutor and the Prey*, 82.

28. There was a certain amount of behind-the-scenes jockeying as to how many preposterous allegations the prisoner had to confess to.

29. Gellately, *Lenin, Stalin, and Hitler*, 272.

30. Schlogel, *Moscow 1937*, 79.

31. Conquest, *The Great Terror*, 381–82.

32. George Orwell, review of "Assignment in Utopia," in *The Oxford Book of Parodies*, ed. John Gross (Oxford: Oxford University Press, 2010), 301–2.

33. Alexis Tolstoy, quoted in Carmichael, *Stalin's Masterpiece*, 14.

34. Trotsky, quoted in Rogovin, *Political Genocide in the USSR*, 344.

35. Gorky, quoted in Gellately, *Lenin, Stalin, and Hitler*, 259.

36. Machiavelli had anticipated this, pointing out centuries earlier: "Occasionally words must serve to veil the facts. But this must happen in such a way that no one become aware of it; or, if it should be noticed, excuses must be at hand to be produced immediately." Niccolò Machiavelli, "Confidential Instructions to Diplomat Raffaello Girolami, Ambassador to the Emperor," cited in Arthur Koestler, *Darkness at Noon*, trans. Daphne Hardy (1941; repr., New York: New American Library, 1961), 143.

37. Koestler, *Darkness at Noon*, 137.

38. Walter Duranty, "Sensation Is Seen in Trial of Radek," *New York Times*, January 21, 1937.

39. David C. Large, *Between Two Fires: Europe's Path in the 1930s* (New York: Norton, 1990), 285.

40. Karl E. Meyer, "The Editorial Notebook: Trench Coats, Then and Now," *New York Times*, June 24, 1990.

41. Harold Denny, "Trotsky Is Called Real Conspirator in Anti-Soviet Plot," *New York Times*, August 21, 1936.

42. J. Davies, quoted in Conquest, *The Great Terror*, 505.

43. J. Davies, quoted in Large, *Between Two Fires*, 314.

44. Charles E. Bohlen, *Witness to History* (New York: Norton, 1973), 51. Others were not so diplomatic. "[Davies] was a pompous, conceited, arrogant man with greater political ambitions than his abilities justified. . . . Stalin brain-

washed him completely." R. Buckner, quoted in Stephen Cox, "The Farthest Shores of Propaganda," *Liberty*, July 2010, 26.

45. Record Group 238, P20, container 9, National Archives, College Park, MD.
46. Schlogel, *Moscow 1937*, 522.
47. Schlogel, *Moscow 1937*, 529–30.
48. Peter Viereck, foreword to Koestler, *Darkness at Noon*, x.
49. The original trial transcript was altered but was recovered by Stephen Cohen in his 1973 biography, *Bukharin and the Bolshevik Revolution: A Political Biography* (New York: Knopf, 1973).
50. Koestler, *Darkness at Noon*, 38, 71.
51. N. Bukharin quoted in Conquest, *The Great Terror*, 126.
52. Getty and Naumov, *The Road to Terror*, 447.
53. One survivor noted that centuries earlier, Michelangelo lauded the blessings of sleep in another time of terror. "Sweet is't to sleep, sweeter to be a stone. In this dread age of terror and of shame, / Thrice blest is he who neither sees nor feels. / Leave me then here, and trouble not my rest." Quoted in Eugenia S. Ginzburg, *Journey into the Whirlwind*, trans. Paul Stevenson and Max Hayward (New York: Harcourt, Brace and World, 1967), 162.
54. Conquest, *The Great Terror*, 141.
55. Sargant, *Battle for the Mind*, 162–63.
56. Schlogel, *Moscow 1937*, 183.
57. Vaksberg, *Prosecutor and the Prey*, 118.
58. Sargant, *Battle for the Mind*, 208–9.
59. Jansen and Petrov, *Stalin's Loyal Executioner*, 111.
60. Vaksberg, *Prosecutor and the Prey*, 74.
61. J. Stalin, quoted in Bohlen, *Witness to History*, 400.
62. George Hodos, *Show Trials: Stalinist Purges in Eastern Europe, 1948–1954* (New York: Praeger, 1987), 67.
63. Hodos, *Show Trials*, 70.
64. Vaksberg, *Prosecutor and the Prey*, 117.
65. Carmichael, *Stalin's Masterpiece*, 97.
66. Carmichael, *Stalin's Masterpiece*, 87; Conquest, *The Great Terror*, 112–13.
67. Vaksberg, *Prosecutor and the Prey*, 111. The defendant was Nikolay Krestinsky, an Old Bolshevik who was at various times a member of the Central Committee and the Politburo and the ambassador to Germany.
68. Carmichael, *Stalin's Masterpiece*, 64.
69. Schlogel, *Moscow 1937*, 463.
70. Vaksberg, *Prosecutor and the Prey*, 95.
71. Yuri Slezkine, *The House of Government: A Saga of the Russian Revolution* (Princeton: Princeton University Press, 2017), 78.

Chapter Three. Extracting Information with Drugs

Epigraph: George Bimmerle, "'Truth' Drugs in Interrogation," Center for the Study of Intelligence, vol. 5, no. 2, approved for release by the CIA Historical Review Program, September 22, 1993, https://www.cia.gov/library /center-for-the-study-of-intelligence/kent-csi/vol5no2/html/v05i2a09p _0001.htm.

1. *Lancet,* May 14, 1853, 453.
2. F. W. N. Haultain and B. H. Swift, "The Morphine-Hyoscine Method of Painless Childbirth, or So-Called 'Twilight Sleep,'" *British Medical Journal,* October 14, 1916, 513.
3. "Twilight Sleep: The Dammerschlaf of the Germans," *Canadian Medical Association* 5 (1915): 805–8.
4. "I will greatly multiply your pain in childbearing; in pain you shall bring forth children." Genesis 3:16. "'Twilight Sleep' Has Come to Stay," *New York Times,* October 19, 1914.
5. Robert E. House, "The Use of Scopolamine in Criminology" (paper presented at the Section on State Medicine and Public Hygiene of the State Medical Association of Texas, El Paso, May 11, 1922).
6. House, "The Use of Scopolamine in Criminology."
7. The scene captured attention worldwide and was portrayed in numerous forensic psychiatry texts as far away as Spain and Latin America. The scholar Alison Winter tracked one famous early instance back to 1932. See Alison Winter, *Memory: Fragments of a Modern History* (Chicago: University of Chicago Press, 2012).
8. House, "The Use of Scopolamine in Criminology."
9. "'Truth Serum' Involves Five in Axe Murders, Clearing Up 44 Crimes in Birmingham, Ala.," *New York Times,* January 8, 1924.
10. "Cleared by Truth Serum: Suspects in Oklahoma Slaying Freed by 'Spite' Admission," *New York Times,* November 29, 1935.
11. I am indebted to the late Alison Winter, who made so many contributions to our understanding of truth serum. See, for instance, "The Making of 'Truth Serum,'" *Bulletin of the History of Medicine* 79 (2005): 500–533.
12. Max Fink, "Rediscovering Catatonia: The Biography of a Treatable Syndrome," *Acta Psychiatrica Scandinavica* 127 (2013): 1–47.
13. Catatonia used to be regarded as a marker of schizophrenia, but today the syndrome is recognized in a number of psychiatric disorders.
14. Elijah Adams, "Barbiturates," *Scientific American* 198 (1958): 60–67. The first barbiturate, barbital, had the brand name Veronal, named after Verona because the chemist who discovered it thought that city was the most peaceful on Earth.
15. W. J. Bleckwenn, "Production of Sleep and Rest in Psychotic Cases: A Preliminary Report," *Archives of Neurology and Psychiatry* 24 (1930): 365–72.

16. Today catatonia is typically treated with a benzodiazepine.

17. L. A. Kirshner, "Dissociative Reactions: An Historical Review and Clinical Study," *Acta Psychiatrica Scandinavica* 49 (1973): 698–711.

18. M. Kanzer, "Amnesia: A Statistical Study," *American Journal of Psychiatry* 96 (1939): 711–16.

19. While drugs or head injury can cause amnesia, the diagnosis of dissociative amnesia is reserved for patients who have no head injury, seizure disorder, or drug intake.

20. *New York Times*, June 2, 1947; October 24, 2006; September 29, 2017.

21. Jonathan Shay, *Achilles in Vietnam: Combat Trauma and the Undoing of Character* (New York: Scribner, 1994).

22. E. Jones and S. Wessely, "Psychiatric Battle Casualties: An Intra- and Inter-war Comparison," *British Journal of Psychiatry* 178 (2001): 242–47.

23. A. Kardner, with the collaboration of H. Spiegel, *War Stress and Neurotic Illness* (New York: Paul Hoeber Books, 1947), 35.

24. E. Jones and S. Wessely, "Battle for the Mind: World War 1 and the Birth of Military Psychiatry," *Lancet* 384 (2014): 1708–14.

25. Erich Lindemann, "Psychological Changes in Normal and Abnormal Individuals under the Influence of Sodium Amytal," *American Journal of Psychiatry* 88 (1932): 1083–91.

26. J. S. Horsley, "Narco-Analysis," *British Journal of Psychiatry* 82 (1936): 416–22.

27. J. S. Horsley, "Narco-Analysis," *Lancet*, January 4, 1936, 55–56.

28. William Sargant, *Battle for the Mind: A Physiology of Conversion and Brain-washing* (1957; repr., Cambridge, MA: Malor Books, 1997).

29. R. R. Grinker and J. P. Spiegel, *War Neuroses in North Africa: The Tunisian Campaign (January-May 1943)* (New York: Josiah Macy Jr. Foundation, 1943).

30. The army felt it was so urgent to distribute this work that it didn't even correct the text. It was so hurriedly produced that it is filled with typographical errors, not the typical ones that appear in any book, but literal strike-throughs of text. Published in wartime, the paper is like old newsprint and the cover is shabby, thin cardboard.

31. Grinker and Spiegel, *War Neuroses in North Africa*, 199–204.

32. The Nazis were trying to formulate reliable suicide pills that would not accidentally activate unless the person intended to die. This issue of arming selected soldiers with cyanide suicide pills resurfaced in 1957 when one American scientist commented: "Just as coding machines may be equipped with explosives to destroy them, on impending capture, . . . so humans storing intelligence would be provided with the means of self-destruction. A possible alternative might be a drug to destroy memories rather than life, if such a compound were ever discovered." James G. Miller, "Brainwashing: Present and Future," *Journal of Social Issues*, no. 3 (1957): 54.

33. U.S. Naval Technical Mission in Europe, technical report no. 331-45, "German Aviation Medical Research at the Dachau Concentration Camp," October 1945, Henry Beecher Papers, box 11, Countway Center for History of

Medicine, Harvard Medical School, Cambridge, MA. After the war, Plöt-ner was brought to the United States and protected from war crimes charges while he worked on classified medical research. He was part of Operation Paperclip, the Cold War program that brought Nazi scientists to the United States to strengthen military research, given the confrontations with Communism.

34. J. H. Anslinger, "Marihuana—Assassin of Youth," *American Magazine*, July 1937, 18–19, 150–52.

35. Interoffice memo, June 21, 1943, Record Group 226, box 346, National Archives, College Park, MD.

36. Memorandum on T.D., June 21, 1943, Record Group 226, box 346, National Archives.

37. Memorandum on T.D., June 2, 1943, Record Group 226, box 346, National Archives.

38. Interoffice memo, June 4, 1943, Record Group 226, box 346, National Archives.

39. Bimmerle, "'Truth' Drugs in Interrogation."

40. J. A. Brussel, D. C. Wilson, and L. W. Shankel, "The Use of Methedrine in Psychiatric Practice," *Psychiatric Quarterly* 28 (1954): 381–94.

41. J. Dimsdale, *Anatomy of Malice: The Enigma of the Nazi War Criminals* (New Haven: Yale University Press, 2016).

42. J. R. Rees, ed., *The Case of Rudolf Hess: A Problem in Diagnosis and Forensic Psychiatry* (New York: Norton, 1948), 88.

43. Even seventy years later, there are continuing calls for court-imposed truth drugs, regardless of their effectiveness or legality. For instance, in 2013, a Colorado judge warned accused mass killer James Holmes that he could be given a narcoanalytic interview with truth drugs if he pled an insanity defense for mass murders at the Aurora movie theater. "Colorado: Massacre Suspect Could Get 'Truth Serum,'" Associated Press, March 11, 2013. Holmes's attorneys initially proposed pleading guilty in return for a life sentence. In all of the ensuing negotiations, the judge did not follow through with the amytal order.

44. Frank Sain was the Cook County sheriff.

45. Oyez, https://www.oyez.org/cases/1962/8 (accessed January 7, 2018); Cornell Law School, Legal Information Institute, https://www.law.cornell.edu /supremecourt/text/372/293 (accessed January 7, 2018).

46. The case went back to Illinois for repeat adjudication but continued to be mired in diverse appeals which, in the opinion of the U.S. Court of Appeals for the Seventh Circuit, had assumed "Jarndycian proportions," referring to Charles Dickens's novel *Bleak House* with its memorable description of the interminable case of *Jarndice vs. Jarndice*. See https://law.justia.com/cases /federal/appellate-courts/F2/452/350/174800/ (accessed January 7, 2018).

47. *Acta Apostolicae Sedis*, November 30, 1953, 735–36, trans. Paul Kleinman.

48. "'Truth Serum' Ban Is Dropped in U.N.," *New York Times*, April 1, 1950.

49. "'Truth Serum' Test Proves Its Power," *New York Times*, October 22, 1924.

50. The Latin expression *In vino veritas* means "In wine, there is truth." There are numerous ancient references along the same lines. In *Germania*, chapter 22, Tacitus observed that Germanic tribes believed that people are more truthful when they are drunk and lack the power to dissemble. "They disclose their hidden thoughts in the freedom of the festivity."

51. F. Redlich, L. Ravitz, and G. Dession, "Narcoanalysis and Truth," *American Journal of Psychiatry* 107 (1951): 586–93.

52. L. D. Clark and H. K. Beecher, "Psychopharmacological Studies on Suppression," *Journal of Nervous and Mental Disease* 125 (1957): 316–21.

53. M. J. Gerson and V. M. Victoroff, "Experimental Investigation into the Validity of Confessions Obtained under Sodium Amytal Narcosis," *Clinical Psychopathology* 9 (1948): 359–75.

54. Louis Gottschalk, "The Use of Drugs in Interrogation," in *The Manipulation of Human Behavior*, ed. A. D. Biderman and H. Zimmer (New York: Wiley, 1961), 96–141.

55. Louis Gottschalk, "The Use of Drugs in Information-Seeking Interviews," in *Drugs and Behavior*, ed. L. M. Uhr and J. G. Miller (New York: Wiley, 1960).

56. Louis Gottschalk, "The Use of Drugs in Interrogation," in *The Manipulation of Human Behavior*, ed. A. D. Biderman and H. Zimmer (New York: John Wiley and Sons, 1961), 134.

Chapter Four. A Cold War Prelude to Korea

Epigraph: Joseph Stalin, "Inevitability of Wars between Capitalism Countries," in *Economic Problems of the USSR* (Moscow: Foreign Languages Publishing House, 1951), Marxists Internet Archive, https://www.marxists.org/reference/archive/stalin/works/1951/economic-problems/index.htm.

1. Winston Churchill, address at Westminster College, Fulton, MO, March 5, 1946.

2. Joseph Stalin, "Concerning the International Situation," in *Works*, January–February 1924 (Moscow: Foreign Language Publishing House, 1953), 6:293–314.

3. John Ranelagh, *The Agency: The Rise and Decline of the CIA* (London: Weidenfeld and Nicolson, 1986), 129.

4. John Dower, *Embracing Defeat: Japan in the Wake of World War II* (New York: Norton, 1999), 526.

5. "Aid Group for Hostages' Families Seeks to Help through 'Lonely Experience,'" *NPR*, November 23, 2018, https://www.npr.org/2018/11/23/670010389/aid-group-for-hostages-families-seeks-to-help-through-lonely-experience.

6. For an excellent description of these early Cold War hostages, see Susan Carruthers, *Cold War Captives: Imprisonment, Escape and Brainwashing* (Berkeley: University of California Press, 2009). North Korea abducted thousands of South Koreans and Japanese, even after the armistice. Hostage taking re-

mains one of the most powerful ways for a regime to command attention. North Korea learned that lesson so effectively in the 1950s that it still employs such actions today.

7. During his asylum, his recurring tirades against Communism irritated the United States, which was attempting a rapprochement with Russia. In some ways, he was like Julian Assange of WikiLeaks fame, an irritant to his hosts in the Ecuadorean embassy.

8. József Cardinal Mindszenty, *Memoirs* (New York: Macmillan, 1974), 94.

9. Mindszenty, *Memoirs*, 152, 154.

10. "The Mindszenty Story," *Time*, December 17, 1956, 47.

11. Albert Hauck, ed., *The New Schaff-Herzog Encyclopedia of Religious Knowledge* (New York: Funk and Wagnalls, 1910), 6:148. Occasionally, *coactus feci* pops up in legal cases such as *State v. Burke* in Missouri, nos. 18181, 18947. John Burke was stopped for speeding in 1990. The state trooper asked him to sign a consent authorizing the trooper to search his car. Burke signed the consent as "John Burke C.F." Marijuana was found. Burke challenged the search as forced and inadmissible by virtue of the abbreviation after his name. He lost the case. Among other arguments, the prosecutor claimed that the trooper could not possibly have understood that Burke was refusing consent by employing an obscure medieval abbreviation. See https://www .leagle.com/decision/1994929896sw2d331927 (accessed November 26, 2018).

12. UK Parliament (Hansard), House of Commons sitting February 14, 1949, vol. 461, cc758.

13. "Mind-Control Studies Had Origins in Trial of Mindszenty," *New York Times*, August 2, 1977.

14. L. E. Hinkle and H. G. Wolff, "Communist Interrogation and Indoctrination of 'Enemies of the State': Analysis of Methods Used by the Communist State Police (A Special Report)," *AMA Archives of Neurology & Psychiatry* 76 (August 1956): 147; Stephen Swift, "How They Broke Cardinal Mindszenty," *Readers Digest*, November 1949, 1–10. Most of us are semi-zombies after long international flights. The cramped seating, limited mobility, poor food, and jet lag from crossing multiple time zones leave us drained. Why is it so hard to believe that months of torture and starvation would make us feel like devitalized automatons?

15. William Shakespeare, *Cymbeline*, act 5, scene 4.

16. Allyn Rickett and Adele Rickett, *Prisoners of Liberation* (1957; repr., San Francisco: China Books, 1981), 126.

17. Rickett and Rickett, *Prisoners of Liberation*, 131, 140.

18. Rickett and Rickett, *Prisoners of Liberation*, 307.

19. Robert Lifton, *Thought Reform and the Psychology of Totalism* (New York: Norton, 1961), 17, 397.

20. Robert Lifton, "Thought Reform of Chinese Intellectuals: A Psychiatric Examination," *Journal of Social Issues*, no. 3 (1957): 9.

21. Lifton, "Thought Reform of Chinese Intellectuals," 14.

22. This proximity is similar to another hot spot in world affairs. Jerusalem and Amman are close neighbors.

23. The Russians did not veto the United Nations' support of the South because they were boycotting the UN over the issue of Taiwan's representation as the legitimate government of China.

24. Congressional Research Service, American War and Military Operations Casualties: Lists and Statistics, updated September 24, 2019, https://crs reports.congress.gov, RL32492. The North lost around 2.5 million people (600,000 civilian dead or missing, 400,000 military dead or missing, and 1.5 million military wounded). The South lost 1.6 million people (1 million civilian dead or missing, approximately 210,000 military dead or missing, and some 430,000 military wounded). United Nations' troops, particularly the Turkish troops, also sustained many casualties. In addition to the Americans killed, about 100,000 more were wounded in the war.

Chapter Five. The Korean War and the Birth of Brainwashing

Epigraph: Edward Hunter, *Brainwashing from Pavlov to Powers* (New York: Farrar Straus and Cudahy, 1956), 203.

1. Ludwig Wittgenstein, *Culture and Value*, trans. Peter Winch (Chicago: University of Chicago Press, 1984), 2.

2. Edward Hunter, *Brainwashing in Red China* (New York: Vanguard, 1951).

3. Edward Hunter, quoted in Lorraine Boissoneault, "The True Story of Brainwashing and How It Shaped America," Smithsonian.com, May 22, 2017.

4. The term *xi nao* has earlier roots, dating back to Chinese intellectuals at the turn of the twentieth century who argued for reforming society, "making the brain new," and "washing away the filth of the past from the brain." In its original sense, the term referred to using rational thought to overcome prejudice and irrationality. In Hunter's hands, its meaning flipped, implying that the individual had no independent rational thought and was in fact controlled by others. See Ryan Mitchell, "China and the Political Myth of 'Brainwashing,'" *Made in China Journal*, October 8, 2019, https://madeinchina journal.com/2019/10/08/china-and-the-political-myth-of-brainwashing/.

5. Edward Hunter, *Brainwashing: The Story of Men Who Defied It* (New York: Farrar Straus and Cudahy, 1956), 257, 259, 22.

6. Hunter, *Brainwashing from Pavlov to Powers*.

7. Communist psychological warfare (brainwashing)—consultation with Edward Hunter, author and foreign correspondent, Committee on Un-American Activities, House of Representatives, 85th Congress, 2nd sess. (March 13, 1958).

8. Joost Meerloo, *The Rape of the Mind: The Psychology of Thought Control, Menticide, and Brainwashing* (Cleveland: World Publishing, 1956).

9. George Goodman Jr., "Dr. Joost Meerloo Is Dead at 73; Was Authority on Brainwashing," *New York Times*, November 26, 1976.
10. Meerloo, *The Rape of the Mind*, chapter 2.
11. David Halberstam, *The Coldest Winter: America and the Korean War* (New York: Hyperion, 2007), 138.
12. John W. Powell, "A Hidden Chapter in History," *Bulletin of the Atomic Scientist* 37, no. 8 (October 1981): 44–52.
13. S. Harris, *Factories of Death: Japanese Biological Warfare, 1932–45, and the American Coverup* (London: Routledge, 1994), 68–69.
14. John Dower, *Embracing Defeat: Japan in the Wake of World War II* (New York: Norton, 1999), 103.
15. Stephen Endicott and Edward Hagerman, *The United States and Biological Warfare: Secrets from the Early Cold War and Korea* (Bloomington: Indiana University Press, 1998).
16. Endicott and Hagerman, *The United States and Biological Warfare*, 163, 155.
17. Endicott and Hagerman, *The United States and Biological Warfare*, 155.
18. Endicott and Hagerman, *The United States and Biological Warfare*, 155.
19. Louis Jolyon West Papers, box 152, folder 10, UCLA Special Collections, Los Angeles.
20. Endicott and Hagerman, *The United States and Biological Warfare*, 157–59.
21. LaRance Sullivan, quoted in Virginia Pasley, *21 Stayed: The Story of the American GI's Who Chose Communist China—Who They Were and Why They Stayed* (New York: Farrar, Straus and Cudahy, 1955), 66.
22. Pasley, *21 Stayed*, 54, 119, 146.
23. Pasley, *21 Stayed*, 106, 100.
24. Pasley, *21 Stayed*, 182.
25. Pasley, *21 Stayed*, 58.
26. Peter Lowe, *The Korean War* (London: Macmillan, 2000).
27. See David Cheng Chang's thoughtful book about the contending forces for prisoners' allegiances, *The Hijacked War: The Story of Chinese POWS in the Korean War* (Stanford: Stanford University Press, 2020).
28. When the two who had thought better of staying returned home, they were nonetheless court-martialed. Three Belgians and one British soldier also chose to remain in China (Dominic Streatfeild, *Brainwash: The Secret History of Mind Control* [London: Hodder and Stoughton, 2006]).
29. Pasley, *21 Stayed*, 206, 204.
30. Pasley, *21 Stayed*, 206.
31. Pasley, *21 Stayed*, 37.
32. Pasley, *21 Stayed*, 43, 44, 50.
33. Pasley, *21 Stayed*, 54, 86.
34. Pasley, *21 Stayed*, 114.
35. Brandan McNally, "The Korean War Prisoner Who Never Came Home," *New Yorker*, December 9, 2013; H. G. Wolff, *Commitment and Resistance*, Spe-

cial Report #3, ARDC Study SR 177-D, Contract AF 18(600)1797 (Washington, DC: Bureau of Social Science Research, 1959), 18.

36. Wolff, *Commitment and Resistance*, 18.

37. Interview with Major William E. Mayer, U.S. Army, "Why Did Many GI Captives Cave In?" *U.S. News and World Report*, February 24, 1956.

38. Major William E. Mayer, "Brainwashing: The Ultimate Weapon" (transcription of address given at the San Francisco Naval Shipyard in the Naval Radiological Defense Laboratory, October 4, 1956), 11.

39. Mayer, "Brainwashing," 9. Mayer did provide an excellent, knowledgeable account of Chinese techniques, but to me he comes across more as *Dr. Strangelove*'s frothing U.S. Air Force brigadier general Jack D. Ripper, concerned about precious bodily fluids. Mayer went on to a successful military career and ultimately became assistant secretary of defense for health affairs in 1983.

40. L. J. West, "Psychiatric Aspects of Training for Honorable Survival as a Prisoner of War," *American Journal of Psychiatry* 115 (1958): 335.

41. Eugene Kinkead, "The Study of Something New in History," *New Yorker*, October 26, 1957.

42. Kinkead didn't seem to consider that malnutrition, disease, exposure, and untreated wounds explained most of the death rate. See Edgar Schein's discussion "Epilogue: Something New in History?" *Journal of Social Issues*, no. 3 (1957).

43. Kinkead, "The Study of Something New in History," 129. Perhaps the Chinese lessons of criticism and informing were well learned by the soldiers.

44. Central Intelligence Agency, "CIA Interrogation Experts Wanted to Use Truth Drugs on American Prisoners of War Returning from the Korean Conflict," https://www.cia.gov/library/readingroom/document/cia-rdp88 -01314r000100060010-8 (accessed February 21, 2019).

45. Eugene Kinkead, "Have We Let Our Sons Down?" *McCall's*, January 1959, 77.

46. Kinkead, "The Study of Something New in History," 160.

47. Kinkead, "The Study of Something New in History," 130, 133.

48. Kinkead, "The Study of Something New in History," 144.

49. George Winokur, "The Germ Warfare Statements: A Synthesis of a Method for the Extortion of False Confessions," *Journal of Nervous and Mental Disease* 122, no. 1 (July 1955): 65–72.

50. Kinkead, "The Study of Something New in History," 158, 169.

51. Dr. Charles W. Mayo, "Destroying American Minds—Russians Made It a Science—World Gets Horrible Truth on Germ-War 'Confessions,'" *U.S. News and World Report*, November 6, 1953, 99.

52. Mayo, "Destroying American Minds," 100.

53. Raymond Bauer, "Brainwashing: Psychology or Demonology?" *Journal of Social Issues*, no. 3 (1957): 47.

54. Julius Segal, "Correlates of Collaboration and Resistance Behavior among U.S. Army POWs in Korea," *Journal of Social Issues*, no. 3 (1957): 37, 36.

55. Edgar H. Schein, "Reaction Patterns to Severe, Chronic Stress in American Army Prisoners of War of the Chinese," *Journal of Social Issues*, no. 3 (1957): 26.

56. I. E. Farber, H. F. Harlow, and L. J. West, "Brainwashing and Conditioning, and DDD (Debility, Dependency, and Dread)," *Sociometry* 20 (1957): 271–85.

57. Albert Biderman, "Communist Attempts to Elicit False Confessions from Air Force Prisoners of War," *Bulletin of New York Academy of Medicine* 33 (1957): 619.

58. Edgar Schein provides an excellent overview of the influence of the social structure on POW behavior. See "Reaction Patterns to Severe, Chronic Stress," 21–30.

59. Segal, "Correlates of Collaboration and Resistance Behavior," 40.

60. Julius Segal provides one of the many descriptions of the army's investigations into prisoner behavior. See "Correlates of Collaboration and Resistance Behavior," 31–40.

61. For a brief discussion of these contradictory observations, see Schein, "Epilogue," 51–60.

62. R. West, *The Meaning of Treason* (New York: Viking, 1945), 245.

63. L. E. Hinkle and H. G. Wolff, "Communist Interrogation and Indoctrination of 'Enemies of the State': Analysis of Methods Used by the Communist State Police (A Special Report)," *AMA Archives of Neurology & Psychiatry* 76 (August 1956): 166.

64. Albert D. Biderman, *March to Calumny: The Story of American POWs in the Korean War* (New York: Macmillan, 1963), 24.

65. Wolff, *Commitment and Resistance*, 11.

66. Lewis H. Carlson, *Remembered Prisoners of a Forgotten War: An Oral History of Korean War POWs* (New York: St. Martin's, 2002), 5.

67. Biderman, "Communist Attempts to Elicit False Confessions," 624.

68. Biderman, *March to Calumny*, 58.

69. Kinkead, "The Study of Something New in History," 102.

70. Biderman, *March to Calumny*.

71. Kinkead, "The Study of Something New in History," 154.

72. Carlson, *Remembered Prisoners of a Forgotten War*, 8; Wolff, *Commitment and Resistance*, 8.

73. Chang, *The Hijacked War*, 130.

74. Biderman, *March to Calumny*, 160.

75. Carlson, *Remembered Prisoners of a Forgotten War*, 13.

76. Wolff, *Commitment and Resistance*, 25.

77. West, "Psychiatric Aspects of Training for Honorable Survival," 329–36.

78. Wolff, *Commitment and Resistance*, 41.

79. The name of the Institute for Social Ecology varied slightly over the years.

80. Hinkle and Wolff, "Communist Interrogation and Indoctrination of 'Enemies of the State,'" 169–70.

Chapter Six. The CIA Strikes Back

Epigraph: J. Doolittle, W. Franke, M. Hadley, and W. Pawley, report of the second Hoover Commission on Organization of the Executive Branch of Government, *Report on the Covert Activities of the Central Intelligence Agency*, submitted to President Eisenhower on September 30, 1954, page 3, https://www.cia.gov › library › readingroom › docs.

1. Allen Dulles, 1953, John Marks Papers, Central Intelligence Agency, MORI #146077, National Security Archives, Washington, DC, The Black Vault, https://www.theblackvault.com/.
2. Doolittle et al., *Report on the Covert Activities of the Central Intelligence Agency*.
3. Anonymous, quoted in John Ranelagh, *The Agency: The Rise and Decline of the CIA* (London: Weidenfeld and Nicolson, 1986), 203.
4. There were countless other program like QKHilltop and MKNaomi, but the names of these programs are not so important seventy years later.
5. John Marks Papers, Central Intelligence Agency, MORI #144829.
6. Christopher Simpson, *Science of Coercion: Communication Research and Psychological Warfare, 1945–1960* (New York: Oxford University Press, 1994), 9. See also Alfred McCoy, *A Question of Torture: CIA Interrogation from the Cold War to the War on Terror* (New York: Metropolitan Books, 2006).
7. John Marks Papers, Central Intelligence Agency, MORI #144686.
8. Harold Wolff, proposal for collaboration between Human Ecology and CIA, Cornell Committee to Investigate CIA Activities, box 1, folder 2, Medical Center Archives of New York-Presbyterian/Weill Cornell, New York.
9. Carl Rogers, quoted in S. P. Demanchick and H. Kirschenbaum, "Carl Rogers and the CIA," *Journal of Humanistic Psychology* 48 (2008): 6–31.
10. John Marks, *The Search for the "Manchurian Candidate": The CIA and Mind Control* (New York: Times Books, 1979), 159.
11. Jo Thomas, "Extent of University Work for C.I.A. Is Hard to Pin Down," *New York Times*, October 9, 1977.
12. Marks, *The Search for the "Manchurian Candidate,"* 160.
13. Helen Goodell, Cornell Committee to Investigate CIA Activities, box 2, Medical Center Archives of New York-Presbyterian/Weill Cornell.
14. Lawrence Hinkle, Cornell Committee to Investigate CIA Activities, box 1, folder 1, Medical Center Archives of New York-Presbyterian/Weill Cornell.
15. J. N. Blau, "Harold G Wolff: The Man and His Migraine," *Cephalalgia* 24 (2004): 215–22.
16. Rebecca Akkermans, "Harold G. Wolff," *Lancet Neurology* 14 (2015): 982–83.
17. Lawrence Hinkle, quoted in Marks, *The Search for the "Manchurian Candidate,"* 131.

18. Harold Wolff, MD, Papers, 2008, Medical Center Archives of New York-Presbyterian/Weill Cornell.
19. L. E. Hinkle and H. G. Wolff, "Communist Interrogation and Indoctrination of 'Enemies of the State': Analysis of Methods Used by the Communist State Police (A Special Report)," *AMA Archives of Neurology & Psychiatry* 76 (August 1956): 159.
20. Carl Rogers, quoted in Demanchick and Kirschenbaum, "Carl Rogers and the CIA."
21. A. M. Gotto and J. Moon, *Weill Cornell Medicine: A History of Cornell's Medical School* (Ithaca: Cornell University Press, 2016), 115–18.
22. Hinkle, Cornell Committee to Investigate CIA Activities, box 1, folder 1.
23. Hinkle, Cornell Committee to Investigate CIA Activities, box 1, folder 1.
24. Hinkle, Cornell Committee to Investigate CIA Activities, box 2, folder "Correspondence."
25. Correspondence between White and Wolff, Harold Wolff, MD, Papers, box 6.
26. Human Ecology Committee to Investigate CIA Activities, box 2, folder 1, Medical Center Archives of New York-Presbyterian/Weill Cornell.
27. Human Ecology Committee to Investigate CIA Activities, box 2, folder 1.
28. Christopher Tudico, *The History of the Josiah Macy Jr. Foundation* (New York: Josiah Macy Jr. Foundation, 2012).
29. H. M. Magoun, "Introductory Remarks," in *The Central Nervous System and Behavior: Transactions of the Third Conference* (New York: Josiah Macy Jr. Foundation, 1960), 13.
30. Harold A. Abramson, "Lysergic Acid Diethylamide (LSD-25): XXII. Effect on Transference," *Journal of Psychology* 42 (1956): 51–98.
31. Louis A. Gottschalk, *Autobiographical Notes of Louis A. Gottschalk* (New York: Nova Science, 2007), 10.
32. Senate Subcommittee on Health and Scientific Research of the Committee on Human Resources, Human Drug Testing by the CIA, 95th Cong., 1st sess. (1977), 85, 90.
33. Marks, *The Search for the "Manchurian Candidate,"* 155.
34. Harold Wolff, Cornell Committee to Investigate CIA Activities, box 1, folder 1, Medical Center Archives of New York-Presbyterian/Weill Cornell. The emphasis in the quotation is mine.
35. H. P. Albarelli Jr., *A Terrible Mistake: The CIA Murder of Frank Olson and the CIA's Secret Cold War Experiments* (Waterville, OR: Trine Da, 2009), 367.
36. Martin Lee and Bruce Shlain, *Acid Dreams: The Complete Social History of LSD: The CIA, the Sixties and Beyond* (New York: Grove Weidenfeld, 1992), 219.
37. Albarelli, *A Terrible Mistake*, 301.
38. Albarelli, *A Terrible Mistake*, 392.
39. Alexander Cockburn and Jeffrey St. Clair, *Whiteout: The CIA, Drugs and the Press* (London: Verso, 1998), 208.

40. Senate Subcommittee on Health and Scientific Research, Human Drug Testing, 115.

41. Memorandum from the CIA inspector general to the director, "Report on MKULTRA," July 26, 1963, cited in Project MKULTRA: The CIA's Program of Research in Behavioral Modification, joint hearing before the Select Committee on Intelligence and the Subcommittee on Health and Scientific Research, Human Drug Testing.

42. Stanley Lovell, quoted in Marks, *The Search for the "Manchurian Candidate,"* 14.

43. Gordon Thomas, *Journey into Madness: The True Story of Secret CIA Mind Control and Medical Abuse* (New York: Bantam Books, 1989), chapter 7.

44. Senator Edward Kennedy, U.S. Senate, joint hearings before Subcommittee on Health of the Committee on Labor and Public Welfare and Subcommittee on Administrative Practice and Procedure, Committee on the Judiciary, Biomedical and Behavioral Research, 94th Cong. (1975), 143–44.

45. Thomas, *Journey into Madness*, 156.

46. S. Kinzer, *Poisoner in Chief: Sidney Gottlieb and the CIA Search for Mind Control* (New York: Henry Holt, 2019), 3.

47. Albarelli, *A Terrible Mistake*, 225.

48. Marks, *The Search for the "Manchurian Candidate,"* 71.

49. Lee and Shlain, *Acid Dreams*, 180.

50. Sidney Gottlieb before Senate Subcommittee on Health and Scientific Research, Human Drug Testing.

51. Vernon Walters, quoted in Ranelagh, *The Agency*, 584.

52. Readers will have noticed certain names recurring throughout this book. Wolff, Abramson, Sargant, West, Gottschalk—they all knew each other from the late 1940s and worked on issues related to coercive persuasion for the rest of their lives.

53. L. J. West, C. Pierce, and W. D. Thomas, "Lysergic Acid Diethylamide: Its Effects on a Male Asiatic Elephant," *Science* 138 (1962): 1100–1103.

54. Louis Jolyon West Papers, box 103, UCLA Special Collections, Los Angeles.

55. L. J. West, "Group Interchange Following Symbolysis," in *The Use of LSD in Psychotherapy*, ed. Harold A. Abramson (New York: Josiah Macy Jr. Foundation, 1960), 185.

56. Abramson, "Psychoanalytic Psychotherapy with LSD," in *The Use of LSD in Psychotherapy*, 62.

57. Abramson, "Psychoanalytic Psychotherapy with LSD" and "Appendix: Resolution of Counter-identification Conflict of Father during Oedipal Phase of Son," in *The Use of LSD in Psychotherapy*, 63, 273.

58. While there are many sources, one must acknowledge in particular John Marks for his extraordinary analysis of the Olson case as well as the MKUltra story in his book *The Search for the "Manchurian Candidate."* Another good source is Albarelli, *A Terrible Mistake*.

59. E. Olson, personal communication, November 26, 2019. See also the

thoughtful Netflix series *Wormwood* and memorandum from Gordon Thomas to Eric Olson, November 30, 1998, Frank Olson Legacy Project, http://frankolsonproject.org/_backup/Statements/Statement-G.Thomas .html.

60. John Marks Papers, Central Intelligence Agency, MORI #144972, MORI #144963.

61. See, for instance, J. Groves, B. Dunderdale, and T. Stern, "Celebrity Patients, VIPs, and Potentates," *Primary Care Companion to the Journal of Clinical Psychiatry* 4, no. 6 (2002): 215–23; and M. Davies, "Do You Know Who I Am? Treating a VIP Patient," *British Medical Journal* 353 (2016): i2857.

62. Harold A. Abramson, John Marks Papers, Central Intelligence Agency, MORI #144981.

63. Bob Vietrogoski, archivist, biographical note, Harold A. Abramson Papers, 2000, Archives and Special Collections, Columbia University Health Science Library, New York.

64. Project MKULTRA, The CIA's Program of Research in Behavioral Modification, 106. For Abramson's consensus panels on LSD research, see, for instance, Abramson, *The Use of LSD in Psychotherapy*.

65. Allen Dulles, John Marks Papers, Central Intelligence Agency, MORI #146416.

66. Carl Rogers, quoted in Demanchick and Kirschenbaum, "Carl Rogers and the CIA."

Chapter Seven. Dead Memories

Epigraph: Allen Dulles, Address to Princeton Alumni meeting in Hot Springs, Virginia, 1953, John Marks Papers, Central Intelligence Agency, MORI #146077. National Security Archives, Washington, DC, The Black Vault, https://www.theblackvault.com/.

1. Penfield described this work to his old professor Charles Sherrington, who commented enthusiastically, "It must have been great fun to put a question to 'the preparation' and have it answer." Sherrington, quoted in Stanley Finger, *Minds behind the Brain: A History of the Pioneers and Their Discoveries* (Oxford: Oxford University Press, 2000), 230.

2. Donald Hebb, "Conditioned and Unconditioned Reflexes and Inhibition" (MA thesis, McGill University, 1932), 1, McGill Library and Collections, http://digitool.library.mcgill.ca/R/-?func=dbin-jump-full&object_id=1192 57&silo_library=GEN01 4/5/19.

3. Milner reported that such lesions had their principal impact on declarative memory (facts and names) but left procedural memory (how to do things) relatively unaffected.

4. P. Solomon, P. H. Leiderman, J. Mendelson, and D. Wexler, "Sensory Deprivation: A Review," *American Journal of Psychiatry*, October 1957, 357–63;

A. H. Riesen, ed., *The Developmental Neuropsychology of Sensory Deprivation* (New York: Academic Press, 1975).

5. Donald Hebb, quoted in Alfred McCoy, "Science in Dachau's Shadow: Hebb, Beecher, and the Development of CIA Psychological Torture and Modern Medical Ethics," *Journal of the History of the Behavioral Sciences* 43, no. 4 (2007): 404.

6. J. C. Pollard, L. Uhr, and C. W. Jackson, "Studies in Sensory Deprivation," *Archives of General Psychiatry* 8, no. 5 (1963): 435–54.

7. Woodburn Heron, "Cognitive and Physiological Effects of Perceptual Isolation," in *Sensory Deprivation: A Symposium Held at Harvard Medical School*, ed. Philip Solomon, Philip Kubzansky, P. Herbert Leiderman, Jack Mendelson, Richard Trumball, and Donald Wexler (Cambridge, MA: Harvard University Press, 1961), 22–23.

8. W. Heron, "The Pathology of Boredom," *Scientific American* 196, no. 1 (1957): 52–57.

9. See, for instance, P. Suedfeld, "Attitude Manipulation in Restricted Environments, I: Conceptual Structure and Response to Propaganda," *Journal of Abnormal and Social Psychology* 68, no. 3 (1964): 242–47.

10. Heron, "Cognitive and Physiological Effects of Perceptual Isolation," 15–16.

11. Jack Vernon, *Inside the Black Room* (New York: Clarkson Potter, 1963).

12. Lawrence Hinkle, quoted in McCoy, "Science in Dachau's Shadow," 407.

13. Joshua Knelman, "Did He or Didn't He? The Canadian Accused of Inventing CIA Torture," *Globe and Mail*, November 17, 2007, updated April 26, 2018; McCoy, "Science in Dachau's Shadow," 401–17.

14. D. O. Hebb, "Introduction to Cognitive and Physiological Effects of Perceptual Isolation by Woodburn Heron," chapter 2, in Solomon et al., *Sensory Deprivation*, 6.

15. Just as LSD research started in interrogation studies and later moved into human growth potential, the same thing happened with sensory isolation. Variants of isolation were developed using flotation tanks, which people found restful, relaxing, and in some instances growth enhancing.

16. Heinz Lehmann, quoted in John Oldham, "Heinz Lehmann Obituary," *Archives of General Psychiatry* 58 (2001): 1178.

17. Alan Gregg, quoted in Anne Collins, *In the Sleep Room: The Story of the CIA Brainwashing Experiments in Canada* (Toronto: Key Porter Books, 1988), 104.

18. Rebecca Lemov, "Brainwashing's Avatar: The Curious Career of Dr. Ewen Cameron," *Grey Room* 45 (Fall 2011): 60–87.

19. Joel Dimsdale, *Anatomy of Malice: The Enigma of the Nazi War Criminals* (New Haven: Yale University Press, 2016).

20. Collins, *In the Sleep Room*, 88–89.

21. Collins, *In the Sleep Room*, 95.

22. Lehmann Collection, box 12, folder 50, UCLA Special Collections, Los Angeles.

23. We owe much to Don Gillmore for his careful research on Cameron's

interaction style. See *I Swear by Apollo: Dr. Ewen Cameron and the CIA-Brainwashing Experiments* (Montreal: Eden, 1987).

24. Gillmore, *I Swear by Apollo*, 321.

25. "Termed Heresy: Humanistic View Scored," Friday, *Windsor Daily Star,* April 27, 1951.

26. Dorothy Trainor, "Looking Back at 21 Years: D. Ewen Cameron, M.D., a Pioneer in Canadian Psychiatry," 1965, folder MG1098/10, 1205A, McGill University Archives, Montreal. Cameron's coworker and successor Dr. Robert Cleghorn thought there was something similar about Cameron's combative relationship with the church and with Penfield. In both instances he acted like a rebellious boy fighting to establish his own autonomy. Robert Cleghorn Diaries ("A Search for Meaning in Hormones and Humans"), Lehmann Collection, box 13, UCLA Special Collections.

27. Gillmore, *I Swear by Apollo*, 5.

28. D. E. Cameron, "The Process of Remembering," *British Journal of Psychiatry* 109 (1963): 325–40.

29. Plato, *Theaetetus and Sophist*, ed. Christopher Rowe (Cambridge: Cambridge University Press, 2015), 191 d1.

30. Dulles was so dashing and bright that when author Rebecca West was asked if she had ever been involved with him, she replied, "Alas, no, but I wish I had been." Stephen Kinzer, "When a C.I.A. Director Had Scores of Affairs," *New York Times*, November 10, 2012.

31. Gordon Thomas, *Journey into Madness: The True Story of Secret CIA Mind Control and Medical Abuse* (New York: Bantam Books, 1989), 90.

32. D. E. Cameron, presentation to third World Congress of Psychiatry, June 4, 1961, folder MG1098, item 5, 1205A, McGill University Archives.

33. Thomas, *Journey into Madness*, 152.

34. R. J. Russell, L. G. M. Page, and R. L. Jillett, "Intensified Electroconvulsant Therapy: Review of Five Years' Experience," *Lancet*, December 5, 1953, 1177–79.

35. D. E. Cameron, "Production of Differential Amnesia as a Factor in the Treatment of Schizophrenia," *Comprehensive Psychiatry* 1 (February 1960): 26–34.

36. Collins, *In the Sleep Room*, 129.

37. Joseph Wortis, *Soviet Psychiatry* (Baltimore: Williams and Wilkins, 1950), 150–51.

38. Harold A. Palmer, "The Value of Continuous Narcosis in the Treatment of Mental Disorder," *Journal of Mental Science* 83 (1937): 636–78.

39. Gillmore, *I Swear by Apollo*, 57.

40. H. Azima, "Prolonged Sleep Treatment in Mental Disorders (Some New Psychopharmacological Considerations)," *Journal of Mental Science* 101 (1955): 593–603.

41. D. E. Cameron, "Psychic Driving," *American Journal of Psychiatry* 112 (1956): 502–9.

42. Aldous Huxley, *Brave New World* (1931; repr., New York: RosettaBooks, 2000), 30.

43. "Learn while You Sleep," https://sleeplearning.com/info/learn-while-you-sleep/ (accessed April 19, 2019).

44. L. Leshan, "Breaking of a Habit by Suggestion during Sleep," *Journal of Abnormal and Social Psychology* 37, no. 3 (1942): 406–8.

45. D. E. Cameron, "Psychic Driving: Dynamic Implant," *Psychiatric Quarterly* 31, no. 4 (1957): 703–12.

46. Sometimes the tapes were in the patient's voice—extracts from psychotherapy sessions; this was called "autopsychic driving." Sometimes other people's voices were on the tapes ("heteropsychic driving"). One of his assistants recorded many of these heteropsychic messages, but his strong Polish accent led to comical effects. A patient recalled countless repetitions of the statement "You are veak and inadequate." When she complained, Cameron rerecorded the message using his familiar Scottish accent. Gillmore, *I Swear by Apollo*, 53.

47. Harvey Weinstein, *Psychiatry and the CIA: Victims of Mind Control* (Washington, DC: American Psychiatric Publishing, 1990).

48. Cameron, "Psychic Driving: Dynamic Implant."

49. Dominic Streatfeild, *Brainwash: The Secret History of Mind Control* (London: Hodder and Stoughton, 2006), 227, 228.

50. Weinstein, *Psychiatry and the CIA*, 42.

51. Streatfeild, *Brainwash*, 229–30.

52. D. E. Cameron, L. Levy, and L. Rubinstein, "Effects of Repetition of Verbal Signals upon the Behavior of Chronic Psychoneurotic Patients," *Journal of Mental Science* 106 (April 1960): 742–56.

53. Cameron, Levy, and Rubinstein, "Effects of Repetition of Verbal Signals."

54. Ludwig Wittgenstein, *Culture and Value*, rev. ed., trans. Alois Pichler (Oxford: Blackwell, 1998), 39e.

55. Gillmore, *I Swear by Apollo*, 93.

56. L. Levi, D. E. Cameron, T. Ban, and L. Rubinstein, "The Effects of Long-Term Repetition of Verbal Signals," *Canadian Psychiatric Association Journal* 10 (1965): 265–71.

57. This is not to say that such behavior does *not* happen in today's environment. When the COVID-19 pandemic struck, some researchers rushed to report that chloroquine treated the illness despite small sample sizes, cavalier decisions about "not counting" some patients in the trial, and patients receiving different doses and combinations of medicines. See Michael Hiltzik, "The Shaky Science behind Trump's Chloroquine Claims," *Los Angeles Times*, April 2, 2020.

58. W. Sargant, quoted in memorandum from Gordon Thomas to Eric Olson, November 30, 1998, Frank Olson Legacy Project, http://frankolsonproject.org/_backup/Statements/Statement-G.Thomas.html.

59. Thomas, *Journey into Madness*, 244; Gillmore, *I Swear by Apollo*, 101.

60. D. E. Cameron, "Adventures with Repetition: The Search for Its Possibilities," presidential address delivered in 1963 and published in P. H. Hoch and J. Zubin, eds., *Psychopathology of Perception* (New York: Grune and Stratton, 1965), 312–22.

61. In describing Cameron's research, Cleghorn drew an interesting analogy to William Gladstone's notable quotation about how governments work: "Government is a messy business, the results are most unsatisfactory."

62. The report also mentioned that 6 percent of the sample were listed as having "severe physical complications."

63. A. E. Schwartzman and P. E. Termansen, "Intensive Electroconvulsive Therapy: A Follow-up Study," *Canadian Psychiatric Association Journal* 12 (1967): 217–18.

64. Donald Hebb, quoted in Joseph Rauth and James Turner, "Anatomy of a Public Interest Case against the CIA," *Hamline Journal of Public Law and Policy* 11 (1990): 336.

65. William Shakespeare, *Macbeth*, act 5, scene 3.

66. Margaret Somerville, "Psychiatry and Ethics: 'The Cameron Effect,'" Lehmann Collection, box 12, UCLA Special Collections.

67. Donald Hebb, quoted in Rauth and Turner, "Anatomy of a Public Interest Case against the CIA," 336.

68. William Sargant wrote his obituary: *British Medical Journal*, September 23, 1967, 803–4.

69. D. E. Cameron, subproject 68 proposal to MKUltra, as abstracted in Orlikow v. United States, court document in the U.S. Direct Court for the District of Columbia, civil action number 80-3163, filed by Joseph Rauh Jr., attorney for plaintiffs, Committee to Investigate CIA Activities, box 1, folder 11, 144F (1979), 9, Medical Center Archives of New York-Presbyterian/ Weill Cornell.

70. Orlikow v. United States, court document in the U.S. Direct Court for the District of Columbia, civil action number 80-3163, filed by Joseph Rauh Jr., 2.

71. Michael E. Parrish, *Citizen Rauh: An American Liberal's Life in Law and Politics* (Ann Arbor: University of Michigan Press, 2010), 273–74.

Chapter Eight. Flash Conversion of Hostages

Epigraph: Jan-Erik Olsson, interviewed by Kathryn Westcott, "What Is Stockholm Syndrome?" *BBC News Magazine*, August 21, 2013, http://www.bbc.com/news/magazine-22447726.

1. Diane Cole, "Why a Hostage Cannot Forget," *Newsweek*, May 19, 1980, 17.

2. Kristin Ehnmark, quoted in Daniel Lang, "A Reporter at Large: The Bank Drama," *New Yorker*, November 25, 1974, 64.

3. Lang, "A Reporter at Large," 63–64, 77.

4. Lang, "A Reporter at Large," 65.

5. Lang, "A Reporter at Large," 73, 74.

6. Lang, "A Reporter at Large," 92, 96.

7. Lang, "A Reporter at Large," 115.

8. Brian Jenkins, Janera Johnson, and David Ronfeldt, "Numbered Lives: Some Statistical Observations from 77 International Hostage Episodes," P-5905, RAND, Santa Monica, July 1977.

9. A. Speckhard, N. Tarabrina, V. Krasnov, and N. Mufel, "Stockholm Effects and Psychological Responses to Captivity in Hostages Held by Suicide Terrorists," *Traumatology* 11, no. 2 (2005): 121–40.

10. "Russian Captives Latest Evidence of 'Stockholm Syndrome,'" *Christian Science Monitor*, June 30, 1995.

11. Interview with Frank Ochberg, "A Case Study: Gerard Vaders," in *Victims of Terrorism*, ed. F. Ochberg and D. Soskis (Boulder: Westview, 1982), 25.

12. "Bombs for Croatia," *Time*, September 20, 1976.

13. Richard Brockman, "Notes while Being Hijacked," *Atlantic*, December 1976.

14. Office of the Inspector General, Special Report: The California Department of Corrections and Rehabilitation's Supervision of Parolee Phillip Garrido, State of California, November 2009, https://www.google.com/url?sa=t&rct=j&q=&esrc=s&source=web&cd=1&cad=rja&uact=8&ved=2ahUKEwiItZ_8tu_jAhWGJTQIHbbaA5UQFjAAegQIABAB&url=https%3A%2F%2Fwww.oig.ca.gov%2Fmedia%2Freports%2FARCHIVE%2FBOI%2FSpecial%2520Report%2520on%2520CDCRs%2520Supervision%2520oof%2520Parolee%2520Phillip%2520Garrido.pdf&usg=AOvVaw2W2jGzk_cto3t4N-VjUuMJ.

15. Sean Dooley, Tess Scott, Christina Ng, and Alexa Valiente, "Jaycee Dugard, Her Daughters Today, and if They Ever Want to See Their Father," *ABC News*, July 18, 2016, https://abcnews.go.com/US/jaycee-dugard-daughters-today-father/story?id=40279504.

16. Jaycee Dugard, interview with Diane Sawyer, *ABC News*, July 9, 2016, https://www.youtube.com/watch?v=C520Vwryn6s.

17. Elizabeth Smart, *Where There's Hope: Healing, Moving Forward, and Never Giving Up* (New York: St. Martin's, 2018), 123, 124.

18. M. Haberman and J. MacIntosh, *Held Captive: The Kidnapping and Rescue of Elizabeth Smart* (New York: Avon Books, 2003), 302.

19. Elizabeth Smart, quoted in Margaret Talbot, "Gone Girl: The Extraordinary Resilience of Elizabeth Smart," *New Yorker*, October 14, 2013.

20. Martin Symonds, "Victim Responses to Terror: Understanding and Treatment," in Ochberg and Soskis, *Victims of Terrorism*.

21. Quoted in Thomas Strentz, "The Stockholm Syndrome: Law Enforcement Policy and Hostage Behavior," in Ochberg and Soskis, *Victims of Terrorism*, 156.

22. Cole, "Why a Hostage Cannot Forget," 17.

23. M. Namnyak, N. Tufton, R. Szekely, M. Toal, S. Worboys, and E. L. Samp-

son, "'Stockholm Syndrome': Psychiatric Diagnosis or Urban Myth?" *Acta Psychiatrica Scandinavica* 117 (2008): 4–11.

24. A. Favaro, D. Degortes, G. Colombo, and P. Santonastaso, "The Effects of Trauma among Kidnap Victims in Sardinia, Italy," *Psychological Medicine* 30 (2000): 975–80.

25. A. A. Slatkin, "The Stockholm Syndrome and Situational Factors Related to Its Development" (PhD diss., University of Louisville, 1997).

26. G. D. Fuselier, "Placing the Stockholm Syndrome in Perspective," *FBI Law Enforcement Bulletin* 68 (1999): 22–25.

27. N. De Farique, V. Van Hasselt, G. M. Vecchi, and S. J. Romano, "Common Variables Associated with the Development of Stockholm Syndrome: Some Case Examples," *Victims and Offenders* 2 (2007): 91–98.

28. Brian M. Jenkins, "Hostages and Their Captors—Friends and Lovers," Defense Technical Information Center, ADA022136, October 1975, RAND, Santa Monica.

29. Frank Ochberg, "The Victim of Terrorism: Psychiatric Considerations," *Terrorism: An International Journal* 1, no. 2 (1978): 160.

30. Thomas Strentz, "The Stockholm Syndrome: Law Enforcement Policy and Ego Defenses of the Hostage," *Annals of the New York Academy of Sciences* 347 (1980): 140.

31. F. Ochberg, personal communication, August 11, 2019.

Chapter Nine. Patricia Hearst

Epigraph: Patricia Campbell Hearst with Alvin Moscow, *Every Secret Thing* (New York: Doubleday, 1982), 1.

1. Bryan Burrough, *Days of Rage* (New York: Penguin, 2015), 275.

2. Stephen Gaskin, quoted in David Talbot, *Season of the Witch: Enchantment, Terror, and Deliverance in the City of Love* (New York: Free Press, 2012), 142.

3. Burrough, *Days of Rage*, 277.

4. Donald DeFreeze, quoted in Hearst and Moscow, *Every Secret Thing*, 66.

5. Burrough, *Days of Rage*, 286.

6. Hearst and Moscow, *Every Secret Thing*, 32.

7. Patricia Hearst, excerpts made by Department of Justice in response to her request for pardon, 2008-1268-F, box 1, folder 4, William J. Clinton Presidential Library, Little Rock, AK.

8. Hearst and Moscow, *Every Secret Thing*, 40.

9. Hearst and Moscow, *Every Secret Thing*, 333, 67.

10. Burrough, *Days of Rage*, 283.

11. Hearst and Moscow, *Every Secret Thing*, 84.

12. Hearst and Moscow, *Every Secret Thing*, 54.

13. Ironically, the Reverend Jim Jones, soon to be known for his own dark persuasive skills, tried to insert himself into this opportunity for publicity,

volunteering himself as a substitute hostage for Patricia and even offering $2,000 to the Hearsts if they were having difficulties meeting the ransom demands. Jeffrey Toobin, *American Heiress: The Wild Saga of the Kidnapping, Crimes, and Trial of Patty Hearst* (New York: Doubleday, 2016), 77; and George Klineman, Sherman Butler, and David Conn, *The Cult That Died: The Tragedy of Jim Jones and the Peoples Temple* (New York: G. P. Putnam's Sons, 1980), 141.

14. Hearst and Moscow, *Every Secret Thing*, 86.

15. Hearst and Moscow, *Every Secret Thing*, 206.

16. Toobin, *American Heiress*, 213.

17. The author Jeffrey Toobin kindly made available his extensive papers on the Hearst case. See Jeffrey Toobin Papers, research material for "American Heiress: The Wild Saga of the Kidnapping, Crimes and Trial of Patty Hearst," box 138, folder "Patty Hearst Statements (Full Set) for Soliah Trial," Harvard Law Library Special Collections, Cambridge, MA.

18. Transcript of taped conversation, September 20, 1975, Jeffrey Toobin "American Heiress" Research Collection, box 117, "PCH Docs, Section 17," Harvard Law Library Special Collections.

19. Hearst and Moscow, *Every Secret Thing*, 369.

20. Toobin, *American Heiress*, 40.

21. Toobin, "American Heiress" Research Collection, box 107, folder "Kidnap Case—Harris Case." There were, after all, only three surviving witnesses to those early events in her captivity: Patricia, Bill, and Emily. Were Bill and Emily minimizing the brutality of Patricia's treatment or was Patricia exaggerating her own victimhood? The court would wrestle with such questions.

22. Toobin, "American Heiress" Research Collection, box 11.

23. Emily Harris, probation officer report filed with County of Alameda, September 22, 1978, Toobin Papers, box 19.

24. Patricia Hearst, shootout statement of Bill, Emily, and Patty, Toobin Papers, box 138, folder "Post 5/17/74."

25. Hearst and Moscow, *Every Secret Thing*, 250, 405, 385. In its review of the case in 2000, the Department of Justice obsessed about whether or not Wolfe had raped Hearst. "The contention that petitioner was raped has been the subject of disagreement . . . but the dispute appears more semantic than substantive. . . . [Hearst] testified at trial that she submitted to sexual intercourse by two of her captors during the time they kept her in a closet. Since incapacitated persons are ordinarily not considered capable of consenting to sexual intercourse and . . . [she] was a kidnap victim, it seems appropriate for her to use the word 'rape' to signify [the] sexual acts. . . . [Her] prosecutors, however, appear to use the word 'rape' in the narrower sense of sexual intercourse accomplished only by overcoming the victim through the use of physical force. . . . [Hearst] never said that the sexual acts against her were the result of her captors' use of physical force to overpower her." Department of Justice, 2000, report to the president on proposed denial of

executive clemency for Patricia Campbell Hearst Shaw, 2008-1268-F, box 1, folder 4, Clinton Presidential Library.

26. Steven Weed with Scott Swanton, *My Search for Patty Hearst* (New York: Crown, 1976), 235, 298.

27. R. Hearst, quoted in Burrough, *Days of Rage*, 349.

28. Hearst and Moscow, *Every Secret Thing*, 412.

29. F. L. Bailey, "Patty Hearst: The Untold Story"; Toobin, "American Heiress" Research Collection, box 117, "PCH Psych Binder."

30. Trial transcript, March 18, 1976, in *The Trial of Patty Hearst* (San Francisco: Great Fidelity, 1976).

31. William Sargant, "How 60 Days in the Dark Broke Patty Hearst," *Times* (UK), January 29, 1976.

32. William Sargant, quoted in Malcolm Macpherson, "A Psychiatrist's Notes," *Newsweek*, February 16, 1976.

33. William Sargant, quoted in F. Hauptfuhrer, "Her British Psychiatrist Says Patty Hearst Is Recovering from 'Conversion,'" *People*, March 15, 1976.

34. L. J. West, testimony in criminal case 74-364, *U.S. v. Patricia Campbell Hearst*, February 23, 1976, trial transcript, in *The Trial of Patty Hearst*.

35. West, testimony, February 24, 1976, in *The Trial of Patty Hearst*.

36. M. Orne, testimony in criminal case 74-364, *U.S. v. Patricia Campbell Hearst*, February 26, 1976, trial transcript, in *The Trial of Patty Hearst*.

37. P. Hearst, quoted in testimony in criminal case 74-364, *U.S. v. Patricia Campbell Hearst*, February 26, 1976, trial transcript, in *The Trial of Patty Hearst*.

38. He was absolutely correct. Louis Gottschalk, whom we have met in previous chapters, received extensive government funding from the NIH, Veterans Administration, and the Defense Atomic Support Agency to study verbal content analysis. See L. A. Gottschalk and G. C. Gleser, *The Measurement of Psychological States through the Content Analysis of Verbal Behavior* (Berkeley: University of California Press, 1969).

39. D. Bourget, P. Gagne, and S. Wood, "Dissociation: Defining the Concept in Criminal Forensic Psychiatry," *Journal of the American Academy of Psychiatry and Law* 45 (2017): 147-60.

40. American Psychiatric Association, *Diagnostic and Statistical Manual of Mental Disorders*, 5th ed. (Washington, DC: American Psychiatric Publishing, 2013), 306. The fact that "brainwashing" made it into the dry compendium of *DSM5* reflects experience in the forty-five years since the Hearst trial with many instances where people had been persuaded to perform acts, often with lethal consequences.

41. R. Lifton, quoted in testimony in criminal case 74-364, *U.S. v. Patricia Campbell Hearst*, February 27, 1976, trial transcript, in *The Trial of Patty Hearst*.

42. Lifton, testimony, February 27, 1976.

43. Dr. Fort viewed the Hearst trial as foolish and told Hearst family members from the outset they should plea-bargain for a lesser charge. He was alleged to have said, "[Defense attorney] Bailey likes to try cases and [prosecutor]

Browning wants to be a federal judge." Testimony in criminal case 74-364, *U.S. v. Patricia Campbell Hearst*, March 4, 1976, trial transcript, in *The Trial of Patty Hearst.*

44. Testimony in criminal case 74-364, *U.S. v. Patricia Campbell Hearst*, March 5, 1976, trial transcript, in *The Trial of Patty Hearst.*

45. J. Fort, testimony in criminal case 74-364, *U.S. v. Patricia Campbell Hearst*, March 8, 1976, trial transcript, in *The Trial of Patty Hearst.*

46. Fort, testimony, March 8, 1976.

47. H. Kozol, testimony in criminal case 74-364, *U.S. v. Patricia Campbell Hearst*, March 15, 1976, trial transcript, in *The Trial of Patty Hearst.*

48. Kozol, testimony, March 15, 1976.

49. Kozol, testimony, March 15, 1976.

50. N. Groth, testimony in criminal case 74-364, *U.S. v. Patricia Campbell Hearst*, March 16, 1976, trial transcript, in *The Trial of Patty Hearst.*

51. A. Johnson, testimony in criminal case 74-364, *U.S. v. Patricia Campbell Hearst*, March 16, 1976, trial transcript, in *The Trial of Patty Hearst.*

52. Robert Jay Lifton, *Witness to an Extreme Century: A Memoir* (New York: Free Press, 2011), 212, 213.

53. O. Carter, testimony in criminal case 74-364, *U.S. v. Patricia Campbell Hearst*, March 19, 1976, trial transcript, in *The Trial of Patty Hearst.*

54. J. Browning, testimony in criminal case 74-364, *U.S. v. Patricia Campbell Hearst*, March 18, 1976, trial transcript, in *The Trial of Patty Hearst.*

55. Browning, testimony, March 18, 1976.

56. F. L. Bailey, testimony in criminal case 74-364, *U.S. v. Patricia Campbell Hearst*, March 18, 1976, trial transcript, in *The Trial of Patty Hearst.*

57. L. Fosburgh, "Hearst Jurors Hoped to Believe," *New York Times*, March 22, 1976.

58. Fosburgh, "Hearst Jurors Hoped to Believe."

59. Hearst and Moscow, *Every Secret Thing*, 441.

60. Toobin, *American Heiress*, 316.

61. John Wayne, quoted in "Miss Hearst's Clemency Plea Gains Wide Support," *New York Times*, December 17, 1978.

62. "Major Issues in Current Presidential Adult Mail," weeks ending February 2, 1979, February 9, 1979, and February 16, 1979, Toobin, "American Heiress" Research Collection, box 19, folder unlabeled.

63. David Bancroft, footnote to report to the president on proposed denial of executive clemency for Patricia Campbell Hearst Shaw, September 24, 1976, 2008-1268-F, box 1, folder 4, Clinton Presidential Library.

64. Nancy Manners, letter to President Clinton, November 9, 1999, 2008-1268-F, box 1, folder 1, Clinton Presidential Library.

65. Robert Mueller, letter to Roger Adams, pardon attorney, U.S. Department of Justice, March 12, 1999, 2008-1268-F, box 1, folder 4, Clinton Presidential Library. The pardon was also opposed by prosecutor David Bancroft in 1988; he noted: "Even after [being] arrested . . . Hearst still expressed revo-

lutionary sentiments; and, her background established her self-propensity for disdain and rebelliousness for which the SLA provided an exotic vehicle." Bancroft, report to the president on proposed denial of executive clemency for Patricia Campbell Hearst Shaw.

Chapter Ten. From Racial Harmony to Death in the Jungle

Epigraphs: William Shakespeare, *The Merchant of Venice*, act 1, scene 3. Jim Jones, last words on "Death Tape," FBI no. Q042, November 18, 1978, transcription in D. Stephenson, ed., *Dear People, Remembering Jonestown: Selections from the Peoples Temple Collection at the California Historical Society* (Berkeley: California Historical Society Press and Heyday Books, 2005), 142.

1. For no apparent reason, there is no apostrophe in Peoples Temple, and this chapter will follow that tradition.
2. For details of survivors, see "How Many People Survived November 18?" Alternative Considerations of Jonestown & Peoples Temple, https://jonestown.sdsu.edu/?page_id=35419 (accessed June 27, 2019). Miraculously, one older woman survived in the midst of Jonestown because she slept through the whole three-hour massacre.
3. Jim Jones, quoted in Tim Reiterman with John Jacobs, *Raven: The Untold Story of the Rev. Jim Jones and His People* (New York: E. P. Dutton, 1982), 149.
4. For estimates, see "How Many People Belonged to Peoples Temple?" Alternative Considerations of Jonestown & Peoples Temple, https://jonestown.sdsu.edu/?page_id=35340 (accessed June 27, 2019).
5. Reiterman and Jacobs, *Raven*, 214.
6. Annie Moore, quoted in Rebecca Moore, *The Jonestown Letters: Correspondence of the Moore Family, 1970–1985*, Studies in American Religion, vol. 23 (Lewiston, NY: Edwin Mellen, 1986), 83.
7. Interview with Laura Johnson Kohl, "Jonestown Survivor: 'Wrong from Every Point of View,'" CNNAccess, November 17, 2003, http://www.cnn.com/2003/US/West/11/17/cnna.kohl/.
8. Jim Jones, sermon, annotated transcript Q987, Alternative Considerations of Jonestown & Peoples Temple, https://jonestown.sdsu.edu/?page_id=63129 (accessed June 26, 2019). The reference is to Acts 2:44–45, King James Version: "And all that believed were together, and had all things common; And sold their possessions and goods, and parted them to all men, as every man had need."
9. Jim Jones, sermon, transcript Q1053-4, Alternative Considerations of Jonestown & Peoples Temple, https://jonestown.sdsu.edu/?page_id=63365 (accessed June 27, 2019).
10. George Klineman, Sherman Butler, and David Conn, *The Cult That Died: The Tragedy of Jim Jones and the Peoples Temple* (New York: G. P. Putnam's Sons, 1980), 64.

11. A professor at Claremont McKenna College was convicted of filing a false police report after she asserted that her tires had been slashed, her windows smashed, and her car covered with racist graffiti. Arlene Martinez and Monte Morin, "Conviction in False Hate Crime Case," *Los Angeles Times*, August 19, 2004. More recently, the actor Jussie Smollett was alleged to have staged a racist and anti-gay attack on himself. Megan Crepeau, Jason Meisner, and Jeremy Gorder, "Judge Scolds Jussie Smollett over Allegations He Staged Racist, Anti-gay Attack: 'Vile and Despicable,'" *Chicago Tribune*, February 21, 2019.
12. Reiterman and Jacobs, *Raven*, 202.
13. Advertisement, *Indianapolis Recorder*, May 19, 1956, Alternative Considerations of Jonestown & Peoples Temple, https://www.flickr.com/photos/peoplestemple/sets/72157706000175671.
14. Klineman, Butler, and Conn, *The Cult That Died*, 145.
15. Deborah Layton, *Seductive Poison: A Jonestown Survivor's Story of Life and Death in the Peoples Temple* (New York: Anchor Books, 1998), 113.
16. Stephenson, *Dear People*, 26.
17. George Moscone, Endorsement of Peoples Temple, FBI RYMUR documents 89-4286-I-1-a-5a-I-1-a-5y, FBI Records: The Vault, https://vault.fbi.gov (accessed June 27, 2019).
18. Moscone, Endorsement of Peoples Temple.
19. Q962 transcript, July 4, 2014, last modified on March 12, 2019, Alternative Considerations of Jonestown & Peoples Temple, https://jonestown.sdsu.edu/?page_id=60680.
20. James Reston Jr., *Our Father Who Art in Hell* (New York: Times Books, 1981), 56.
21. Reiterman and Jacobs, *Raven*, 110.
22. Klineman, Butler, and Conn, *The Cult That Died*, 191.
23. Reiterman and Jacobs, *Raven*, 125, 173.
24. Klineman, Butler, and Conn, *The Cult That Died*, 281.
25. Government of Guyana, "Findings, Analysis and Inventory of the Peoples Temple Agricultural Settlement," appendix K, 1979, Alternative Considerations of Jonestown & Peoples Temple, https://jonestown.sdsu.edu/?page_id=69387.
26. Nate Thayer, "Comrades in Mass Murder: The Secret Alliance between Suicide Cult Leader Jim Jones and North Korea," October 22, 2018, Alternative Considerations of Jonestown & Peoples Temple, https://jonestown.sdsu.edu/?page_id=80857.
27. Reston, *Our Father Who Art in Hell*, 148.
28. Jim Jones, quoted in Reiterman and Jacobs, *Raven*, 405.
29. Larry Schacht on cyanide, RYMUR document 89-4286-EE-1-S-55—EE-1-S-56, Alternative Considerations of Jonestown & Peoples Temple, https://jonestown.sdsu.edu/?page_id=13207 (accessed June 26, 2019).

30. Jonestown tape transcript Q734, December 18, 2014, Alternative Considerations of Jonestown & Peoples Temple, https://jonestown.sdsu.edu/?page_id=27567.

31. "What Were the Disciplines and Punishments in Jonestown?" May 24, 2014, Alternative Considerations of Jonestown & Peoples Temple, https://jonestown.sdsu.edu/?page_id=35333.

32. Jonestown tape transcript Q734, December 18, 2014, Alternative Considerations of Jonestown & Peoples Temple, https://jonestown.sdsu.edu/?page_id=27567.

33. Layton, *Seductive Poison*, 175.

34. Annie Moore, quoted in Moore, *The Jonestown Letters*, 78.

35. Advertisement from Concerned Relatives, reprinted in Stephenson, *Dear People*, 93–94.

36. Charles Garry, quoted in Stephenson, *Dear People*, 95.

37. Charles Garry, "I Have Been to Paradise," *Sun Reporter*, November 10, 1977, Alternative Considerations of Jonestown & Peoples Temple, https://jonestown.sdsu.edu/?page_id=86603.

38. Angela Davis, radio broadcast, September 10, 1977, Alternative Considerations of Jonestown & Peoples Temple, https://jonestown.sdsu.edu/?page_id=19021.

39. Layton, *Seductive Poison*, 278.

40. Stephenson, *Dear People*, 86.

41. Ryan, quoted in Reiterman and Jacobs, *Raven*, 494.

42. For details of her harrowing experience and protracted recuperation from her multiple gunshot wounds, see Jackie Speier, *Undaunted: Surviving Jonestown, Summoning Courage, and Fighting Back* (New York: Little A, 2018). Cults don't immediately evaporate when their leader dies or is dethroned. Even weeks after the Jonestown shootings, Speier required round-the-clock protection from U.S. marshals because of continuing death threats from isolated pockets of Peoples Temple adherents (80).

43. For transcriptions, see the extensive site Alternative Considerations of Jonestown & Peoples Temple, https://jonestown.sdsu.edu/.

44. Jim Jones, quoted in Stephenson, *Dear People*, 129.

45. Stephenson, *Dear People*, 131, 132.

46. Dianne Wilkinson, Q245 transcript, FBI Records: The Vault, Alternative Considerations of Jonestown & Peoples Temple, posted August 31, 2020, https://jonestown.sdsu.edu/?page_id=27394.

47. FBI audiotape Q245, transcribed in Rebecca Moore, *Understanding Jonestown and Peoples Temple* (Westport, CT: Praeger, 2009), 85.

48. Tish Leroy, FBI FOIA doc. 89-4286-484, cited in Moore, *Understanding Jonestown and Peoples Temple*.

49. RYMUR 89-4286-1894, FBI Records: The Vault; see also Rebecca Moore, "The Forensic Investigation of Jonestown Conducted by Dr. Leslie Moo-

too: A Critical Analysis," May 18, 2020, Alternative Considerations of Jonestown & Peoples Temple, https://jonestown.sdsu.edu/?page_id=80811.

50. Klineman, Butler, and Conn, *The Cult That Died*, 363.

51. Excerpts from the tape in Stephenson, *Dear People*, 137–41.

52. Richard Tropp, FBI FOIA doc. X-1-A-54, also published in Stephenson, *Dear People*, xv–xvii.

53. Reston, *Our Father Who Art in Hell*, 41.

54. Elazer ben Yair, as recounted by Josephus, *The Jewish War*, trans. G. A. Williamson, rev. E. Mary Smallwood (New York: Dorset, 1981), 398–403.

55. Annie Moore, quoted in Moore, *The Jonestown Letters*, 286.

56. While the Jonestown living conditions were primitive and the food in short supply, it is incorrect to believe that the colony had no money. In fact, Jones had saved millions of dollars from real estate transactions and Social Security payments to his congregation. He apparently believed that such funds would help the community move, if necessary, from Guyana.

57. Michael Prokes, RYMUR document 89-8286-2035, February 8, 2018, 3, FBI Records: The Vault, Alternative Considerations of Jonestown & Peoples Temple, https://jonestown.sdsu.edu/?page_id=13683.

58. Laura Johnston Kohl, *Jonestown Survivor: An Insider's Look* (Bloomington, IN: iUniverse, 2010).

59. United States v. Laurence John Layton, 855 F.2d 1388 (9th Cir. 1988) Court of Appeals, docket number 87-1071, https://www.courtlistener.com/opinion/510998/united-states-v-laurence-john-layton/.

60. Larry Layton, as quoted in "Former Aide of People's Temple Confessed 5 Killings at Guyana Airstrip," *New York Times*, April 2, 1981.

61. Reston, *Our Father Who Art in Hell*, 25.

62. Jay Matthews, "Layton Is Called 'Inside' Man as Peoples Temple Trial Opens," *Washington Post*, August 19, 1981.

63. U.S. v. Layton 90 F.R.D. 520 (N.D. Cal. 1981), https://casetext.com/case/us-v-layton-11/.

64. U.S. v. Layton, https://casetext.com/case/us-v-layton-6.

65. Moore, *The Jonestown Letters*, 62.

66. "Layton, Jones Had Sexual Relationship, Lawyer Says," *Los Angeles Times*, April 24, 1987.

67. Matthews, "Layton Is Called 'Inside" Man"; "Cult Member Cries over Plea to Jury," *New York Times*, September 17, 1981.

68. Charles Garry, quoted in Spencer Sherman, "Jones Statements Not Admitted," United Press International, August 1, 1981.

69. Robert Strand, "Jonestown Survivor Goes to Prison," United Press International, June 16, 1987.

70. Dan Morain, "Layton Sentenced to Life in Ryan's Death," *Los Angeles Times*, March 4, 1987.

71. Moore, *Understanding Jonestown and Peoples Temple*, 108.

72. "Larry Layton Released from Federal Prison," January 15, 2020, Alterna-

tive Considerations of Jonestown & Peoples Temple, https://jonestown.sdsu
.edu/?page_id=32946.

73. John Moore, quoted in Moore, *The Jonestown Letters*, 365–70.

Chapter Eleven. Heaven's Gate

Epigraph: Eugene Zamiatin, *We*, trans. Gregory Zilboorg (New York: Dutton, 1924), 171.

1. It is *proximity* to a cult that compels attention. For the neighbors of the Order of the Solar Temple in Quebec, Western Switzerland, and France, that group's murders and suicides were unforgettable. Similarly, Tokyo subway riders will always remember the sarin gas attacks of Aum Shinrikyo.

2. R. W. Balch and D. Taylor, "Seekers and Saucers: The Role of the Cultic Milieu in Joining a UFO Cult," *American Behavioral Scientist* 20, no. 6 (1977): 839–60.

3. At various times they had other names, such as Bo and Peep, an intentional reference to their being space-age shepherds.

4. "The Next Level," *Newsweek*, April 7, 1997, 31.

5. Barry Bearak, "Eyes on Glory: Pied Pipers of Heaven's Gate," *New York Times*, April 28, 1997.

6. Stmody, quoted in Benjamin Zeller, *Heaven's Gate: America's UFO Religion* (New York: New York University Press, 2014), 187.

7. James Brooke, "The Day a Cult Shook a Tiny Town," *New York Times*, March 30, 1997.

8. Gibson, quoted in Douglas E. Kneeland, "500 Wait in Vain on Coast for 'The Two,' UFO Cult Leaders," *New York Times*, October 10, 1975.

9. "Statements That Heaven's Gate Released over the Years," *New York Times*, March 28, 1997, https://www.nytimes.com/1997/03/28/us/statements-that-heaven-s-gate-released-over-the-years.html.

10. "Overview of Present Mission," by Jwnody, a student, Heaven's Gate, April 1996, http://heavensgate.com/misc/ovrview.htm.

11. Such millenarian beliefs were common as the year 2000 approached. There were society-wide concerns about "Y2K" and the anticipated failure of all computers—a kind of secular millennialism.

12. Bearak, "Eyes on Glory."

13. "'88 Update—The UFO Two and Their Crew—A Brief Synopsis," October 18, 1988, http://heavensgate.com/book/3-3.htm.

14. Robert Balch and David Taylor, "Salvation in a UFO," *Psychology Today*, October 1976, 61.

15. "Do's Intro: Purpose—Belief," Heaven's Gate, http://heavensgate.com/misc/intro.htm (accessed September 19, 2017).

16. "Last Chance to Advance beyond Human," Heaven's Gate, January 16, 1994, http://heavensgate.com/misc/lastchnc.htm.

17. "'95 Statement by an E.T. Presently Incarnate," section 9, Heaven's Gate, January 1977, https://www.psywww.com/psyrelig/hg/95upd96.htm.

18. Joshuah Bearman, "Heaven's Gate: The Sequel," *LA Weekly*, March 21, 2007.

19. George Johnson, "Comets Breed Fear, Fascination and Web Sites," *New York Times*, March 28, 1997.

20. Quoted in Barry Bearak, "Time of Puzzled Heartbreak Binds Relatives," *New York Times*, March 30, 1997.

21. "Earth Exit Statement," by Chkody, a student, Heaven's Gate, http://heavens gate.com/misc/exitchk.htm (accessed September 19, 2017).

22. "Earth Exit Statement," by Glnody, a student, Heaven's Gate, http://heavens gate.com/misc/exitgln.htm (accessed September 19, 2017).

23. *Heaven's Gate Class Exit Videos*, Heaven's Gate, https://video.search.yahoo .com/search/video?fr=yset_chr_syc_oracle&p=heaven%27s+gate+cult#act ion=view&id=20&vid=d9305e905b2dcca26bef49388bd61b1b (accessed August 12, 2017). All subsequent quotations from the exit videos come from this source.

24. GAP Report for the Advancement of Psychiatry, formulated by the Committee on Psychiatry and Religion, report number 132, *Leaders and Followers: A Psychiatry Perspective on Religious Cults* (Washington, DC: American Psychiatric Press, 1992).

25. Mark Muesse, "Religious Studies and 'Heaven's Gate': Making the Strange Familiar and the Familiar Strange," in *Heaven's Gate: Postmodernity and Popular Culture in a Suicide Group*, ed. G. K. Chryssides (Burlington, VT: Ashgate, 2011), 54.

26. Values and Beliefs Poll, Gallup Poll Social Series, Gallup Organization, Princeton, March 2004.

27. Claire Gecewicz, "'New Age' Beliefs Common among Both Religious and Nonreligious Americans," Pew Research Center, October 1, 2018, https:// www.pewresearch.org/fact-tank/2018/10/01/new-age-beliefs-common-among -both-religious-and-nonreligious-americans/.

28. Even mainstream religions occasionally espouse peculiar and harmful beliefs. On June 15, 2017, Pope Francis declared that gluten-free wafers will not transubstantiate and thus cannot be used in Communion, thereby posing a painful dilemma for those Catholics (around 1 percent) who have celiac disease.

29. Zeller, *Heaven's Gate*, 57.

30. Winston Davis, "Heaven's Gate: A Study of Religious Obedience," in Chryssides, *Heaven's Gate*, 78.

31. See the thoughtful analysis by Benjamin Zablocki: "Exit Cost Analysis: A New Approach to the Scientific Study of Brainwashing," *Nova Religio: The Journal of Alternative and Emergent Religions* 1, no. 2 (1998): 216–49.

32. Benjamin Zablocki, "The Blacklisting of a Concept: The Strange History of the Brainwashing Conjecture in the Sociology of Religion," *Nova Religio: The Journal of Alternative and Emergent Religions* 1, no. 1 (1997): 96–121.

33. Although there is debate whether he truly self-castrated.
34. Daniel F. Caner, "The Practice and Prohibition of Self-Castration in Early Christianity," *Vigiliae Christianae* 51 (1997): 396–415. I should add, parenthetically, that two thousand years ago religiously inspired castration was not limited to the Catholic Church. The Hellenistic Jewish author Philo (20 BC–AD 50) thought there was value in castration because eunuchs are able "to escape wickedness and to unlearn passion." Sean D. Burke, "Eunuchs," in *Queering the Ethiopian Eunuch: Strategies of Ambiguity in Acts* (Minneapolis: Fortress, 2013), 111.
35. Frank Rich, "Heaven's Gate-gate," *New York Times*, April 17, 1997.
36. American Psychiatric Association, *Diagnostic and Statistical Manual of Mental Disorders*, 5th ed. (Washington, DC: American Psychiatric Publishing, 2013), 93.
37. Daniel Freeman and Philippa Garety, *Paranoia: The Psychology of Persecutory Delusions* (Hove, UK: Psychology Press, 2004), 2.
38. Freeman and Garety, *Paranoia*, 4; M. Olson et al., "Psychotic Symptoms in an Urban General Medicine Practice," *American Journal of Psychiatry* 159 (2002): 1412–19.
39. David Laporte, *Paranoid: Exploring Suspicion from the Dubious to the Delusional (No, This Book Is Not about You)* (Amherst, NY: Prometheus Books, 2015).
40. Freeman and Garety, *Paranoia*, 82.
41. Richard Mullen, "The Problem of Bizarre Delusions," *Journal of Nervous and Mental Disease* 191 (2003): 546–48.
42. Michael Flaum, Stephen Arndt, and Nancy Andreasen, "The Reliability of 'Bizarre' Delusions," *Comprehensive Psychiatry* 32 (1991): 59–65.
43. If there are more than two people involved, the term is *folie plusieurs*.
44. American Psychiatric Association, *Diagnostic and Statistical Manual of Mental Disorders*, 122.

Chapter Twelve. The Beleaguered Persistence of Brainwashing

Epigraph: Søren Kierkegaard, *Works of Love*, trans. Howard V. Hong and Edna H. Hong (Princeton: Princeton University Press, 1995), 5.

1. B. Spinoza, *Tractatus Theologico-Politicus* (1670), trans. R. H. M. Elwes (New York: Dover, 1951), 257.
2. Protagonists referred to Pavlov in every chapter in this book.
3. Even Skinner was a Pavlov devotee. Skinner originally wanted to be a novelist but changed his mind after reading an article about Pavlov in 1927. Skinner proudly displayed a signed photograph of Pavlov in his office. M. Specter, "Drool: Ivan Pavlov's Real Quest," *New Yorker*, November 24, 2014.
4. B. F. Skinner, quoted in Peter Schrag, *Mind Control* (New York: Pantheon Books, 1978), 10.

5. This issue of deprogramming the brainwashed comes up repeatedly. It was originally considered as a possible strategy to use on American POWs returning from Korea. The "deprogramming" of former POWs or cult members could be considered the same as brainwashing, only in the service of more traditional beliefs.

6. Joseph H. Fichter, *Autobiographies of Conversion*, Studies in Religion and Society, vol. 17 (Lewiston, NY: Edwin Mellen, 1987), 86–87.

7. Report of the Task Force on Deceptive and Indirect Techniques of Persuasion and Control, November 1986, Center for Studies on New Religions, https://www.cesnur.org/testi/DIMPAC.htm.

8. APA Memo to Members of the Task Force on Deceptive and Indirect Techniques of Persuasion and Control, May 11, 1987, Center for Studies on New Religions, https://www.cesnur.org/testi/APA.htm.

9. M. Dittmann, "Cults of Hatred," *APA Monitor* 33 (November 2002): 10.

10. The lengthy Hoffman report is summarized in an APA document dated July 10, 2015: "Press Release and Recommended Actions: Independent Review Cites Collusion among APA Individuals and Defense Department Official in Policy on Interrogation Techniques," https://www.apa.org/news/press/releases/2015/07/independent-review-release.

11. Hamburg was head of the Institute of Medicine and president of the Carnegie Corporation.

Chapter Thirteen. The Future of Brainwashing in Neuroscience and Social Media

Epigraph: W. B. Yeats, "The Second Coming" (1921), in *Modern Poetry*, 2nd ed., ed. M. Mack, L. Dean, and W. Frost (Englewood Cliffs, NJ: Prentice-Hall, 1961).

1. T. Holbrook, J. Anderson, W. Sieber, et al., "Outcome After Major Trauma: 12-Month and 18-Month Follow-up Results from the Trauma Recovery Project," *Journal of Trauma and Acute Care Surgery* 46, no. 5 (1999): 765–73.

2. M. Stein, C. Kerridge, J. Dimsdale, and D. Hoyt, "Pharmacotherapy to Prevent PTSD: Results from a Randomized Controlled Proof-of-Concept Trial in Physically Injured Patients," *Journal of Traumatic Stress* 20, no. 6 (2007): 923–32.

3. W. Qi, M. Gevonden, and A. Shalev, "Prevention of Post-traumatic Stress Disorder After Trauma: Current Evidence and Future Directions," *Current Psychiatry Reports* 18 (February 2016): 20; S. Horn, D. Charney, and A. Feder, "Understanding Resilience: New Approaches for Preventing and Treating PTSD," *Experimental Neurology* 284 (2016): 119–32.

4. P. Broks, M. Preston, M. Traub, et al., "Modelling Dementia: Effects of Scopolamine on Memory and Attention," *Neuropsychologia* 26, no. 5 (1988): 685–700.

5. G. Preston, C. Brazell, C. Ward, et al., "The Scopolamine Model of Demen-

tia: Determination of Central Cholinomimetic Effects of Physostigmine on Cognition and Biochemical Markers in Man," *Journal of Psychopharmacology* 2, no. 2 (1988): 67–79.

6. G. Preston, C. Ward, P. Broks, M. Traub, and S. Stahl, "Effects of Lorazepam on Memory, Attention and Sedation in Man: Antagonism by Ro 15-1788," *Psychopharmacology* 97 (1989): 222–27.

7. H. Nomura, H. Mizuta, H. Norimoto, et al., "Central Histamine Boosts Perirhinal Cortex Activity and Restores Forgotten Object Memories," *Biological Psychiatry* 86, no. 3 (2019): 230–39.

8. Shakespeare referred to a classic technique used in Elizabethan falconry. Adult hawks are made tractable through sleep deprivation. Training manuals note that the hawk "must be watched or kept awake at night till by sheer weariness she settles down into tameness and docility." G. Lascelles, "Falconry," in *Shakespeare's England: An Account of the Life & Manners of His Age* (Oxford: Clarendon, 1950), 2:351–66. In *Othello*, Desdemona comforts Cassio, saying that she will influence Othello to trust him again. The term "watch him tame" refers to a technique for taming hawks.

> I'll watch him tame and talk him out of patience,
> His bed shall seem a school, his board a shrift.
> I'll intermingle everything he does
> With Cassio's suit. (Act 3, scene 3)

J. Dimsdale, "Sleep in *Othello*," *Journal of Clinical Sleep Medicine* 5, no. 3 (2009): 280–81.

9. S. Diekelmann et al., "Sleep Loss Produces False Memories," *PLoS One* 3, no. 10 (2008): e3512.

10. S. Frenda et al., "Sleep Deprivation and False Memories," *Psychological Science* 25, no. 9 (2014): 1674–81; J. C. Lo et al., "Sleep Deprivation Increases Formation of False Memory," *Journal of Sleep Research* 25 (2016): 673–82.

11. J. A. Hausser et al., "Sleep Deprivation and Advice Taking," *Scientific Reports* 6 (2016): 24386.

12. See, for instance, E. F. Loftus and K. Ketcham, *Witness for the Defense: The Accused, the Eyewitness, and the Expert Who Puts Memory on Trial* (New York: St. Martin's, 1991).

13. S. Frenda et al., "Sleep Deprivation and False Confessions," *PNAS* 113, no. 8 (2016): 2047–50.

14. C. Walsh et al., "Weaker Circadian Activity Rhythms Are Associated with Poorer Executive Function in Older Women," *Sleep*, December 1, 2014, 2009–16; T. Endo, D. Kripke, and S. Ancoli-Israel, "Wake Up Time, Light, and Mood in a Population Sample Age 40–64 Years," *Psychiatry Investigation* 12, no. 2 (April 2015): 177–82.

15. A. Huhne, D. Welsh, and D. Landgraf, "Prospects for Circadian Treatment of Mood Disorders," *Annals of Medicine* 50, no. 8 (December 2018): 637–54;

L. Friedman et al., "Brief Morning Light Treatment for Sleep/Wake Disturbances in Older Memory-Impaired Individuals and Their Caregivers," *Sleep Medicine* 13, no. 5 (May 2012): 546–49.

16. I. Pavlov, *Lectures on Conditioned Reflexes*, vol. 2, *Conditioned Reflexes and Psychiatry*, trans. Horsley Gantt (New York: International, 1941), 26.

17. As an aside, this question about specificity cuts both ways. If the intervention is too broadly targeted, more tissue will be destroyed, resulting in more functional impairment. On the other hand, if the intervention is too precisely targeted, one may inadvertently miss the target. One encounters this exact dilemma in contemporary radiation oncology.

18. J. Delgado, *Physical Control of the Mind—Toward a Psychocivilized Society* (New York: Harper, 1971).

19. V. Mark and F. Ervin, *Violence and the Brain* (New York: Harper and Row, 1970).

20. J. Olds, "Pleasure Centers in the Brain," *Scientific American* 185 (1956): 105–16.

21. R. G. Heath, "Electrical Self-Stimulation of the Brain in Man," *American Journal of Psychiatry* 120, no. 6 (1963): 571–77.

22. R. G. Heath, "Pleasure and Brain Activity in Man," *Journal of Nervous Mental Disease* 154, no. 1 (1972): 3–18.

23. R. G. Heath, quoted in L. Frank, *The Pleasure Shock: The Rise of Deep Brain Stimulation and Its Forgotten Inventor* (New York: Dutton, 2018), 142.

24. M. P. Dandekar et al., "Deep Brain Stimulation for Treatment-Resistant Depression: An Integrative Review of Preclinical and Clinical Findings and Translational Implications," *Molecular Psychiatry* 23, no. 5 (May 2018): 1094, 1112; Frank, *The Pleasure Shock*. There have been contemporary reports of using DBS to treat severe OCD and anxiety. See, for instance, M. Synofzik, T. Schlaepfer, and J. Fins, "How Happy Is Too Happy? Euphoria, Neuroethics, and Deep Brain Stimulation of the Nucleus Accumbens," *AJOB Neuroscience* 3, no. 1 (2012): 30–36.

25. Margaret Thaler Singer with Janja Lalich, *Cults in Our Midst* (San Francisco: Jossey-Bass, 1995), 114.

26. P. Cappellen et al., "Effects of Oxytocin Administration on Spirituality and Emotional Responses to Meditation," *Social Cognitive and Affective Neuroscience* 11, no. 10 (2016): 1579–87; J. Jouret, "The Sport Hormone?" *Lancet Diabetes & Endocrinology*, August 1, 2013, S8–S9; M. Nagasawa et al., "Oxytocin-Gaze Positive Loop and the Coevolution of Human-Dog Bonds," *Science* 348, 6232 (2015): 333–36.

27. K. Carsten et al., "Oxytocin Promotes Human Ethnocentrism," *Proceedings of the National Academy of Science* 108, no. 4 (2011): 1262–66.

28. Keeping in mind George Hunter White's failed experiments with inhaled psychedelics when the wind blew the wrong way.

29. Asch reported that the idea came to him while reflecting about his childhood experience attending a Passover Seder. An extra glass of wine was poured for

Elijah and the seven-year-old Solomon asked if Elijah would really come. His uncle replied, "Oh, yes. You just watch," and Solomon thought he saw the wine level diminish slightly in the glass. David Tout, "Obituary—Solomon Asch Is Dead at 88: A Leading Social Psychologist," *New York Times*, February 29, 1996.

30. Singer and Lalich, *Cults in Our Midst*, 76.

31. S. Milgram, *Obedience to Authority: An Experimental View* (New York: Harper and Row, 1974).

32. V. Packard, *Hidden Persuaders* (New York: David McKay, 1957), 4.

33. Packard memorably recounted that prune farmers, concerned about declining markets, hired motivational researchers to understand how to improve sales. They learned from word association tests that the word *prune* had no positive connotations; it brought forth associations such as *old maid*, *dried up, old prune face*, and a cheap laxative floating in black liquid. As Packard described it, the solution was to start talking about the *taste* of prunes and to use brightly colored advertisements emphasizing prunes as a wonder fruit for dynamic young people (Packard, *Hidden Persuaders*, 136).

34. S. Matz, M. Kosinski, G. Nave, and D. Stillwell, "Psychological Targeting as an Effective Approach to Digital Mass Persuasion," *PNAS* 114, no. 48 (2017): 12714–19.

35. Previous generations worried about a different form of surreptitious targeting. Tachistoscopes project images so rapidly that they are not consciously perceptible. Many worried that these devices could be used to influence viewers. Subliminal advertising is threatening because it is intentional, methodical, and its targets are unaware of it. In fact, tachistoscope-mediated advertising is not an effective tool in brainwashing because it has such a small effect. See, for instance, C. Trappey, "A Meta-analysis of Consumer Choice and Subliminal Advertising," *Psychology and Marketing* 13, no. 5 (1996): 517–30; and William M. O'Barr, "Subliminal Advertising," *Advertising & Society Review* 13, no. 4 (2013), https://muse.jhu.edu/article/193862. Some people nonetheless are convinced that advertisements have hidden images of breasts and penises—messages to excite their viewers and persuade customers to associate companies' products with sex. It is akin to finding images of the Virgin Mary on a tortilla or seeing animals in clouds. It reminds me of Stalin's director for literary and publishing affairs, who advised censors to scrutinize all works of art with a magnifying glass to find counterrevolutionary content. See Yuri Slezkine, *The House of Government: A Saga of the Russian Revolution* (Princeton: Princeton University Press, 2017), 818. The internet doesn't need a tachistoscope in order to be persuasive.

36. N. Cousins, "Smudging the Unconscious," *Saturday Review*, October 5, 1957, 20.

37. A. Bandura, D. Ross, and S. A. Ross, "Transmission of Aggression through the Imitation of Aggressive Models," *Journal of Abnormal and Social Psychology* 63, no. 3 (1961): 575–82.

38. See, for instance, "Boy Who Tried to Fly 'Like Superman' Dies," *New York Times*, February 12, 1979; and "5-Year-Old Dies After Falling from 10th Floor while Pretending to be Superman," January 13, 2019, https://www.news24 .com/World/News/5-year-old-dies-after-falling-from-10th-floor-20190113.

39. American Psychiatric Association, "Suicide Deaths, Calls to Hotlines Increased Dramatically Following Robin Williams' 2014 Suicide," *Psychiatric News Alert*, May 1, 2019.

40. Serah Wanza, "Countries That Drink the Most Gin," World Atlas, May 16, 2018, https://www.worldatlas.com/articles/countries-that-drink-the-most -gin.html.

41. Similar stories could be told of other newly introduced intoxicants (for example, alcohol to the New World, opium to China). In such instances, people obsessively reoriented their lives around a new North Star, seeking comfort from that which was actually destroying them, obsessively circling around their drug like a moth around a flame.

42. L. M. Maruschak, "DWI Offenders under Correctional Supervision," Bureau of Justice Statistics, June 1999, https://www.bjs.gov/content/pub/ascii /dwiocs.txt. For a more current analysis reporting similar findings, see Office of Behavioral Safety Research, Traffic Safety Facts Research Note, "Results of the 2013–2014 National Roadside Survey of Alcohol and Drug Use by Drivers," DOT HS 812 118, February 2015, https://www.nhtsa.gov /behavioral-research/2013-14-national-roadside-study-alcohol-and-drug -use-drivers. Although it has decreased, drunk driving remains an extremely common problem; in 2010, there were 1.4 million arrests for drunk driving in the United States. M. Chambers, M. Liu, and C. Moore, "Drunk Driving by the Numbers," Bureau of Transportation Statistics, 2017, https://www .bts.gov/archive/publications/by_the_numbers/drunk_driving/index.

43. H. Cash et al., "Internet Addiction: A Brief Summary of Research and Practice," *Current Psychiatry Reviews* 8, no. 4 (November 2012): 292–98.

44. See, for instance, the Brookings Report "How to Combat Fake News and Disinformation," December 18, 2017, https://www.brookings.edu/research /how-to-combat-fake-news-and-disinformation/.

45. S. Vosoughi, D. Roy, and S. Aral, "The Spread of True and False News Online," *Science* 359 (2018): 1146–51.

46. Callum Borchers, "A Harsh Truth about Fake News: Some People Are Super Gullible," *Washington Post*, December 5, 2016.

47. Catherine Rampell, "Americans—Especially but Not Exclusively Trump Voters—Believe Crazy, Wrong Things," *Washington Post*, December 28, 2016. See also K. Frankovic, "Belief in Conspiracies Largely Depends on Political Identity," YouGov, December 27, 2016, https://today.yougov.com /topics/politics/articles-reports/2016/12/27/belief-conspiracies-largely -depends-political-iden. The 2020 election in the United States provides continuing evidence of the effects of social media to incite violence.

48. Millennia ago, Thucydides (460–400 BC) pointed this out: "It is a habit of

mankind to entrust to careless hope what they long for, and to use sovereign reason to thrust aside what they do not fancy." Thucydides, *The Peloponnesian War*, trans. Richard Crawley, book IV, 108. More recently, Yogi Berra observed, "I wouldn't have seen it, if I hadn't believed it."

49. G. King, J. Pan, and M. Roberts, "How the Chinese Government Fabricates Social Media Posts for Strategic Distraction, Not Engaged Argument," *American Political Science Review* 111, no. 3 (2017): 484–501. China is certainly not alone with its use of troll farms. The Philippines, Turkey, Russia, and many other countries are also prominent in this regard, either for promoting their own states or for being paladins for hire. See Shibani Mahtani and Regine Cabato, "Why Crafty Internet Trolls in the Philippines May Be Coming to a Website Near You," *Washington Post*, July 25, 2019, https://www.washingtonpost.com/world/asia_pacific/why-crafty-internet-trolls-in-the-philippines-may-be-coming-to-a-website-near-you/2019/07/25/c5d42ee2-5c53-11e9-98d4-844088d135f2_story.html. See also Fruzsina Eordogh, "The Russian Troll Army Isn't the Only One We Need to Worry About," *Forbes*, April 11, 2018, https://www.forbes.com/sites/fruzsinaeordogh/2018/04/11/the-russian-troll-army-isnt-the-only-one-we-need-to-worry-about/#2d2446602334.

50. U.S. Senate, Report of the Select Committee on Intelligence, Russian Active Measures Campaigns and Interference in the 2016 U.S. Election, 116th Cong., 1st sess. 1:5.

51. Jane Mayer, "How Russia Helped Swing the Election for Trump," *New Yorker*, September 24, 2018.

52. U.S. Department of Justice, *Report on the Investigation of Russian Interference in the 2016 Presidential Election* (Washington, DC, 2019), https://www.justice.gov/storage/report.pdf.

53. P. Beinart, "The U.S. Needs to Face Up to Its Long History of Election Meddling," *Atlantic*, July 22, 2018.

54. Jason LeMiere, "Who Is Michelle Carter? Verdict Reached in Texting Suicide Trial Involving Death of Conrad Roy III," *Newsweek*, June 16, 2017, https://www.newsweek.com/michelle-carter-verdict-conrad-roy-626649.

55. Dalton Main, "'Such Unusual Circumstances': Here's What Michelle Carter's Appeal Hinges On," *Boston25 News*, updated July 8, 2019, https://www.boston25news.com/news/-such-unusual-circumstances-here-s-what-michelle-carter-s-appeal-hinges-on/846074193.

56. Joey Garrison, "Former Boston College Student Charged in Suicide Death of Boyfriend, Echoing Michelle Carter Case," *USA Today*, October 28, 2019, https://www.usatoday.com/story/news/nation/2019/10/28/former-boston-college-student-charged-suicide-death-boyfriend/2484454001/.

57. Mark Pratt, "Woman in 'Total Control' of Boyfriend Charged in His Suicide," Associated Press, October 28, 2019.

58. L. Coviello, Y. Sohn, A. Kramer, C. Marlow, M. Franceschetti, N. Christakis, and J. Fowler, "Detecting Emotional Contagion in Massive Social Net-

works," *PLOS One* 9, no. 3 (March 2014): e90315; R. Bond, C. Fariss, J. Jones, A. Kramer, C. Marlow, J. Settle, and J. Fowler, "A 61-Million-Person Experiment in Social Influence and Political Mobilization," *Nature*, September 13, 2012, 295–98.

59. William Shakespeare, *Henry IV, Part 2*, Induction.
60. C. Paul and M. Matthews, "The Russian 'Firehose of Falsehood' Propaganda Model," RAND Corporation Perspectives, 2016, https://www.rand .org/pubs/perspectives/PE198.html.
61. Plato, *The Republic*, chapter IX.

Afterword

1. See, for instance, D. Seed, *Brainwashing: The Fictions of Mind Control— A Study of Novels and Films since World War II* (Kent: Kent State University Press, 2004).
2. George Orwell, *1984* (1949; repr. in ebook edition, Columbus, OH: Biblios, 2017), part 3, chapter 3.
3. H. G. Wells, "What This World Might Be Were Men United in a Common Peace and Justice," in *Outline of History: Being a Plain History of Life and Mankind* (New York: Macmillan, 1920), 2:594.

Index

*Note: Page numbers in **bold** refer to tables; numbers in italics refer to a photograph or illustration.*